THE TUDOR &
JACOBEAN
COUNTRY HOUSE
A Building History

The Triangular Lodge, Rushton, Northamptonshire (Megan Parry).

THE TUDOR &
JACOBEAN
COUNTRY HOUSE
A Building History

MALCOLM AIRS

Bramley Books

A Sutton Publishing Book

This edition published in 1998 by Bramley Books, an imprint of
Quadrillion Publishing Limited,
Godalming Business Centre, Woolsack Way,
Godalming, Surrey GU7 1XW

ISBN 1 85833 833 6

This book was designed and produced by
Alan Sutton Publishing Limited, an imprint of Sutton Publishing Limited,
Phoenix Mill · Thrupp · Stroud · Gloucestershire GL5 2BU

Typeset in 11/12 Erhardt.
Typesetting and origination by
Sutton Publishing Limited.
Printed in Great Britain by
WBC Limited, Bridgend, Mid-Glamorgan.

To Thomas
for bringing me more happiness than I ever imagined
and to Megan
for making it all possible.

Contents

Foreword

I suspect that most people, if asked to nominate 'The Age of the English Country House', would choose the eighteenth century, but it is arguable that the Tudor and Jacobean period has a better claim to the title. Not only were country houses built in greater numbers than ever before or since in England, but they dominated their age to a greater extent even than in the eighteenth century. There was virtually no church building of any importance, and little royal building after Henry VIII; town and market halls and government buildings were small and unpretentious, and most of them were replaced in later centuries; industrial architecture was negligible; the amount of new domestic architecture in the towns was considerable, but much of it went up in flames in the great fires of the seventeenth and eighteenth centuries, or has been remodelled and redeveloped. But the country houses of the age, presiding over their subordinate fringe of mud-and-wattle cottages, long since vanished, and substantial yeoman houses, many happily surviving, still exist in an amazing wealth and variety of type and scale, from the great 'prodigy' houses, with their fantastic skylines of turrets and obelisks, to modestly lovable manor houses, rising gently above the mellow brick of their garden and forecourt walls.

The houses did indeed rise gently. Sir Christopher Hatton was described in his lifetime as a 'mere vegetable of the court that sprung up at night and sank again at his noon', and his enormous mansion at Holdenby in Northamptonshire rose almost as quickly and had all but disappeared a hundred years later. But the general picture, as so skilfully and vividly pieced together by Malcolm Airs, was a very different one, for large house and small. It was one of gradual growth, conditioned by practical and financial constraints. First came the slow accumulation of materials next to the intended site: rough-hewn stone, seasoning timber, heaped-up bricks and tiles baked from local clay. I love the thought of these pregnant piles, each a kind of architectural kitchen garden, from the raw materials of which the house was going to be concocted, with no-one quite sure what the end result would be.

A plan perhaps came down from a fashionable London surveyor, or an official of the Royal Works, along with a fireplace or two from a London sculptor's yard. A copy of Serlio's *Architecture* or a sheaf of continental engravings were handed to the workmen, and free copies from them incorporated in the detail, but much of what was built was rooted in long-standing traditions of craftsmanship. The owner-builder was firmly in command, with no architect, touchy about his professional status, to argue with him; he may have had a vivid idea of what he was after, often some ingenious visual gimmick, or features from someone else's house which he wanted to incorporate, and sent one of his workmen to look at; but he (or she) was often away for long periods, much was left to the man in charge on the spot, there were no precise drawings, and so bit by bit over a ten or twenty-year period, with constant discussions, decisions and changes of mind on site, the house moved to completion.

This slow and multi-faceted gestation had its obvious disadvantages, and yet one can look back on it with a little envy: perhaps it was more likely to end with a satisfied client, and perhaps the special love which I and others have for houses of the period derives at least in part from the results which it led to: buildings of slow growth, rooted in tradition and in their local landscape and local society, and yet at the same time filled with a sense of delight for new features, new devices and new shapes.

It was not all a rosy picture, however. Malcolm Airs makes clear how heavily weighted the scales were in favour of the employer, how little security the workmen had, how hard an unfeeling employer could make their lives. Sir John Thynne, although presiding over the creation of one of the most magnificent prodigy houses, emerges as a thoroughly nasty piece of work. How dearly one would like to hear Robert Smythson, the brilliant young mason who came to work at Longleat, give his opinion of Thynne, and of his other employers: Francis Willoughby of Wollaton, neurotic intellectual and would-be industrial tycoon, or Bess of Hardwick who, tough nut though she was, was remarkably generous to her workpeople.

Such accounts cannot be hoped for. The personalities of the patrons rise from a sea of anonymity, the inevitable result of the lack of relevant archives. But in spite of these constraints it is a remarkably vivid picture that Airs builds up: of hierarchies of labourers and craftsmen, of where they came from, and how they lived when on the job; of costs and methods of accounting; of the influence of the seasons, and of winter and summer work; of quarries leased or opened up, of stone moving in slow boatloads up and down the rivers, or being painfully dragged or carted across country; a whole forgotten world quantified or brought to life, to deepen our understanding of the Tudor and Jacobean country house.

Mark Girouard

Introduction

The decline of the private castle and its replacement by the country house as the seat of power and the centre of hospitality for the elite was one of the great achievements of the Tudor age. By any standards, this was a remarkable social change which irrevocably transformed the appearance of the English landscape and which had essentially been completed by the time of the Civil War. The first flowering of the country house was founded on a variety of complex economic and political factors, including rampant price-inflation, the establishment of a bureaucratic state, the dissolution of the monasteries, economic growth and political isolation from much of the rest of Europe. It culminated with the unique and exciting cultural achievements of the Elizabethan and Jacobean era: the age of Shakespeare, Ben Jonson and Inigo Jones.

The scholarly appreciation of the architectural legacy of that momentous period has been slow to mature. Despite the pioneering publications of J.A. Gotch around the turn of the century and the more considered approach of Sir John Summerson in the decades after the Second World War, the implicit belief that the buildings of the Tudors and the early Stuarts represented some kind of primitive aberration before the inevitable adoption of classical rules in the eighteenth century has shaped the critical response ever since Sir Roger Pratt castigated the 'glaring through lights' of the magnificently fenestrated houses of his father's generation. The turning point came with the publication in 1966 of Mark Girouard's *Robert Smythson and the Architecture of the Elizabethan Era*, which convincingly reinterpreted the architecture of the period in the light of its own intrinsic merits, unencumbered by the false dialectic of historical determinism. Since that date, Girouard has consolidated the seminal position of the sixteenth-century great house in a broader architectural perspective through his *Life in the English Country House* (1978), and Maurice Howard has established the importance of *The Early Tudor Country House* (1987). It is now generally accepted that the English country house in the period between 1500 and 1640 was the product of enthusiastic and genuine architectural creativity and a worthy contribution to the culture of a dynamic age.

Although the architecture provides the background to this work, its principal concern is with the people who created these monuments to a vanished society. It examines the motives that inspired them to build and the choices that they were faced with. Without the hopes and aspirations, the piety and the arrogance, the generosity and the meanness, the vision and the flair of the patrons, the houses themselves would never have existed. Of equal importance are the craftsmen, labourers and administrators who by their individual skill and knowledge turned the architectural dreams of their employers into solid reality. This study is as much a testament to the unsung workforce as it is to their more celebrated patrons. The insecurity of their employment, the homes that they lived in and the diet that sustained them are explored, as well as their hours of work, their financial rewards and their individual foibles and failings. Technical matters are considered only in so far as they relate to the practical problems of construction. The principal sources are the building accounts of the houses themselves and the correspondence of their builders, and these are fully documented in the notes. In the interests of historical accuracy, quotations are given in their original spelling and sums of money are expressed as *£.s.d.* The research on which this book is based was first published in 1975 under the title of *The Making of the English Country House, 1500–1640.* This revised edition takes into account the substantial body of literature published since that date and summarized in the select bibliography. Its main themes, however, remain unchanged in seeking to understand how the country houses of the period were commissioned and the ways in which their construction was organized and executed.

One of the great pleasures of working in the field of architectural history is the generosity and encouragement provided by fellow enthusiasts. Over the last twenty years or so Howard Colvin, Mark Girouard, John Newman, John Summerson, Andor Gomme and Nicholas Cooper have all kindly shared their discoveries with me and discussed various aspects of the buildings of the period. Maurice Howard has given me many fresh insights and has been particularly generous with his time and support. In Oxford the Architectural History Seminar founded by Edward Chaney and Geoffrey Tyack has provided me with constant intellectual stimulus and the informal Wednesday gatherings of archaeologists and conservationists at the Queens' Arms and other congenial venues has offered good company and the wisdom of John Ashdown, John Steane, Julian Munby, Brian Durham, Malcolm Graham, Edith Gollnast and many others. I am particularly grateful to my colleagues in the Department for Continuing Education and Kellogg College for creating such an agreeable atmosphere in which to promote the cause of historic conservation, and to Anthony Quiney for his constant friendship and encouragement. Janet Grimsdale typed the manuscript in difficult circumstances with great patience and efficiency, and I would like her to know how much I value her support in every aspect of my work. I have attempted to express my gratitude to Megan Parry and our son Tom (as he prefers to be known) in the dedication but the words remain inadequate.

Malcolm Airs
Dorchester-on-Thames

Part I

THE BUILDERS

Burghley House

Everie man almost is a builder . . .

WILLIAM HARRISON, 1577

CHAPTER 1

The Motives for Building

The sixteenth century was a period of extraordinary building activity. As early as 1549, Sir Thomas Smith drew attention to 'our buildings that we have here in England of late days, far more excessive than at any time here before' and by 1577 William Harrison, an Essex clergyman, was driven to comment that:

> Everie man almost is a builder and he that hath bought any small parcell of ground, be it never so little, will not be quiet till he have pulled downe the old house (if anie were there standing) and set up a new after his own devise.

This impression was given added emphasis by an anonymous critic of Southampton society who wrote, in 1582, 'Then began costly apparel. Then down with old houses, and new set in their places: for the houses where the fathers dwelt could not content their children'.[1] This frenzy of construction reached its height in the reign of James I, of whom Bishop Goodman commented, 'no kingdom in this world spent so much in building as we did in his time'.[2] The surviving evidence for such unprecedented architectural creation is visible throughout much of England and provides a unique contribution to our cultural heritage.

In the county of Essex alone, to choose one example, there are well over a hundred country houses still standing which can be dated to the sixteenth century. When the amount of materials and labour involved in building these houses are considered, the powerful effects that their construction had on the local community can be readily appreciated. And yet, these are only the survivors. In 1594 John Norden counted no less than 354 houses belonging to the nobility and gentry in Essex, the majority of which must have been built or substantially altered during the preceding century.[3] The number of country houses built in the early decades of the seventeenth century was equally noteworthy. If only the firmly dated examples are included, then seven major country houses were built in Warwickshire between 1500 and 1560, whereas twenty were erected in the period from 1560 to 1630,[4] and Professor Stone has estimated that the amount of country house building between 1570 and 1620 far exceeded that of any subsequent half-century.[5]

This remarkable building boom was not confined to the builders of large country houses. It was partly initiated by a continuous period of rising food prices which enabled all primary producers with security of tenure to accumulate the necessary capital to rebuild, and it went hand-in-hand with a general improvement in living standards discernible at all levels of society. The yeoman and the husbandman were remodelling the family home or building themselves a new house at the same time as their lord in the manor house was recruiting his labour force and contemplating his own more ambitious building schemes. The tangible evidence is all there in the buildings themselves, and it is easy in the mind's eye to draw up a picture of much of England resounding to the noise of the carpenter's adze and the mason's chisel.

Although the impetus for what W.G. Hoskins has described as the Great Rebuilding was felt throughout society, this study is only concerned with the houses of the gentry and their social superiors. At this level there were a number of additional influences at work which emphasized the obsolescence of the medieval house and inspired many owners to become builders.[6]

The establishment of the Tudor state, and the change in social relationships that it implied, had a profound influence on the way that they built. The end of civil discord after the Wars of the Roses meant that it was no longer necessary, or indeed politic, to build houses that were primarily defensive in character. Even houses that were called castles, such as Thornbury Castle, Gloucestershire, begun in about 1511 by the Duke of Buckingham, were fortified in name alone and could never have been designed to withstand a serious attack. Increasingly throughout the sixteenth century the great feudal magnates were becoming courtiers and office-holders, tied to the crown by a mutual self-interest which effectively eliminated armed conflict. There were, of course, still personal and family feuds which sporadically erupted into bloody clashes, but they were never on a scale sufficient to justify a return to private castle building.

Parallel with this development was a change in the relationship between the great landowners and the peasantry on their estates. Direct farming of the demesne was becoming less significant for many of them, as increasingly the bulk of their wealth came mainly from rents. The less personal landlord–tenant relationship meant that the planning of their houses was no longer conditioned by their possible function as a centre of economic activity, and the gradual decline in the importance of a communal life centred on the great hall allowed a greater concentration of architectural effect on more private apartments such as the great chamber and the long gallery.[7]

The abolition of such restrictive factors as the need for defence and the community role of the great house made many men discontented with the accommodation that had served their fathers. There was a growing emphasis on domestic comfort that could only be satisfied by a new house, or the extensive remodelling of an older house, to provide better sanitation and heating arrangements, more light, and suites of rooms that could be adapted to a more private way of life. As soon as men began to translate these ideals into bricks and mortar, houses inevitably became symbols of status. New features, such as a deliberately contrived symmetry or a vast expanse of window, drew attention to the builder's modernity and the prosperity of his estate. Architecture became a fashionable talking-point and the subject of much fulsome prose in the

The lavishly fenestrated garden elevation of the Privy Lodgings range at Thornbury Castle contrasts deliberately with the bellicose air of the outer towers.

correspondence of the day. Sir Thomas Heneage, for example, wrote to Sir Christopher Hatton in 1583:

> For my own opinion Holdenby is altogether even the best house that hath been built in this age; and it more showeth the good judgement and honour of the builder than all the charge that hath been bestowed upon stones by the greatest persons and the best purses that hath been in my time.[8]

They were not always so complimentary in their comments. In 1560 Sir Nicholas Bacon felt free to offer Cecil the practical advice that in his newly built London house

> Mary me thynkes ye prvye in ye west end ys wt ye lest and to nere ye logyng, to nere an hoven and to nere a lytle lardre. I thynk you had been better to have offendyd yor yey [eye] owtward then yor nose inward.[9]

But no matter what tone these observations took, they were intensely interested in each other's buildings, and this reflected esteem and social rivalry were powerful motives for many to build themselves.

The title page of Geoffrey Whitney's
A Choice of Emblemes *(1586).*

Building could be inspired by a competitive determination to give visible proof of the builder's prosperity and social standing to all who cared to look, but it could equally be used to demonstrate their wit and intelligence to those who were capable of understanding. The cultured mind of the sixteenth century delighted in anything that could be called 'curious' or 'ingenious'; anything whose true meaning was obscure enough to require some thought before intellectual satisfaction could be achieved by arriving at its correct interpretation. This fascination can be seen in the preoccupation with allegory and metaphor which characterize much of the literature and painting of the period. It is reflected in the pleasure that the sixteenth century derived from emblems and devices, in which a philosophical truth or a line of conduct was reduced to an allegorical picture supported by a cryptic motto or some lines of verse. Geoffrey Whitney in his book, *A Choice of Emblemes*, published in 1586, defined an emblem as

> having some wittie devise expressed with cunning woorkemanship, somethinge obscure to be perceived at the first, whereby, when with further consideration it is understood, it maie the greater delighte the behoulder,

and his definition can be extended to embrace the contemporary meaning behind such words as 'conceit' and 'device', and their concomitant adjectives, 'curious' and 'ingenious'.[10] When John Chamberlain referred to the Queen's House as 'some curious devise of Inigo Jones',[11] or the 9th Earl of Northumberland announced his intention, now that he was a builder, to 'borrow of my knowledge somewhat out of Tibballs, somewhat out of every place of mark where curiosities are used',[12] they were expressing just such an intellectual concept.

Both the major contemporary collections of architectural drawings contain examples that demonstrate this almost childlike concern with artful ingenuity in building. In the Thorpe collection there are designs based on circles, squares, triangles, and combinations of these geometrical forms, together with a whimsical plan and elevation for a house formed from his own initials and inscribed

these 2 letters I and T
ioyned together as you see
Is mete for a dwelling howse for mee

John Thorpe.[13]

In the Smythson collection there is an ingenious unexecuted design for a house in the shape of a Greek cross with an open central courtyard, and a number of other plans which were actually built, such as that for Hardwick Hall, which are clearly based on the deliberate disposition of various geometrical elements.[14] Similarly, in the architectural drawings collected by William and Robert Cecil there is 'a plat how to mak a hows in form of a Cross', and another plan, apparently for a fortification, but which is endorsed 'for a place of pleasure'.[15] This latter is related to yet another manifestation of the curious and ingenious conceit, whereby gardens as well as buildings were used as an opportunity for cerebral fun. John Chamberlain graphically described such a garden when he visited Sir Henry Fanshawe at Ware Park, Hertfordshire, in October 1606 and found more than forty workmen transforming the grounds of the house:

And in the midst of it, instead of a knot, he is making a fort in perfect proportion, with his ramparts, bulwarks, counterscarps and all other appurtances, so that when it is finished it is like to prove an invincible piece of work.[16]

Most of the executed buildings that were deliberately designed to display the builder's intellectual ingenuity date from the latter part of the sixteenth and the first half of the seventeenth century. They include the triangular Longford Castle in Wiltshire, begun in about 1580 for Sir Thomas Gorges, and a whole series of buildings which were characterized by three wings arranged in the form of the letter Y. One of these, Newhouse, near Redlynch, Wiltshire, is said to have been built for the same Sir Thomas Gorges, although it is likely that the house was already in existence when he bought the estate from William Stockman in 1619. Another, built as a parsonage at Goodrich, Herefordshire, for the Revd Thomas Swift (the grandfather of Jonathan Swift), in 1636, is similarly named Newhouse.[17] The triadic form of all these buildings was possibly inspired by the religious symbolism that John Thorpe assumed for Longford when he drew the house some years after its completion and added the sign of the Holy Trinity to one of his plans,[18] but of the deliberate spiritual motive for Sir Thomas Tresham's Triangular Lodge at Rushton,

John Thorpe's plan of a triangular house on a circular terrace (by courtesy of the Trustees of Sir John Soane's Museum).

John Thorpe's plan for a house based on his own initials (by courtesy of the Trustees of Sir John Soane's Museum).

Northamptonshire, there can be no doubt. Tresham was brought up as a Protestant, but was converted to Catholicism in 1580 and for the remaining years of his life he defiantly practised his new faith in the face of continual official persecution. Two of his buildings were undoubtedly little more than public proclamations of this faith. The Triangular Lodge, built for his warrener between 1594 and 1597, is a most delightful allegory on the Trinity, which, in its consistent pursuit of the mystic properties of the figure three, can still provide the onlooker with immense intellectual satisfaction.[19] Each of its three sides is a third of a hundred feet long. It has three storeys with three trefoiled windows on each face, and is capped by nine gables and a triangular chimney-shaft. Even the inscription on the frieze above the upper storey is thirty-three letters long. The building is decorated with a wealth of religious emblems and inscriptions, and over the entrance doorway is the motto *Tres Testimonium Dant*, a characteristic pun on both the Trinity and Tresham's own name. In 1604 he began another decorative lodge as part of an elaborate garden scheme on his estate at Lyveden. The New Build was designed on the plan of a Greek Cross, symbolizing the Passion of Christ, and its polemical purpose was further underlined by the Catholic ciphers that adorn its external walls and proclaim the faith to all who pass.[20]

The religious belief that inspired the Triangular Lodge and Lyveden New Build can be clearly discerned from the buildings themselves, but there were other buildings of the period where a similar expression of faith would have been all but lost were it not for the chance survival of explicit documentary evidence.

*John Thorpe's survey plan of Longford Castle, Wiltshire (*by courtesy of the Trustees of Sir John Soane's Museum*).*

Newhouse, Goodrich, Herefordshire, of 1636 on a Y plan.

Plan by Robert Smythson for a house in the form of a Greek cross imposed on a quatrefoil and set within a square enclosure (British Architectural Library, RIBA, London).

Inscription over the entrance to the Triangular Lodge.

Lyveden New Build, begun in 1604 on a Greek cross plan as a symbol of Sir Thomas Tresham's Catholicism.

The E-shaped plan, which was a commonplace of sixteenth and seventeenth-century architectural design, was specifically intended as a religious conceit at Chantmarle House, Dorset, built between 1612 and 1623 by John Strode, who noted that

> Constructa est in forma, de Littera (E) sc.
> Emmanuel. id est, Deus nobiscum in Eternum.[21]

And the amateur poet and antiquary, Henry Oxinden, who had erected a circular lodge on his estate in Kent in 1631, only explained its significance in a doggerel verse composed during an illness some thirty-six years later:

> *A Query why I made the house on top of the Hill round?*
> Tell me how Henry in thy minde it came
> Upon the Hill thy House so round to frame
> *Answere*
> I imitated the great Architector, Loe
> Both Earth & Heaven, hee hath framed soe.[22]

In essence, the use of classical elements in English architecture in the sixteenth century was merely another aspect of this intellectual delight in the curious.

Emmanuel inscribed over the entrance to Chantmarle House, Dorset.

With the exception of a few builders, such as the Duke of Somerset, Sir John Thynne, and Sir Thomas Smith, they were adopted as a novelty and for the intrinsic pleasure to be derived from their design, and not from any philosophical concept of ideal aesthetic perfection. John Shute referred to classical architecture as the 'new facion', and it was accepted as such by most of his contemporaries, who simply absorbed its more striking motifs into their eclectic repertory of decorative elements. As a fashion it was liable to be superseded by other trends, such as the mannerism of Germany and the Low Countries, and the revival of interest in gothic forms in the later sixteenth century, and consequently to provide a motive for further alteration and rebuilding. At Burghley House, for example, the unmistakably gothic-inspired west front, and possibly the hammer-beamed great hall, seem to have succeeded the chastely classical courtyard in Burghley's complicated scheme of building which extended from the 1550s into the 1580s.[23]

The underlying theme behind this preoccupation with ingenuity and passing fashion was a determination to draw attention to a builder's architectural achievement. It was not simply a matter of intense social rivalry, although elements of this were undoubtedly present. It was more a reflection of a contemporary concern with mortality, and of ways to outwit its effect, which can be seen in such literary expressions as the 'time' sonnets of Shakespeare. Sonnet LXV, with its belief in the immortal qualities of artistic creation, provides a good example of the effect that many builders seem to have been striving to achieve.

The ceiling of the gothic great hall at Burghley House.

The courtyard loggia at Burghley House.

Since brass, nor stone, nor earth, nor boundless sea,
But sad mortality o'ersways their power,
How with this rage shall beauty hold a plea,
Whose action is no stronger than a flower?
O, how shall summer's honey breath hold out
Against the wreckful siege of battering days
When rocks impregnable are not so stout,
Her gates of steel so strong, but time decays?
O fearful meditation! Where, alack!
Shall Time's best jewel from Time's chest lie hid?
Or what strong hand can hold his swift foot back?
Or who his spoil of beauty can forbid?
O none, unless this miracle have might,
That in black ink my love may still shine bright.

The need to believe that when you died, your name and something of your deeds would continue to live, could be satisfied before the Reformation by the conspicuous adornment of the parish church, but after the break with Rome some more secular monument was required. The wealth of initials, dates, heraldic devices and mottoes to be found emblazoned on buildings of Elizabethan and Jacobean date are sufficient testimony to their builders' desire for immortality.

However, despite the intellectual impetus of the age, most builders had a more personal motive before they engaged in large-scale expenditure on building. It might be enforced retirement from public life caused by exclusion from Court, as in the examples of Sir Thomas Smith and, in the following century, the Earl of Holland. Smith had been one of Somerset's protégés during the reign of Edward VI. With the eclipse of his patron he retired to Eton and built himself a house in the nearby manor of Ankerwicke. He returned to political life with the accession of Elizabeth and sat in her first parliament. However, disappointed in his hopes of office, he concentrated much of his energies on rebuilding Hill Hall on his Essex estates. Building work came to a halt when he was appointed ambassador to France in 1562. He returned in 1566 and between 1568 and 1569 he remodelled the north and west ranges of the courtyard with a design incorporating some of the startling new architectural motifs he had seen in France. Progress on the new house was temporarily suspended by his return to Court in 1571 where he was appointed to the Privy Council, and in the following year succeeded Burghley as Secretary. Between 1574 and 1575 he turned his attention to the reconstruction of the south and east ranges. In 1576, a serious illness led to his retirement, and he spent the remaining months of his life in a vain attempt to complete the work.[24]

Henry Rich, 1st Earl of Holland, was 'a handsome man of lovely and winning presence'. He had enjoyed a successful career at Court, being appointed Gentleman of the Bedchamber to Prince Charles and conducting the negotiations for his marriage to Henrietta Maria. On the accession of Charles to the throne he remained in high favour with the queen, but in 1637 he was openly frustrated in his ambitions when the post of Lord High Admiral was granted to the Earl of Northumberland. According to his biographer, he 'retired to his house at Kensington in disgust', where he consoled himself by embarking upon an extensive building programme. Between 1638 and 1640 he spent more than £6,500 on a magnificent new stable block and added a new wing to the house that his father-in-law had built fewer than thirty years earlier.[25]

Social aspirations provided another powerful motive for building, especially for those whose wealth derived from trade or business. It was a common pattern for younger sons of the landed gentry to enter commerce, make sufficient money to invest in land, and then return to the ranks of the landed gentry themselves. Clement Sysley, for example, was the younger son of Richard Sysley of Sevenoaks, Kent. In 1557 he bought a farm called Eastbury, near Barking, Essex, from another London merchant, Sir William Denham. By 1560 he had taken up residence in the parish and begun to build. Soon after its completion in 1572, Sysley began to refer to it by the socially impressive title of Eastbury Hall, a name that it retained until it declined once more into a farmhouse in the eighteenth century.[26]

Successful lawyers were another class of builder desirous of the social esteem provided by landed estates and an impressive country house. Such a man was John Strode, Reader at the Middle Temple, member of parliament, and knighted in 1623. In 1606 he bought the Dorset estates of the Cheverells, a local gentry family in financial difficulties, and at Chantmarle he remodelled and enlarged the existing house on a grand scale.[27]

The building career of another lawyer illustrates the influence exerted by political success. Educated at Cambridge, Nicholas Bacon was admitted to Gray's

Holland House, enlarged 1638–40 by the Earl of Holland when he was out of favour at court.

Inn in 1532. In 1537 he was appointed to the position of Solicitor with the Court of Augmentations, and ten years later he was made an attorney in the Court of Wards. Both these positions provided ample opportunity for considerable financial gain. In 1545 he began to build a modest country house at Redgrave in Suffolk. It was finished by 1554 at a cost of less than £1,500. Four years later Bacon was created Lord Keeper of the Great Seal and was assigned York House as his London residence. Redgrave, as originally conceived, was clearly inadequate for his new status, and between 1560 and 1562 he spent over £400 on building two additional wings. Still dissatisfied, the following year he began a completely new house at Gorhambury, near St Albans, leaving Redgrave as a residence for his recently married son. The cost of Gorhambury was more than double the amount that he had spent on his first house. Completed in 1568, it was

Eastbury House, Essex. Built by Richard Sysley out of the proceeds of a successful commercial career.

visited by Elizabeth I on one of her progresses in 1572, when she is reputed to have told her host, 'My Lord, what a little house have you gotten'. Bacon, so legend would have it, made the telling reply, 'Madam, my house is well, but it is you that have made me too great for my house'.[28] Whether this story is apocryphal or not, shortly after 1572 considerable additions were made to the house, including a loggia with a gallery above it.[29]

The anecdote of the queen's visit to Gorhambury shows Bacon to have been one of that small class of builders motivated by a more expensive reason than their own personal or social needs. Close to the Court was a small group of men dependent on the Crown for their jobs, or looking to it for the rewards of patronage. The summer progresses, when the monarch toured a part of the country living off the hospitality of the nobility and showing herself to her loyal subjects, provided an opportunity – or, more correctly, a necessity – for those anxious to preserve or increase their favour at Court, to entertain her lavishly. But, in order to accommodate the queen and her retinue of privy councillors, courtiers and retainers, it was in the interests of those likely to be visited frequently to build on a scale far exceeding their normal requirements. The result was that group of what Sir John Summerson has so aptly called 'Prodigy Houses': houses such as Burghley, Theobalds and Holdenby of Elizabeth's reign, and Hatfield and Audley End in the following reign. Such houses were envisaged more as occasional palaces for the monarch than as dwellings for her noble subjects. William Cecil, Lord Burghley, made explicit their inspiration when he stated in 1585 that Theobalds 'was begun by me with a mean measure but encreast by occasion of her majesty's often coming'.[30] His anonymous contemporary biographer confirms that

> He buylt three houses. One in London for necessity. Another at Burghley of computency, for the mansion of his barony. And another at Waltham for his younger sonne. Which at the first, he ment but for a little pile, as I hard him saie. But, after he came to entertayne the quene so often there, he was inforced to enlarge it, rather for the quene and her greate traine, and to sett poore on worke, than for pomp or glory. For he ever said 'it would be to big for the small living he cold leave his sonne'.[31]

Even under Charles I, when the custom of royal progresses had declined in the face of the growing isolation of the Crown, there were still those who sought to ingratiate themselves with the monarch by building on a grand scale. Thomas Wentworth, Earl of Strafford, appointed Lord Deputy of Ireland in 1632, wrote to Archbishop Laud in 1637 about the house that he was building there:

> they say I build unto the sky. I acknowledge that were myself only considered in what I built it were not only to excess but even to folly . . . but his Majesty will justify me that, at my last being in England, I acquainted him with a purpose I had to build him a house at the Naas, it being uncomely that his Majesty should not have one there of his own, capable to lodge him with moderated conveniency (which in truth he has not) in case he might be pleased sometime hereafter to look upon this kingdom.[32]

It should be emphasized, however, that the royal influence exerted its hold over a comparatively small circle of ambitious subjects. There were others who did not look to the Court for aggrandizement, for whom the expense of playing host to a royal progress was a somewhat doubtful honour. Sir William More, a man of limited political ambition, was threatened with a visit from the queen in 1567 when his house near Guildford was still only half finished. With the aid of friends at Court he was able on this occasion to dissuade her by reason of 'what fewe smal romes and howe unmete' his house was; but even so, Loseley House was visited by the queen on three subsequent progresses.[33] Sir Thomas Arundell is said to have been reluctant to have the name of Wardour Castle even mentioned at Court during progress time for fear of being visited by the queen, and Lord Spencer went to the length of feigning illness to avoid entertaining Queen Henrietta Maria in 1626.[34]

Apart from some highly individual reasons for building such as that attributed to Thomas Cecil, Lord Exeter, who, according to Thomas Fuller, built Wothorpe

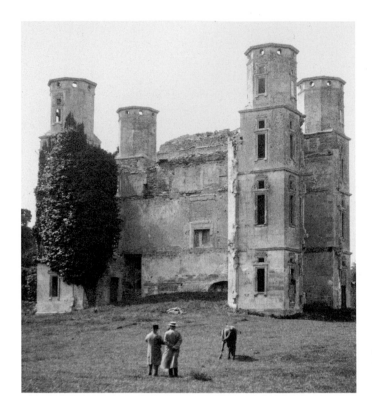

Wothorpe Lodge, as photographed in 1911 by J.A. Gotch (RCHME © Crown Copyright).

Lodge, Northamptonshire, 'to retire to out of the dust while his great house of Burghley was a-sweeping', there remain to be considered those men who can only be described as compulsive builders: men whose passion for building pursued them throughout their adult life; men who continued to build, to alter and to remodel, long after their basic housing requirements had been satisfied. Some of them have already been mentioned in other connections. Sir Nicholas Bacon is one who, in addition to his houses at Redgrave and Gorhambury, built Stiffkey Hall in Norfolk for his son Nathaniel, a London house for his son, Edward, and a chapel for Corpus Christi College, Cambridge. From 1545, when he began his first house at Redgrave, he was engaged in building during at least twenty-seven of the remaining thirty-four years of his life. Sir John Thynne devoted an even longer period of time to just one building. He began to build at Longleat in about 1546, and at his death in 1580 the house was still unfinished. During that time he had been building almost continuously and the design of the house had been developed through three distinct phases before the final architectural masterpiece was begun.

Other public figures were driven by a similar restless compulsion. Burghley, who had built Theobalds, Burghley and Cecil House in the Strand, was succeeded in office by his son Robert Cecil, whose buildings included two London houses, a new exchange to rival that of Gresham in the City, Cranborne

Kirby Hall, Northants.

House in Dorset, and Hatfield House in Hertfordshire, on which he spent nearly £40,000 and in the event only lived long enough to spend a few nights in the completed building.[35] The list of houses owned and built by the Earl of Shrewsbury and his wife, Bess of Hardwick, ran well into double figures.[36] After Bess was estranged from her husband she retired to her father's house at Hardwick. Between 1587 and 1589 she devoted herself to a major remodelling of the house and then in 1590, with the death of her husband, she abruptly stopped, leaving it unfinished, and began the new and even more magnificent Hardwick Hall only a few yards away.[37] The partly built Kirby Hall in Northamptonshire was bought in 1575 by Sir Christopher Hatton, even though he was already engaged in building Holdenby in the same county. The building of these two great houses, less than twenty-five miles apart, continued simultaneously throughout the decade. Despite the massive expenditure involved, Hatton wrote to Sir Thomas Heneage in 1580 that he was going to see his new house at Kirby for the first time 'leaving my other shrine, I mean Holdenby, still unseen until that holy saint may sit in it to whom it is dedicated'.[38] That holy saint, the inspiration for so much conspicuous expenditure on building, was, needless to say, Queen Elizabeth herself. It is sufficient to add that these are no more than outstanding examples of men of high social or political rank who built with a compulsion that seemed to spring from deeper reasons than mere ostentation or competitiveness.

The same sort of passion for building can be seen in a more limited form among less prominent men, such as Edward Pytts, who was almost fifty when he purchased the ruined castle at Kyre, Worcestershire, in 1586. By 1595 he had completely transformed the building. He then built himself a house in London, and in 1611 at the age of seventy-five he turned his attention once again to his country house. The second phase of building at Kyre was undertaken with the advice of some of the most sought-after craftsmen of the day, including John Bentley of Yorkshire and Oxford, and was still in progress when Pytts died in 1618.[39] Sir Thomas Tresham was another man with an insatiable urge to build which he indulged in the face of the most daunting personal circumstances. Most of his building activity was concentrated in the decade after 1593 when he was released from imprisonment for his recusancy. Despite further spells of imprisonment from 1596 to 1597 and 1599 to 1603, the payment of substantial marriage portions for his six daughters, and the imposition of irregular and hefty fines for his continued recusancy, he made important additions to his country seat at Rushton, built the Triangular Lodge, the Hawkfield Lodge and Lyveden New Build, altered the old house at Lyveden, improved the church at Rushton, and undertook a number of other minor works on his estate, including new bridges at Rothwell and Rushton, and a dam at Pipewell.[40] The frenzy with which he built is almost frightening in its intensity, and yet, in the final analysis, it is little more than an extreme form of an enthusiasm for building which was highly characteristic of the age in which he lived.

Part II

THE BUILDING PROCESS

Rushton Hall

Every mans proper Mansion House, being the Theater of his Hospitality, the Seate of Self-fruition, the Comfortablest part of his owne life, the Noblest of his Sonnes Inheritance, a kinde of private Princedome; Nay, to the Possessors thereof, an Epitomie of the whole World: may well deserve by these Attributes, according to the degree of the Master, to be decently and delightfully adorned.

SIR HENRY WOTTON, *1624*

CHAPTER 2

Sites

The first stage in the building process was the selection of an appropriate site. There was a general belief that the orientation of a house and its precise location had a fundamental effect in ensuring a healthy life, and there was no shortage of published advice on the best ways to achieve this. William Horman, the Headmaster of Eton, wrote in *Vulgaria*, published in 1519:

> A mannys dwellynge shulde be chosen out: if it maye be where is an holsome soyle bothe wynter and sommer. It is not good dwellynge on the see costis . . . The hylley countrey rounde about us kepeth awey parellous wyndis and pestylent infections.

Dr Andrew Boorde devoted several chapters to the requirements necessary for selecting the ideal location in his popular book, *A Compendyous Regyment or a Dyetary of Helth*, first published in 1542. The provision of an adequate water supply and sufficient wood for fuel and repairs were considered essential, as was the correct orientation of the house 'so that the pryncypall and chefe prospectes may be Eest and West . . . for the South wynde doth corrupt and doth make evyl vapours'. A cursory examination of surviving houses makes it clear that this advice on aspect was not always followed in practice, but there must have been some general agreement with the conclusion of Francis Bacon wryly expressed in his essay *Of Building* that 'He that builds a fair house upon an ill seat, committeth himself to prison'.

The chosen site could be somewhere on the builder's existing demesne, but often it seems that the final impetus to build was provided by the acquisition of a new estate. In either case it frequently happened that the best position for the new house was already occupied by an earlier building. Thus when Sir William Petre bought the manor of Ingatestone in 1539 he had to pull down 'an old house scant meet for a farmer to dwell upon' before he could begin to build the following year.[1] At Blickling in Norfolk, which the Lord Chief Justice Sir Henry Hobart purchased in 1616, the decision was taken to incorporate part of the medieval moated mansion in the design for the new house on which work was commenced in 1619, and this had a curious asymmetrical effect on the north and west elevations which was only rectified in the eighteenth century.[2] Such a piecemeal approach was not unusual. Maurice Howard found that 'the great majority of new early Tudor country houses were built on pre-existing sites and involved the renewal of older buildings rather than an original construction',[3] and there is evidence that the practice continued throughout the century and later, although this is not always immediately obvious from the appearance of the finished fabric. When in 1573 Sir William Petre's son, John, purchased the seat of the Mordaunt family at West Horndon in Essex, he began almost immediately to remodel it in a leisurely fashion, working from room to room. It was over twenty years before he was finished but, in external appearance, his house now showed no signs of its fifteenth-century core.[4] After acquiring the manor of Kyre Wyard in Worcestershire from Lord Compton in 1586, Edward Pytts began in 1588 'the newe buildinge the house of Kyer Court now ruyned'.[5] Work was still in progress at his death in 1618 and, when his son James had completed it, only a single wing of the fourteenth-century house remained. Similarly, John Strode's new work at Chantmarle in Dorset in the early seventeenth century was

> so fitly adjoyned to the old buildings by the care & direction of old Gabriell Moore (a skilful architect) as that they have good use of, and passages to the chambers over the old chapell & the Dairy houses, and likewise to ye Chambers over the old cellar & Brewhouses as if they had been built together with them.[6]

Occasionally the main structure of the old house was demolished but the foundations were retained and partly incorporated in the new building, presumably for reasons of economy. Stiffkey Hall, Norfolk, begun in August 1576, contains the cellars of the house that existed on the site when Sir Nicholas Bacon bought the manor in 1571, and Hadham Hall in Hertfordshire was built about 1572 by Henry Capell using part of the original foundations of the house erected by Thomas Baud in the mid-fifteenth century.[7]

Sometimes the new house was built at a distance from the existing house, as at Gorhambury where Sir Nicholas Bacon used materials from the old house on the site that he had bought in 1561 for his new building begun in 1563.[8] Similarly at Wollaton Sir Francis Willoughby deserted the valley site of his ancestral home to build his new house on the top of a hill, where Camden saw it 'standing bleakly but offering a very goodly prospect to the beholders far and near'.[9] At Gorhambury Bacon demolished the existing house before commencing to build the new house, but this was not always common practice. Besides acting as an easy source of material, a habitable building on the site could fulfil a number of useful functions while the actual building operation was going on, and in certain circumstances could even prove a permanent asset after the completion of the work. As Sir Edward Hext wrote to John, Lord Petre, in March 1610, describing the site of the proposed Wadham College at Oxford. There is:

> a fyne newe house which cost cc *li.*, a backesyde cont. half an acre, which ys most necessary to lay yn our tymber & stone, & about yt many hangyng houses which will serve to hewe our stones in or work in tymber in all weathers, & the house necessary for our workemen and his wyef to be yn, that he may contynually attend the worke, & after will serve for a landry or many other uses for the Colledge, or lett out for a rent.[10]

Sir William Cecil used the old moated manor house for occasional residence while his new house at Theobalds was being built,[11] and his son Robert, although he pulled down much of the Bishop's Palace at Hatfield, retained part of the hall range which was converted into stables in 1628 and used as such until early in the present century. At Denton Court in Kent, Captain Percivall adopted a similar practical approach in 1640 when he 'builded the new farme house against the Mansion house & converted that which was the farme house before into stables etc'.[12] It was exceedingly fortunate that when Francis Bacon began to build Verulam House in about 1617 in the grounds of Gorhambury, he left his father's house still standing. In the event, Verulam House was demolished within fifty years, while Gorhambury remained in use as a residence until the latter part of the eighteenth century.[13]

The purchase of a new estate was often the stimulus to become a builder, and the land market created by the dissolution of the monasteries made an enormous number of potential building sites available. In addition to the actual monastery buildings themselves, there were also large numbers of monastic manors and other dependent buildings which passed into lay hands. Maurice Howard, in his important book, *The Early Tudor Country House*, has fully documented what he describes as the 'highly opportunistic and forthright action on the part of most beneficiaries' in exploiting their former monastic estates for building purposes, and the influence that this had on the planning of the country house.[14] In general it was the more powerful men, and those officials who played a leading part in the actual process of dissolution, who were the first to make use of the new opportunities for building provided by the alienated ecclesiastical property. Although it was always an expensive option, some were brazen enough to convert the monastic church itself to domestic use, as for example at the Augustinian priory of Mottisfont in Hampshire where Lord Sandys divided the nave horizontally and added brick wings shortly after he acquired the property at the dissolution. Also in Hampshire, Thomas Wriothesley, Earl of Southampton, had adapted and completed his work on the Premonstratensian abbey church of Titchfield as early as 1542, while in Wiltshire, Sir William Sharington began his alterations to Lacock Abbey shortly after 1540, although in this case he demolished the church first. However, Richard Rich, Chancellor of the Court of Augmentations, who was granted the Augustinian priory of Little Leez in Essex as early as the spring of 1536, incorporated part of the nave in the great hall, which he began to build almost immediately.

Some of the early builders with monastic sites, however, perhaps daunted by the sacrilegious implications of using the church for secular purposes, preferred to incorporate only the domestic buildings and offices. Somerset used part of the buildings of the Bridgettine convent at Syon, while Sir John Thynne incorporated a part of the house of the Austin canons at Longleat.

John Cheney, who was granted a lease of Harrold Priory in Bedfordshire, in 1537, the year after its surrender, seems to have done little beyond simply adapting the buildings to basic domestic use. Despite the erection of a new house in the early years of the seventeenth century, the monastic buildings were still standing in 1614, when they were described as 'the auncient mancion howse of the said Priory or Mannor of Harrold with the outhowses thereunto belonging'.[15]

An early thirteenth century capital which survived the remodelling of Mottisfont Abbey by Lord Sandys in 1536–40.

Titchfield Abbey, Hants., as remodelled by the Earl of Southampton in 1538–42 (Anthony Quiney).

Leez Priory, Essex, remodelled by Lord Rich after 1536.

A number of the owners of dissolved monastic land seem to have been reluctant to build on their new sites. No doubt this was partly the result of caution bred by an uncertainty about the future course of the religious settlement. It was only the most confident who were prepared to indulge in large capital expenditure on land which might eventually be restored to the church. The potency of a basic religious faith, and the fear of committing sacrilege, must also have played a significant part. In the early years after the dissolution, it was just as common for monastic buildings to be used as a source of material for buildings being erected elsewhere. Sir Thomas Kytson, whose house at Hengrave in Suffolk was nearing completion by the time of the dissolution, was buying ex-monastic stone as early as July 1535 from Bromehill Abbey in Norfolk.[16] In 1536 and 1537 he bought additional stone from monastic sources at Ixworth and Thetford in addition to lead and iron from the former and from the Benedictine abbey at Bury St Edmunds. Nicholas Bacon, in addition to the monastic materials already existing on the site of the abbey hunting lodge which he purchased at Redgrave, also used stone from Ixworth and Bury and, after the act of Edward VI ordering the removal of altars from parish churches, he used the 'Altur-stones' from the four local churches of which he was patron.[17] John Hynde built the kitchen range of Madingley Hall, Cambridgeshire, in the 1540s, of stone from Anglesey Abbey which he had been granted at the dissolution.[18] But even the re-use of monastic materials elsewhere seems to have been met with a certain amount of reluctance on the part of many of the new owners, and often a generation elapsed before they fully exploited the assets that they had acquired at the dissolution.

With the death of Mary and the accession of Elizabeth, the holders of monastic lands probably felt secure in their possessions for the first time. In addition, having paid off the purchase price of the land, they were able to consider further capital expenditure in the form of building. It is only in the 1570s and '80s that the full

The church at Buckland Abbey, Devon, converted to a house by Sir Richard Grenville in the 1570s.

effects of the dissolution of the monasteries on building activity is apparent, and it is surely more than coincidence that it was in these same years that the strong incentives to build already noted were growing in intensity. It is possible to see the late exploitation of monastic property as just one of the effects of this powerful social trend, but this would be an incomplete reading of the situation. Some of the beneficiaries of the dissolution were indeed conserving their monastic resources against a time when they might wish to build. In 1574, Edward Paston of Binham Priory, Norfolk, for example, refused Nathaniel Bacon stone from the priory to help in the building of the neighbouring Stiffkey Hall, on the grounds that he was possibly going to use it for a new house for himself.[19] But on the whole, the evidence that remains suggests that for many builders the impropriety of putting former ecclesiastical possessions to secular use, and the lingering uncertainty of their tenure, meant that they were prepared to wait for a period before beginning to realize their potential. Often the property was sold or had passed to later generations before it was exploited, and it is not unreasonable to suggest that this further transaction helped to free it from the inhibitions arising from its religious associations. Buckland Abbey in Devon had been granted to Sir Richard Grenville in 1541, but it was his grandson, another Sir Richard, who carried out the conversion of the church into a domestic dwelling in the 1570s. Eastbury in Essex was a demesne tenement of Barking Abbey before the dissolution. In 1539 it was granted to Sir William Denham, who continued the lease on the farm that Nicholas Stoddard had taken out with the Abbess of Barking in 1543, and it was only after 1557 when Clement Sysley had bought the property from Denham's son-in-law that a new house was built on the site.[20] When considering houses occupying former monastic sites, it is significant that many were not begun before the last quarter of the sixteenth century and some, such as Trentham Hall, Staffordshire, were not built until well into the seventeenth century.

CHAPTER 3

Design and Designers

Once a site had been settled upon, the appearance and planning of the new house could be addressed. Unfortunately the surviving evidence relating to the processes of design and the role of the designer in the sixteenth century is of a very fragmentary nature. Few of the building accounts even mention the subject, and in order to draw tentative conclusions it is necessary to refer to more circumstantial evidence, such as contemporary correspondence and literary references, and to the few facts that are known about the lives of the individual craftsmen themselves. What is clear is that the architect, in Sir Nikolaus Pevsner's definition,

> one who plans buildings as opposed to one who executes them, and furthermore one who plans with a view to aesthetically as well as functionally satisfactory results, as opposed to one who concerns himself only with the technical requirements of building – in short, the architect as opposed to both the mason and the builder[1]

hardly existed in the sixteenth century.

In the latter part of the century the word 'architect' is encountered with increasing frequency, but it is used in a vague and imprecise way. James Baret, in his *Alvearie or Quadruple Dictionarie* of Latin, Greek, French and English, published in 1580, translated the word as 'the maister mason, the maister carpenter, or the principall overseer and contriver of any work'. In its Latin form, the word 'Architector' is sometimes found in English medieval accounts, with a meaning considerably removed from its later sense. Salzman gives examples of it being used to mean thatcher or tiler,[2] and in the fifteenth-century accounts of St John's Hospital at Winchester it was applied to ordinary carpenters.[3]

In England the intellectual basis of Renaissance architecture was not fully appreciated before Inigo Jones, and even then, as a result of the prevailing political climate, it was confined to a small group immediately surrounding the Court. The sixteenth-century approach to Renaissance architecture was to treat it as a conceit, a new fashion, to be grafted on to the indigenous building tradition. For a brief period around the middle of the century a small number of public men, all connected in some way with the Duke of Somerset, showed indications of a deeper understanding of the architectural implications of the Renaissance, but their influence was small and of too short a duration to have any radical effect

John Shute's First and Chief Groundes of Architecture, *published in 1563.*

on the development of the English architectural tradition. Somerset's brother, the Duke of Northumberland, went so far as to send one of his household, John Shute, to Italy, 'there to confer wt the doinges of y skilful maisters in architectur, & also to view such auncient Monumentes herof as are yet extant'[4] but, as far as it is known, Shute was never given the opportunity to design any buildings on his return. The derivative treatise on architecture that he published in 1563, the year of his death, although significant as the first English architectural book, is also noticeably reticent about contemporary Roman architects and architecture, and contains little that could not be gleaned from the existing continental architectural books. On the title page of his book, Shute styled himself 'Paynter and Archytecte', but this latter title was probably more a wishful reference to his Italian experience than an exact statement of his accomplishments.

Another early use of the word 'architect' was by Sir Thomas Smith who, in his will of 1576, left £20 to Richard Kirby, his 'chief architect'.[5] Smith, one of the men associated with Somerset, was a scholar of considerable reputation. His interest in classical architecture, stimulated by his foreign travels as ambassador to France and his service with Somerset, is reflected in the six separate editions of Vitruvius that he owned. Of all the men surrounding Somerset, Smith was the most intellectually able, and the one with the greatest first-hand knowledge of Renaissance ideas, but his use of the term 'architect' was more a demonstration of pedantic scholarship than an accurate description. Richard Kirby was strictly an artisan who can be identified with the Richard Kyrbe employed by Sir Thomas Kytson as a mason and bricklayer at Hengrave Hall, Suffolk, in 1537.[6] The overall supervision of the work at Hill Hall was carried out by John Dighton, Smith's household steward.[7] It was in a similar academic fashion that another craftsman, Ralph Symons, was described in the inscription to his portrait which hangs in Emmanuel College, Cambridge, as 'architecti sua aetate peretissimi'. Symons always called himself 'freemason'[8] and although he is known to have made drawings for King's College and St John's, and provided a model for the hall of Trinity College, his work on St John's, which is the best documented of all his Cambridge work, was clearly undertaken in accordance with the detailed instructions of the College.[9] He also apparently took part as a working craftsman, for he was said to have lost the use of one of his hands as a result of an accident during the course of the building.

At the University of Oxford the title of 'architect' was used in an equally loose way when John Bentley was described as 'architectus peritissimus' of the Schools and Thomas Holt was also called 'scholarum publicarum architectus', although it seems that if any single person provided the design it was John Akroyd, who was merely described as 'chief builder'.[10] Akroyd, however, had previously been called 'the architect' of the new quadrangle at Merton College for which he had contracted to 'be the stone mason' in January 1609.[11]

Ralph Symons, freemason, fl. *1585–1605* (The Master and Fellows of Emmanuel College Cambridge).

The word 'architect', as used at Oxford and Cambridge and elsewhere, seems to have had the general meaning of supervisor of the works, rather than implying the designer of the building, and it was in this sense that Sir John Strode wrote that his new buildings at Chantmarle 'are so fitly adjoyned to the old buildings by the care & direcion of old Gabriell Moore (a skilful architect)', who, he adds, was employed 'only to survey & direct the building to the forme I conceived & plotted it'.[12] A similar meaning was probably intended when Robert Liming was buried at Blickling in Norfolk in 1628 and the parish register recorded that he was 'the architect and builder of Blicking Hall', and even the inscription on Robert Smythson's tomb in Wollaton Church that he was the 'Architect and surveyor unto the most worthy house of Wollaton' was probably originally of little greater significance.

However, even though the term 'architect' was loosely used in the sixteenth century, with a meaning that was not synonymous with that which it has now, many of the men to whom it was applied were clearly able to make designs. But most of them remained 'mechanics', employed as wage earners and servants of the builder. None of them had the social status that a few years later was to enable Nicholas Stone to write of 'my very nobell frind Ser David Cuningham',[13] or which allowed John Webb in the 1650s to sign his letters to Sir Justinian Isham, for whom he had designed an addition to Lamport Hall, Northamptonshire, 'Your assured ffreind'.[14] Almost without exception their background was that of a working craftsman, and although a few rose in the social hierarchy, none was in a position to address his employers on anything approaching equal terms. This social inequality did not, of itself, mean that their role as designers was necessarily

Blickling Hall, Norfolk.

unimportant. But it did mean that their opinions, apart from those concerned with purely technical matters, were wholly subservient to those of the men who employed them. Even now, of course, architecture invariably represents a compromise between the opinions of the architect and the wishes of the client; but it is a compromise that recognizes the architect's professional knowledge and skill in interpreting the client's desire. In the sixteenth century, however, the inferior social status of the craftsmen designers meant that their influence was of importance only in so far as their patrons or employers allowed it to be. In some cases they were given considerable freedom, but more frequently the personal interest taken by the builder strictly curtailed their independence in matters of design.

The influence of the craftsmen was further restricted by reasons related to the development of architectural design in England. Connected as they were with opportunities of education and patronage which were largely outside the craftsman's own control, they had a crucial influence on the shape in which the architectural profession eventually emerged in the latter half of the seventeenth and the early part of the eighteenth century, and explain the reasons why it is necessary to consider at such length the processes by which designs were made in the sixteenth century. In the medieval period considerations of defence and safety acted as powerful limitations on the development of domestic planning and, generally speaking, it is only in architectural and constructional details that any clear sense of change can be discerned. Development in roof forms and window mouldings, for example, took place within a continuing craft tradition, and innovations, perhaps initiated by a few master craftsmen, were quickly absorbed into that tradition and spread by example from their place of origin throughout the rest of the country.[15] Medieval architectural styles are primarily identified by their details of form which, as John Harvey has written, were 'matters governed by the individual knowledge and creative imagination of the designer (the master craftsman), and not a part of the programme (plan, proportions, functional arrangements) largely or even wholly dictated by the needs of the client'.[16] It is on these grounds that the same author has been able to describe many of the medieval master craftsmen as architects.[17]

The changed social circumstances of the sixteenth century already discussed had far-reaching effects on country house building. The greater freedom in planning that resulted and, more especially, the gradual infiltration of Renaissance ideas in decorative detail, radically altered the importance and position of the craftsmen designers. The ultimate inspiration for the 'new fashion' in design was foreign. Originating in Italy and France it reached England mainly via the free interpretations of the Low Countries. Initially, access to it was to be had in two ways: by travel into Europe where the buildings themselves could be seen, or by study of the growing number of illustrated treatises and books on architecture. With the sole exception of John Shute's *The First and Chief Groundes of Architecture*, first published in 1563, the latter were exclusively foreign. A number of the more architecturally advanced buildings of the sixteenth century were built for men who had spent some time abroad. Sutton Place, Surrey, one of the earliest country houses to exhibit Renaissance forms of ornamentation, was built by Sir Richard Weston who had travelled in France and accompanied Henry VIII to the Field of Cloth of Gold in 1520. Hill Hall, Essex, was built by Sir Thomas Smith who had been ambassador to France between 1562 and 1566. John Trevor, the builder of the symmetrical Trevalyn Hall in Denbighshire, had spent several periods abroad in the service of Sir Thomas Sackville who was on a grand tour in France and Italy from about 1563 to 1566, and who was again in France in 1568 and 1571.

Some of the men who had been on the continent also took the opportunity to build up their own libraries of books on architecture. Smith possessed over twelve important architectural books, including six editions of Vitruvius. Others, who had no first-hand experience of continental buildings themselves, were able to learn about Renaissance architecture from books imported from Italy, France, Switzerland, Germany and Flanders. The first illustrated edition of Vitruvius had been published in 1511. The highly influential volumes of Serlio had come out in 1537, 1540, 1545, 1547, 1551, and, posthumously, in 1575. Hans Blume's book on the Orders was published in Zurich in 1550. Vredeman de Vries brought out his *Architectura* in Antwerp in 1563, and his *Compertimenta* in 1566. The number of other foreign books known and used by Englishmen, such as those of Philibert de l'Orme, du Cerceau, Palladio, Alberti and Wendel Dietterlin, are far too numerous to mention in detail. At home the popularity of Shute's thin volume on architecture led to subsequent editions in 1579, 1580, 1584 and 1587. At least some knowledge of architecture must have formed part of the education

The title page of the 1619 edition of Serlio, once owned by Inigo Jones.

of most gentlemen. William Harrison, for example, knew the names, if not the writings, of 'old Vitruvius, Leo Baptista, and Serlo'.[18] However, the interest of some of these men in the theory of architecture was far from superficial. A number of notable builders of the period are known to have had extensive architectural libraries, and there were undoubtedly others. Sir Francis Willoughby of Wollaton owned books by Vitruvius, du Cerceau and Alberti, and the library of Sir Thomas Smith has already been mentioned. Although large for the period, it cannot compare with the remarkable collection made by Sir Thomas Tresham who owned well over twenty books on architecture, including three editions of Vitruvius, two editions of Serlio, one of which was the lavishly illustrated Frankfurt edition of 1575, Alberti, de l'Orme, de Vries, Shute, Palladio, and several other treatises, including those of du Cerceau, Labacco and Cataneo.[19] Henry Percy, 9th Earl of Northumberland, is known to have owned at least a dozen books on architecture,[20] and several of his contemporaries clearly possessed similar collections. Lord Burghley asked Sir Henry Norris to send him de l'Orme's *Nouvelles Inventions* from Paris, and almost certainly owned other architectural books, for his interest, and that of his son Robert, in the subject led them to make a large collection of original plans and designs.[21] In the seventeenth century, Sir James Pytts, finishing the house that his father had begun at Kyre Park, Worcestershire, is known to have owned at least one 'book of Architecture';[22] and in November 1619 Sir Roger Townshend purchased three (unnamed) 'bookes of architecture' for £1.13s.6d. in preparation for commencing work on his new house at Raynham in Norfolk.[23] Sir Roger Pratt later testified that Townshend owned 'many Italian and French books of Architecture'. Similarly, Sir Edward Peyto, who built a classical watermill and a circular windmill in 1632 on his estate at Chesterton in Warwickshire, possessed a notable collection of architectural works.[24] As the ownership of books expanded in the late sixteenth and early seventeenth centuries, the subject of architecture was clearly well represented.

However, for the majority of artisans, the methods of access to Renaissance designs presupposed opportunities which were ordinarily denied them: the ability to travel abroad, and the formal education necessary to enable them to read and understand the essential source books. John Shute, of course, had been sent to Italy by Northumberland specifically to meet Italian architects and to study their buildings, but insufficient is known of his background to enable him to be confidently called an artisan. The only documented example of a craftsman being taken abroad by his master, presumably to study building, occurs well into the seventeenth century, when Sir Roger Townshend took his leading mason with him to the Low Countries for much of the summer of 1620 shortly after he had begun to build Raynham Hall, Norfolk.[25] Nicholas Stone, the son of a Devonshire quarryman, had lived and worked in Amsterdam between 1606 and 1613, but he initially went abroad simply to work for Henrik de Keyser, the Dutch mason and sculptor, and probably without any strong educational motives.[26]

The majority of building craftsmen were illiterate and thus unable to acquire a knowledge of the principles governing Renaissance design from literary sources. However, James Pytts lent his 'book of Architecture' to his mason, presumably to

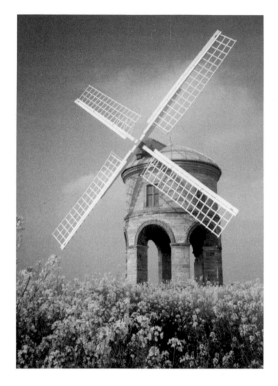

Chesterton Windmill, Warwickshire.

enable him to make copies from the illustrations that it contained.[27] In a similar fashion, some the plans in the Thorpe collection were traced from Palladio's *Quattro Libri*[28] and others were based on du Cerceau,[29] while the drawings of Robert Smythson include copies of details from Vredeman de Vries which he used in his designs for Wollaton Hall, Nottinghamshire.[30] In addition, the sketch books compiled by the Abbott family of Devon plasterers show that relatively provincial craftsmen could be fully conversant with current books of engravings.[31]

But the true basis of Renaissance architecture was intellectual, and an understanding of its rules necessarily implied book-learning. It was one thing to copy attractive motifs from the published wood-cuts, but it was something else entirely to make truly classical designs. Even men from craft backgrounds who managed to give themselves some sort of education such as John Thorpe, who prepared an unpublished translation of du Cerceau's *Leçons de Perspective Positive*, certainly knew some Latin and possibly also translated Hans Blume's book on the Orders for the English edition of 1608,[32] showed little appreciation of the philosophy underlying the writings of the foreign architects. They looked to them for inspiration in forms, but they were ignorant of – or unsympathetic to – the spirit that they represented. In this respect it is unfortunate that insufficient details of the life of Robert Stickells have survived, for he seems to have been a craftsman with greater intellectual aspirations than the majority of those connected with the building industry at the time. The editors of the 1631 edition

The Chateau de Madrid as published by J. Androuet du Cerceau in le Premier Volume des Plus Excellents Bastiments de France *(1576) and copied by John Thorpe* (by courtesy of the Trustees of Sir John Soane's Museum).

Method of framing a floor, illustrated in Serlio's Tutte l'Opere d'Architettura.

of Stow's *Chronicle* even called him, posthumously, 'the excellent Artichect [sic] of our time'. Employed in a lowly administrative position in the Office of Works for much of his working life, he also had a reputation as an engineer, worked as a joiner, and called himself freemason in his will. He is known to have supplied designs to private builders on at least two occasions – in 1605 to Sir Thomas Tresham for Lyveden New Build and in 1613 to Sir Edward Pytts – and probably designed a lodge in Richmond Park for the Crown.[33] His knowledge of classical architecture was competent, as a letter to Tresham noting the importance of modular proportion in the Doric Order, and a drawing by him, also among the Tresham papers, illustrating a method of floor-framing based on Serlio, make clear.[34] What is more noteworthy, however, is that his approach to architecture was, at least in part, intellectual and that he attempted to record some of his ideas on the subject in a literary form. The two obscure and confused papers that he left behind, although firmly in the Elizabethan architectural tradition in their conclusion that 'the bookes of Architecktur, Victriuces [Vitruvius] and all thoos Authers have taken the wronge sence; their inwardes woorkes ar dead when theay shewe no lif in ther outward doweings',[35] are important as the only known commentary on architecture as a serious art by a working designer before the middle of the seventeenth century. But Stickells is, at best, a shadowy and elusive

Robert Stickell's design for the base of the lantern at Lyveden New Build (redrawn from the original in the British Library).

figure who, lacking the consistent private patronage accorded to men such as Smythson, never achieved social status, and his contemporary importance was probably slight.

With these few notable exceptions, it follows that the one social class that had the ability and the opportunity to study the sources was the country house builders themselves, and consequently that their potential influence on the design of their own houses was of great importance. In practice, their contribution was limited by the amount of time they were prepared to devote personally to acquiring a knowledge of architecture or to attending at the building site, and by their technical ability to represent their ideas on paper in a form capable of being translated into a three-dimensional building. Even William Cecil, who was accustomed to making sketches to guide his workmen at Burghley, was capable of making only the most elementary drawings, as a letter that he wrote to Sir William More at Loseley in 1591 indicates:

> Sr, this other daie at my being at Guildford, when I vewed the Priorie theare, I made a rude trick thereof, in a manner of a platt wth mine own hand, at wch time a servant of yors or Mr Wolleis beinge present, and being a mason, as I remember, he offered him to mak the same more parfitlie.[36]

Only a minority of the builders, men such as Sir Thomas Smith and Sir John Thynne, were willing to subject themselves to the discipline necessary to achieve sufficient expertise in the new architecture. The majority of them, as has already been suggested, thought of it as just another fashion, like the changing modes of dress or the contemporary enchantment with the 'ingenious device', and in consequence never had more than a superficial understanding of the principles governing Renaissance design. As a result, they delegated much of their personal responsibility for their buildings to the men who were in charge of the day-to-day supervision of operations and to the leading craftsmen who carried out the actual works. They were, of course, subject to the will of the builder at every stage of the enterprise, but in many cases they seem to have been given considerable freedom of action within this framework, as when Nicholas Stone noted in his agreement with Sir Robert Pye for two chimney-pieces, in 1636, 'he hath left the forme to my decresion and allso the prices he referes himself unto me'.[37] In this way the design of many sixteenth-century buildings emerged as a combination of a number of influences ranging from the builder, through the supervisor or surveyor, to the more important artisans. Of these, the will of the builder was ultimately of sole importance, but the influence of the others in interpreting and arriving at the final form was far from neglible.

To understand how the buildings of the sixteenth century were designed it is therefore necessary to consider in closer detail these influences. As suggested above, that of the builder was potentially the most important. The surviving correspondence of Sir John Thynne gives some indication of the technical expertise and personal involvement that must have been characteristic of many of the builders. During the 1540s while work was going ahead on the first Longleat, Thynne was actively following his career as secretary to the Duke of Somerset. Yet, although he was rarely in Wiltshire to see his building at first hand, he kept a tight control over all its aspects by means of a comprehensive correspondence with his steward, John Dodd, and by regular consultations with his leading craftsmen who were sent up to London for that purpose. No matter how busy his public life kept him, he always found time to write at length to Dodd, sometimes as often as five times a week, and occasionally two letters in one day. Thynne, as befitted a man who administered Somerset's extensive buildings works, was well aware of many of the practical aspects of building, and his correspondence contains many references to minutiae, such as the necessity for seasoning wainscot and even the method of doing it.[38] Thynne's close personal involvement in every stage of the building is clear enough, but his exact role as a designer is rather more obscure. For the first Longleat at least, there seems to have been little more than a vague overall conception of what the completed building would look like. Individual features were considered as they arose. In April 1547, when he wrote asking for Berryman, his chief mason, to be sent to London, it was 'to thentent I may show him my pleasur in suche things as I wolde have doon this year at my house'.[39] When he arrived, early in May, Thynne explained to him his 'mynd for the two gats at the lane ends to be mad and for altering my chamber over the parler and for the paving of my haull, chapell, buttry, pantry, kchyn, larder and other placs'.[40] The instructions that Thynne gave were probably only verbal, and it is likely that they were not very precise. It was Berryman's responsibility to use them as a basis for drawings which were then submitted back to Thynne. Thus in June 1547 Thynne wrote to Dodd, 'when Beryman may have tyme I wold be glad to have the plat of myn outhouses and the rest set forth as hertofore I did apoint & to be sent unto me'.[41]

The key to the whole problem of design is related to the question of just how much freedom the craftmen were given in making such drawings. Thynne's instructions extended as far as writing that

> I wol have my walles from the first floor upward to be but two briks length in thicknes as hertofore I declaryed to Berryman,[42]

but this was only a technical specification which, although important, still left open the matter of appearance. On occasion Dodd was forced to write to Thynne for more precise advice about decorative treatment,[43] and the craftsmen themselves were not afraid to suggest alterations to approved plans. In 1546 Dodd reported to Thynne that

> The oppenion of William Love ys that the Chapell weyndow in the South syde wh you appointyd to stand will do very yll and much disvigure yor building wherfore he wold you shuld make an new weyndoo ther wh coold be but litle more cost to you.[44]

Love, who was the principal mason before the employment of Berryman, went on to advise several other changes in the design and made drawings incorporating his suggestions. However, the conclusion of this part of the letter, 'that your pleasure may be knowen herin with sped or ells he must go in hand according as you last appointed', makes it clear that these were only suggestions, and that the initiative for any action remained solely with Thynne. Unfortunately, it is no longer possible to see whether he followed Love's advice. It can only be assumed from the manner in which the advice was offered that it was not considered out of place for the leading craftsmen to prepare amendments to the schemes which were drawn up for the builders. Indeed, the initial schemes seem to have been so vague and lacking in essential detail that it would be surprising if they were not modified in the light of practical, and even aesthetic, conditions apparent only on the site.

Thus, the design of the first Longleat emerges as the rather flexible result of a continuous dialogue between Thynne and his master mason, with the initial and dominant impetus coming from Thynne but with his ideas being rendered into practical form and to a certain extent modified by his principal executive.

The evidence from Thynne's three later remodellings of Longleat is not as informative on questions of design, for with the fall of Somerset in 1549 and his ultimate execution in 1552, Thynne retired from public life to live on his estates, and consequently it was no longer necessary for him to correspond at length with his building officials. What evidence that remains, however, suggests that the basic methods of design differed little from those used in his earlier building, although his employment of more competent and sophisticated workmen led to a corresponding increase in their influence over his ideas. By the time that the design for the fourth and final Longleat had been evolved, the French sculptor Allen Maynard and the English mason Robert Smythson were able to claim that 'the ordenanse therof cam frome us'.[45] Maynard's known skill in the classical idiom and Smythson's genius for architectural composition, convincingly documented in his drawings and embodied by his later buildings, are reason enough to accept the substance of their claim, but it is difficult to conceive of their achievement without the inspiration and drive of Thynne. There can be no doubt that he remained the dominating influence, in the words of William Darell, the builder of Littlecote, 'musing many a tyme with great care and now and then pulling downe this or that parte . . . to enlardge sometyme a foote, or some few inches, upon a conceyt, or this or that man's speech, and by and by beat downe windows for this or that fault here or there'.[46] Longleat is a monument to his fanatical search for perfection, and its final form is as much a result of Thynne's own architectural development as it is a testimony to the skills of the exceptional artisans that he employed.

The evidence from Longleat, especially the correspondence of the early years, is the most important surviving source for the processes of architectural design in the sixteenth century. Other sources are more fragmentary, but the overall picture that they present differs only in detail from the situation at Longleat. In general the differences seem to result from the individual personalities and capabilities of the men involved, and in this context it is significant that some builders who were unable to make their own designs turned for help to friends of their own social class rather than to their building craftsmen. Thus, the lodge that Sir Richard Carew built on the fishpond at Antony in Cornwall was 'devised for me by that perfectly accomplished gentleman, the late Sir Arthur Champernowne'.[47] In 1569 the Duke of Somerset's son, Lord Hertford, applied to Sir John Thynne for architectural advice, and was supplied with plans provided by Thynne with the help of his leading craftsmen.[48] Sir Nicholas Bacon sent his son, Nathaniel, plans for Stiffkey that he had drawn himself,[49] while another of his sons, Francis, made a note in his notebook on 28 July 1608, 'To give directions of a plott to be made to turn ye pond yard into a place of pleasure and to speak of them to my L. of Salisbury'.[50] Salisbury's father, Lord Burghley, had been consulted in a similar manner by other builders. In August 1577, for example, the Earl of Shrewsbury wrote to him, 'I have sent Greves a plat of a front of a lodge that I am building, which, if it were not for troubling your Lordship, I would wish your advice theron'. Nathaniel Bacon, in turn, provided constant advice to his grandson, Sir Roger Townshend, in the early stages of the building of Raynham Hall from 1618 onwards and he supervised the work when Sir Roger was away from the site.[51]

Many builders were forced by domestic reasons or by the demands of public life to spend long periods away from the sites of their new buildings, and as a result of these prolonged absences their administrative officers were given an opportunity to exercise an influence on the design of the building. In Cecil's absence, Peter Kemp, his steward at Burghley, played an important part in modifying the design for the house. Usually he sought Cecil's permission before

The hall chimney-piece at Longleat carved by Allen Maynard.

he actually initiated any changes, as for example, in October 1561 when he wrote, 'I thynck it good to lay the flore over the pantre somwhat hegher than the flore of my ladyes chamber', and added, 'I pray yo let me know yor plesur herin shortlye becawse it is in hande precelye'. But on occasion, he carried out alterations on his own initiative, and merely reported to Burghley, 'I do not prosed after the tryck I sent yo'. Although in May 1562 Kemp was prepared to support his suggestion for lowering the ground table of the loggia with his own aesthetic judgement that it would be 'no fowle syght but rather a bewte', the alterations that he was concerned with were mainly restricted to those necessitated by practical considerations which became apparent as the building progressed, and his recommendations were taken in consultation with the leading craftsmen.[52] The influence of the steward seems to have been similarly restricted to practical matters in the realization of the design on the other documented building projects of the period. Such considerations could have a profound effect on the final form of a building, but they were largely accidental, and in the majority of cases only resulted in minor modifications to the external design. The conscious designing role of the steward must have been considerably less important than that of the principal craftsmen.

Although the position of the builder as the predominant influence on architectural design has been strongly emphasized, it is equally clear that the working craftsmen's advice was crucial in the drawing up of a feasible scheme. In 1610 when the Earl of Salisbury was building at Cranborne, William Arnold, his master mason, was said to have spent 'every day a whole houre in private with him' discussing the work.[53] It has already been noted that the craftsmen at Longleat had regular consultations with Sir John Thynne and that the vagueness of his instructions must have transferred some of the responsibility for detailed designs to them.

Sometimes the advice was sought of craftsmen who were unconnected with the work. In a letter of May 1617 to the master of Jesus College, Cambridge, Fulke Greville wrote from London,

> Let me entreat you farther, that a Plat may be drawne to shewe the contrivinge of the lights, stayre-cases, chimneyes and studies, with the severall charges of them, to the intent, that by conference with some workmen here, I may see if anie thinge may be altered for the better.[54]

Although these independent craftsmen were called upon only to make revisions and comments to an existing scheme, the practice was only a short step away from commissioning them to initiate completely new schemes. From the end of the sixteenth century there are indications of the emergence of a class of professional designing craftsmen who, although still connected with the mechanical side of building, were of sufficient reputation as designers for their services to be occasionally used in that way. Many smaller country houses, outside those of the nobility, were probably partly designed by these working craftsmen. These were men such as the mason Walter Hancock, of whom the parish register of Much Wenlock, Shropshire, stated when recording his burial in 1599 that he was skilful in the art of masonry, in setting of plottes for buildinges & perfominge of the same, ingravinge in ale blaster and other stone or playster, and in divers other giftes that belonges to that art as dothe appeare by his workes which may be seene In divers parts of England & Walles, moste sompteouse buildinges, moste stately tombes, moste curyouse pictures . . . .[55]

It is clear from this that not only did Hancock have a local reputation as a designer in several allied fields, but that he was also a building contractor and working mason as well. He is known to have worked as a craftsman on Condover Hall, Shropshire, and to have been employed by Sir Francis Newport, the builder of High Ercall and Eyton-on-Severn. Newport thought highly of him, for he recommended him to the bailiffs of Shrewsbury in 1595 as a suitable mason for their new market house,[56] but it was for his expertise as a workman that he was praised and not his skill as a designer. His ability in the 'setting of plottes for buildinges' was, no doubt, considered to be an exceptional talent for what was a basic part of his craft.

This talent was recognized in other craftsmen, but the designs that were commissioned from them were subject at every stage to the ideas of the builder; and most builders were sufficiently conscious of architecture to impress their

The banqueting house at Eyton-on-Severn and Shrewsbury Market House, two of the 'sompteous buildinges' where Walker Hancock performed his 'art of masonry'.

personalities on their own buildings. This is apparent from the various stages in the construction of Kyre Park, Worcestershire. In 1588, on one of his visits to London, Sir Edward Pytts employed John Symonds, one of the leading craftsmen of the Royal Works, to make a design for the house. Shortly afterwards Pytts changed his mind about the design and paid 'the same John Symons for drawing my latter platt according to my newe purpose'. Symonds never visited the site, and his only connection with the building was in providing designs, but it is clear that these designs were no more than an articulate expression of Pytts' requirements and ideas. Pytts, having completed the first stage of his building in 1595, again turned to a well-known craftsman in 1611 when he decided to enlarge the house. In the early summer of that year he

> brought John Bentley, freemason, from Oxford (where he wrought the newe addition to Sir Thomas Bodleigh his famous library) with me as I came from London to Kyer,

but Bentley's contribution was strictly defined. He was

> to take instructions from me by veinge the place to draw me a newe platte for I altered my first intent because I wold not encroche on the churchyard.

'The newe addition to Sir Thomas Bodleigh his famous library' which commended the freemason John Bentley to Sir Edward Pytts of Kyre Park.

At the same time Pytts brought Thomas Sergianson, a prominent mason from Coventry, to discuss the design, 'though he died nothing in that busynes'. Despite the comparatively large sums that Pytts spent on architectural advice, there can be little doubt that he exercised a very strong influence over the layout and appearance of his building. Symonds and Bentley were something more than draughtsmen, but they were certainly not the architects of the house in any modern sense of the word. His patronage of outstanding workmen and the regularity with which he altered his original schemes was not confined to his country house, for an entry in his accounts of December 1613 notes £3, 'Paid to Stickles of London for drawing the platt of my house anewe'. This was almost certainly Robert Stickells, and probably refers to Pytts' London house for which he had previously paid £2 to Francis Carter for an elevation.[57] Carter was a leading London carpenter who in 1614 was to become Chief Clerk of the King's Works.

Stickells is known to have provided designs for Sir Thomas Tresham, and it is conceivable that he had other patrons among the gentry. Other prominent employees of the King's Works, such as Robert Adams and Lawrence Bradshaw, were certainly commissioned to make designs for private builders or for the private use of public figures.[58] However, their relationship with their patrons probably differed little from that of Sir Edward Pytts and the various craftsmen that he consulted. It is possible that in time these superior craftsmen eventually would have achieved the function and status of architects. Nicholas Stone, although primarily a monumental mason, achieved this status through the patronage and friendship of his noble clients. But the majority of craftsmen-designers failed to rise above the artisan level. Instead, social and intellectual trends in the early part of the seventeenth century resulted in the emergence of a new type of architectural designer. Once the principles of Renaissance thought had been accepted, it was possible to design a building based on the rules and proportions of the classical orders, without any previous experience of the practical aspects of building; and this divorce from the mechanical side gave the study of architecture the status of a 'liberal' art. As such it was a pursuit fit for a cultured gentleman, and it was even socially acceptable for the gentry to practise it professionally, much as younger sons might have gone into the law or commerce. This social acceptance was a gradual achievement, and it was not won without a struggle. The well-known dispute between Inigo Jones and Ben Jonson was partly a reflection of this battle for the status of the architect.[59]

The ability of Jones, and the opportunity provided by his royal patronage, were influential factors in gaining respectability for the architect, but the notion also received indirect support from men of higher birth who were beginning to consider intellectual as well as aesthetic aspects of architecture. In 1570 Henry Billingsley's translation of *The Elements of Geometrie of Euclid* had been published with a long introduction by John Dee, in which Dee asserted the primacy of architecture over all the other mathematical arts and carefully explained the Renaissance idea of the architect. He supported his argument with long quotations from Vitruvius and Alberti, and lamented that few 'in our days' had attained the excellence of a true architect.[60] Dee's remarkably advanced views seem to have met with little immediate response and it was only with the following generation that they began to gain acceptance. By 1607 James Cleland in *The Institution of a Young Noble Man* was able to refer to 'the principles of architecture: which I think necessary also for a gentleman to be known', and by 1660 John Webb confidently stated that 'most gentry in England at this day, have some knowledge in the Theory of Architecture'.[61]

In terms of literary output, this certainly seems to be true. Francis Bacon published his essay on architecture in 1623, and according to Aubrey was 'the chiefest architect' of his own house near St Albans.[62] Sir Henry Wotton, who was ambassador in Venice and later became Provost of Eton, published an influential treatise on the *Elements of Architecture* in 1624. Sir Balthazar Gerbier, the courtier and diplomat, was designing buildings for the Duke of Buckingham in the 1620s, and in 1662 published *A Brief Discourse Concerning the Three Chief Principles of Magnificient Building*, following this with *Counsel and Advise to all Builders . . .* in 1663.

The discovery of the noble qualities inherent in the pursuit of architecture had its first practical flowering among the gentry in the person of Sir Roger Pratt. Although he did not design his first building until 1650, his career and his writings are important as an indication of the new influences on English architecture that were emerging during the seventeenth century. Born in 1620, he was educated in a way common to many of his social class. In 1637 he matriculated at Magdalen College, Oxford, and in 1639 entered the Middle Temple. Between 1643 and 1649 he travelled extensively in Europe, visiting Italy and France and building up a considerable library of architectural books. The year after his return to England, he designed and supervised the building of Coleshill House, Berkshire, for a relative, Sir George Pratt. This was his first architectural work, and he was assisted in his task by the advice of Inigo Jones. It established a reputation for Pratt as an architect, and in 1662 he was simultaneously engaged on Kingston Lacy, Dorset, for Sir Ralph Bankes, and Horseheath, Cambridgeshire, for Lord Allington. In 1664 he began work on Clarendon House in Piccadilly for Edward Hyde, the Lord Chancellor. In 1667 Pratt inherited the family estates at Ryston in Norfolk and, apart from serving as one of the commissioners for rebuilding the City of London, retired to live the life of a country gentleman. In 1669 he rebuilt his own house. As far as is known, these five buildings represent his total output over a period covering almost twenty years. Their influence on domestic design was considerable, but they are equally important in showing that the actual practice of architecture was a suitable occupation for a gentleman by the time of the Restoration.

The attitude of Pratt's class to the process of architectural design is summarized in the unpublished advice to prospective builders that he wrote in 1660:

First resolve with yourself what house will be answerable to your purse and estate, and after you have pitched upon the number of the rooms and the dimensions of each, and desire in some measure to make use of whatsoever you have either observed, or heard to be excellent elsewhere, then if you be not able to handsomely contrive it yourself, get some ingenious gentleman who has seen much of that kind abroad and been somewhat versed in the best authors of Architecture: viz. Palladio, Scamozzi, Serlio etc. to do it for you, and to give you a design of it in paper, though but roughly drawn, (which will generally fall out better than one which shall be given you by a home-bred Architect for want of his better experience, as is daily seen) . . .[63]

It is probable that Pratt originally intended to publish his writings as an architectural treatise, and in that context this passage is clearly an advertisement for his own services, but it is also revealing as a statement of architectural practice in the middle of the seventeenth century. The initiative was still necessarily with the builder, but the accomplishment of his requirements was, if not by himself, by one of his social equals. It was not simply a coincidence that many of the leading Restoration architects were of gentle birth. Hugh May was the seventh son of John May, esq., and cousin of Baptist May, the Keeper of the Privy Purse to Charles II,[64] and Roger North was the sixth and youngest son of Dudley, 4th Lord North.[65] The craftsmen designers remained, and continued to be patronized, but the gentleman architect had taken his place alongside them, and it was his taste that was to be the predominant factor in English architecture during the following hundred years.

However, the importance of the gentlemen architects before the Restoration must not be over-emphasized. The seeds of their eventual predominance were certainly present in the years before 1640, but, considered on a quantitative basis, the most influential men were still the craftsmen designers. It remains now to explain how they gained their knowledge of architectural design, and how the styles that they helped create were disseminated thoughout the country.

Masons are known to have made collections of drawings and plans, which they valued highly, and which they bequeathed with care to their sons or apprentices along with the tools of their trade.[66] Cornelius Brownstone, for example, a master mason of Westminster who died in 1562, left John Sparrowe, his apprentice, 'all my plats and patterns', as well as his tools, a gown, and a compass.[67] Sometimes the collections of drawings were divided up. William Cure bequeathed some of his 'paternes' to his son-in-law, and the remainder he gave to his son, Cornelius.[68] The Thorpe collection probably began in this way, for it contains a number of early plans and elevations that John Thorpe inherited from his mason father, Thomas Thorpe. The plans are all of upper floors, and only one of them has a corresponding elevation. The missing plans and elevations were presumably divided up among John's brothers.[69] The collections were not confined simply to buildings that the craftsmen themselves had worked on but included notable buildings, both ancient and modern, that they had seen and wished to remember. On a journey from the Midlands to London in 1609, Robert Smythson made a large number of drawings, including a plan of King's College chapel, Cambridge, and details of the window tracery in Henry VII's chapel in Westminster Abbey, as well as a plan and elevation of the New Exchange in the Strand which had only been opened in April of that year.[70] He recorded what was new and what was of interest to him among the old. What he saw had little influence on his own work

The New Exchange in the Strand drawn by Robert Smythson on his visit to London in 1609 (British Architectural Library, RIBA, London).

The panelling in the Great Chamber at Theobalds drawn by John Smythson on his way to London in 1618 (British Architectural Library, RIBA, London).

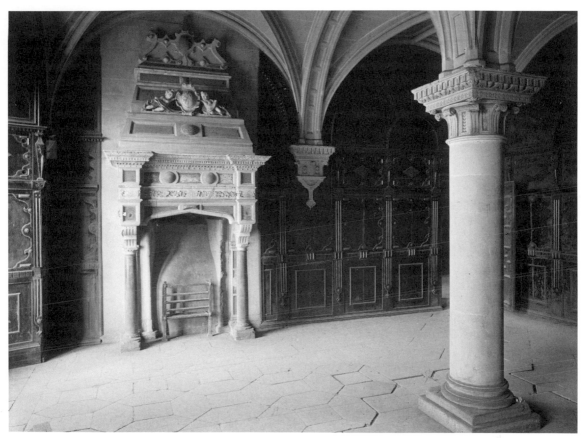

Panelling in the Pillar Parlour, Bolsover Castle, Derbyshire (RCHME © Crown Copyright).

for he was already an old man when he visited London and he was to die shortly afterwards. But when his son John made a similar trip ten years later and drew details of many of the newest buildings in London, including the incomplete Banqueting House; the 'Holborn gables', the 'pergulas', and the rustication that impressed him were incorporated in his subsequent work at Bolsover Castle. On his way to London, John had also visited Theobalds and made a drawing of some of its panelling, which he later used as a model when he came to design the panelling of the Pillar parlour at Bolsover.[71]

The Smythson drawings are just such a collection as were mentioned in the wills of other masons. The presence of three late gothic drawings suggests that, as with Thorpe, Robert Smythson inherited the nucleus of the collection. They passed from Robert to his son, John, and from him to his grandson. They were used by the family as a working tool, and they show the Smythsons' readiness to absorb and use new influences. They demonstrate in a particularly clear way how the novel architectural features in one part of the country rapidly spread to other areas. It is reasonable to assume that the collections by other craftsmen were used in a similar fashion as practical working aids, and were equally influential in the dissemination of new ideas.

The craftsmen's first-hand architectural knowledge was also on occasion supplemented by information derived from books. A number of masons certainly possessed their own books, and bequeathed them along with their drawings and tools. The will of John Multon dated 1546 mentions 'all my portatures, plaates, books with all other my tooles and instruments,'[72] and William Cure left all his 'books, paternes, toles and other necessaryes' to his son in 1579.[73] At his death in 1634, John Smythson had a room in his house at Bolsover which he called the library,[74] and examples have already been mentioned of drawings in both the Thorpe and the Smythson collections which were direct copies from architectural books, and of craftsmen being lent such books by their employers. Undoubtedly it was the illustrations rather than the text which were of most practical use to the craftsmen, and they used them simply as pattern books. The books of Serlio, de Vries, and Dietterlin were particularly influential on architectural decoration in the late sixteenth and early seventeenth centuries. The first recorded English pattern book was *A Booke of Sundry Draughtes principally serving for glasiers: and not impertinent for plasterers, and gardiners; besides sundry other professions* by Walter Gedde. Published in 1615, it contained over a hundred different designs, and was specifically intended as an aid to the craftsmen, 'Knowing the expert maister is not unfurnished of these usuall draughts, though each workeman have not all of them'.

However, although printed books played a demonstrable part in the creation of a national architectural style, they were only rarely a direct influence. More frequently they provided a basic inspiration on which the craftsmen exercised their individual ingenuity, and the process of adaptation was further extended by the widespread practice of seeking inspiration from existing buildings. This has already been inferred from the drawings in the Smythson collection, and can be supported by a large body of documentary evidence. Several surviving building contracts specify that certain features were to be modelled on those of other buildings, and there is evidence, other than the well-known letter of 1603 from Northumberland to Cecil already quoted,[75] of builders going to see comparable buildings before starting work themselves. Usually they were accompanied on these journeys by their principal craftsmen. Before commencing the design of the hall at Trinity College, Cambridge, in 1604, the supervisor of the works took his carpenter to London where they paid a total of 10s. to 'Carpenters and keepers of dyvers Halles to viewe and measure them', and the hall that they built was of exactly the same dimensions as the hall of the Middle Temple.[76] In the early years of the seventeenth century Northumberland had his carpenter, John Dee, compile 'A Booke of Computations for Buildings', which included a collection of notes on the size of the main rooms of ten important contemporary buildings.[77] The principal carpenter working on Little Saxham Hall, Suffolk, in 1505, was instructed to copy the roof of Horham Hall, Essex, which had only recently been begun, and the same carpenter was also sent to look at the house in Tower Street, London, of the wealthy merchant Angel Donne. In 1506, when the bricklayer was preparing to make a bridge across the moat, he had his expenses paid 'to se a

Horham Hall, Essex (RCHME © Crown Copyright).

bruge in Essex', and similarly in 1509 the glazier, like the carpenter four years previously, was sent to Horham before starting the chapel window.[78] Sir Roger Townshend visited a wide range of contemporary buildings in the company of his principal mason when the design for Raynham Hall was in a formative stage in 1619. He seems to have been particularly interested in the work of Inigo Jones, but he also inspected more conventional houses such as Wimbledon, Hatfield and Audley End.[79]

Another factor leading to the diffusion of general stylistic trends throughout the country was the itinerant nature of many of the craftsmen's jobs. The maxmium length of time that they might be employed on one house was something like ten years. They would then have to move on elsewhere to find employment, and they would take with them their own particular skills and stylistic preferences. Sometimes they continued to find employment within the same locality, and in consequence it is possible to find particular architectural motifs confined to a relatively small area. In Essex, for example, the fireplaces in at least three houses built in the latter half of the sixteenth century showed a curious variation on what was basically a common type. They were all of freestone with moulded jambs and flat pointed arches, but their shoulders were cut obliquely in a straight line rather than the usual rounded form, and the decorative frieze of alternate circles and lozenges filled with roses and leaves was substantially similar in each case. The houses for which they were made, Eastbury House, Little Belhus, and Albyns, were all within a few miles of each other, and it seems reasonable to postulate that the fireplaces were all executed by the same craftsmen.

Often, however, they travelled a considerable distance to their next job, as when many of the Longleat craftsmen moved on to Wollaton in Nottinghamshire in 1580, and their influence was inevitably felt over a wide area. In combination with the practice of viewing other buildings as models, it meant a rapid diffusion of architectural innovations throughout the country.

With each successive job the craftsmen themselves were open to new influences from their fellow craftsmen, the majority of whom had invariably been employed on a number of different houses. The later work of Robert Smythson probably owes much to the experience that he gained from working with the gifted French mason and carver, Allen Maynard, and similarly Smythson must have inspired and influenced some of the craftsmen working for him at Wollaton, Worksop and Hardwick. They, in turn, eventually moved to other building sites where their accumulated experience was able to influence, and be influenced by, other craftsmen. In this way the peculiar conditions of English house design, whereby considerable freedom was given to the executive craftsmen, produced a distinct national architectural style which was freely eclectic and basically unsympathetic to the rigid rules of the Court architecture of Inigo Jones. By the end of the seventeenth century, however, the gentlemen and professional architects had imposed their intellectual discipline on the mainstream of English architecture. The basis for this domination had been laid down by the end of our period.

CHAPTER 4
Methods of Undertaking

In 1681, Sir Christopher Wren advised the Bishop of Oxford that 'There are 3 ways of working: by the Day, by Measure, by Great',[1] an observation that could have been made with equal validity for the period with which this study is concerned. Even before the detailed planning of the building enterprise had begun, the builder had to decide which of these three main methods should be employed. The administrative arrangements depended on the decision, as did, indeed, the extent to which the builder was likely to be personally involved in the work.

The most direct method of organization was for the builder to supply all the materials, arrange for their transport, provide the necessary equipment and accommodation for the working of the materials, and to hire the workmen by the day to work on the materials in accordance with instructions. This method of direct labour, which was synonymous with Wren's first category of working, was suited to projects where the size of the labour force was comparatively small and could be effectively administered by a household official, or even the builder in person. The building of many country houses was organized by this method throughout much of the sixteenth century, but by the early seventeenth it had been largely superseded by other methods and its use was mainly confined to minor repair work on existing fabrics. Although it was a practical system for smaller houses, such as William Dickenson's house at Sheffield in 1575 and Dr William Griffith's house at Carreglwyd, Anglesey, in 1636, or for those houses which were built over a long period of time with a small labour force, such as Old Thorndon Hall, Essex, the builders of larger houses were faced with considerable administrative problems. Responsible officials were necessary to arrange for the supply, carriage, storage and issue of materials and equipment, the workmen had to be closely supervised and instructed, their attendance checked and their wages paid. Sometimes they had to be accommodated and fed. Accounts had to be kept, and the whole enterprise had to be co-ordinated and planned so that it would not be delayed through lack of labour or materials, or so that expenditure did not exceed the money currently available. All these functions were capable of being discharged by one or two household officials on smaller country house sites, although it must have meant an inconvenient disruption of their regular duties, but where the labour force was large and the materials had to come from varied and sometimes more distant sources, the number of administrative officials invariably increased and the overall supervision became more complex. The

Hengrave Hall, Suffolk. Begun by direct labour but completed by contract (RCHME ©
Crown Copyright).

majority of country house builders only built one house in their lifetime, and the
temporary establishment of a large administrative body must have seemed
impractical to many of them. Thus in 1530, when Sir Thomas Kytson decided to
enlarge Hengrave Hall, Suffolk, he partly abandoned the direct labour method
that he had employed exclusively for the previous five years and put much of the
new work out to contract.[2] Similarly, Sir John Thynne contracted with a mason
for a large new range at Longleat in 1559 rather than undertake it on the direct
labour basis that had characterized his earlier, less ambitious, work.[3]

The Royal Works were predominantly carried out by direct labour, but the
existence of a permanent administration and the power of coercion available to
the Crown enabled it to overcome the problems that the system posed to the
private builder. The Duke of Somerset, who was building Somerset House, Syon
House, and Wulfhall between 1548 and 1551, in addition to work at Banbury,
Odiham, and Reading, also largely relied on direct labour, but his powerful public
position allowed him to set up a works organization similar in its hierarchical
complexity to that of the Royal Works.[4] There were not many other private
builders who possessed such power or who built in so many different places
simultaneously, to justify such an organization. By the time that the Cecils came
to engage in their building activity in the late sixteenth and early seventeenth
centuries, the advantages of the contract and piece-work systems had been
recognized, and their reliance on direct labour was correspondingly less.

One way by which a builder could avoid the administrative problems of the direct labour system was to let the work out to contract. This might take the extreme form of an agreement with a single contractor for a complete building, under the terms of which he would be responsible for every aspect of the work in return for a fixed sum of money agreed in advance. Such was the contract made by Joseph Wood with a builder for a new wing to his house in Illingworth, near Halifax, in April 1648.[5] Most private builders, however, seem to have been reluctant to make comprehensive contracts for all the work with one contractor, and generally they entered into separate agreements with contractors from each of the crafts involved. Certainly there were craftsmen who were capable of organizing a complete building enterprise, such as the glazier Bernard Dinninghof, who offered to undertake all the work including the provision of designs for the rebuilding of Sheriff Hutton Castle, Yorkshire, in 1618, for Thomas Lumsden,[6] and Gilbert Wigge and Ralph Symons, who built the second court of St John's College, Cambridge, between 1598 and 1602, for £3,605,[7] but the opportunities available to them on country house sites were almost invariably restricted to their own trades. Thus Henry Hunt, an Arundel freemason, was contracted with Giles Garton for all the stone and brickwork for a new wing to his house at East Lavington, Sussex, in 1586, but no mention was made in the contract of the necessary carpentry, plastering and roofing, which were clearly arranged by separate agreements with other craftsmen.[8] Hunt subsequently executed both the stonework and the woodwork for the Earl of Northumberland's new work at Petworth in 1595 and 1596, but again the plumbing, plastering, and tiling were undertaken by other craftsmen.[9] Most of the surviving contracts relate to a single craft, such as that made by Roger Palmer, mason, for 'alle . . . masones worke' on Mount Edgcumbe, Cornwall, in 1547,[10] or William Spicer's contract at Longleat in 1559 for

al maner of stone worke, fremasonrye, Rowmasonrye and bryckworkes.[11]

Sometimes the responsibility was divided even further by making separate contracts with different craftsmen within the same trade. This seems to have been the case at Thorpe Hall, Northamptonshire, in 1653, when two masons agreed to make the thirty-eight windows for the house, the other masonry presumably being carried out by other masons,[12] and at Harrold House, Bedfordshire, between 1608 and 1610, where the fabric was executed by Thomas Harris, and some of the decorative masonry by Thomas Grumbold.[13]

Within the framework of the system there was a great deal of variety between the conditions attached to individual contracts. Most contractors bound themselves to provide all the necessary labour, and, in view of the difficulty that some builders experienced in attracting sufficient skilled workmen, it is possible that this was one of the prime motives for many builders to place part of their work in the hands of contractors. Materials were sometimes provided by the contractor and sometimes by the builder. Generally, masons supplied their own stone, while the builder arranged for the supply of more easily accessible materials, such as timber or sand for mortar. Clearly, where the builder was able to provide the necessary material from his own estates, he did so. Most contracts contained a clause specifying the date by which the work was to be completed, but it was only rarely that this was accompanied by a penalty for failure. In the few cases where a specific financial penalty was written into the contract it usually represented a substantial proportion of the total payment, as at Illingworth, Yorkshire, where the house was to be finished by 31 May 1649 under penalty of £2 on the £11 contract,[14] and at Hengrave Hall, Suffolk, in 1538, where Sir Thomas Kytson retained £20 out of an agreed sum of £116 until the joiner had successfully completed his contract.[15] In addition to a time limit for the completion of the work, some contractors also entered into a maintenance clause for the restitution of any defects that might appear within a specified period of time. Thus Henry Hunt was to be responsible for the new wing at East Lavington for twelve months after its completion.

In 1662, Sir Balthazar Gerbier warned that if

> Builders put their design to Master Workmen by the Great, or have it Wrought by the Day, either the Workmen will over-reach themselves, or the Builder will be over-reached.[16]

Although he perhaps over-emphasized the financial danger to the builder of the direct labour system, adequate costing of the proposed work must have been a very arbitrary process when it was to be carried out either by contract or direct labour, and a number of contractors seem to have got into difficulties through unrealistic estimating. Spicer failed to complete his contract at Longleat, although he received most of the money for the work, and at Hardwick Old Hall, Derbyshire, Ralph Smith, a carpenter who had contracted to make the roof of the Great Chamber in March 1589, was forced to mortgage his house to Bess of Hardwick in November of that year, when another craftsman was paid for the 'bargain that Smith should have done'.[17] The massive contract undertaken by Wigge and Symons for St John's College, Cambridge, was completed within the specified time, but 'in a manner ruinous to the undertakers and not over advantageous to the college'. A year after the end of the work, the contractors were still in debt to the college to the sum of £200, and a further £156 had been spent by the college in repairing some of the defects already apparent in the building.[18]

The builder was unlikely to obtain adequate recompense from a contractor who had got into financial difficulties during the course of the work, and he invariably had to make alternative arrangements at his own expense for the completion of the contract. A similar situation was liable to arise should the contractor decide to leave the site before the work was finished. At Ashley Park, Surrey, in the early seventeenth century, the builder contracted all the carpentry for the house with a carpenter called Parsons for £90. Having received £78.16s.0d. on the contract, Parsons suddenly disappeared and the builder was forced to employ direct labour for the remainder of the work at a cost of £36.3s.0d. A contract which had been originally estimated at £90 therefore cost the builder £114.19s.0d. before the work was successfully completed. John Coke experienced similar difficulties with his

Hall Court, Herefordshire, where the building programme was disrupted by a dispute with the masons.

contracting masons at Hall Court, Much Marcle, Herefordshire, in 1608 and 1609, when they walked out and severely disrupted the building programme.[19]

Another deficiency inherent in the contract system was the possibility that the chosen contractor should prove incompetent. If his shortcomings did not become apparent until the work was well under way, the builder was faced with a considerable dilemma as to the action he should take to remedy the situation. Whatever he did invariably involved additional expenditure before a satisfactory result was obtained. The problem is well illustrated by the documentation for Little Saxham Hall, Suffolk, where Thomas Lucas contracted most of the bricklaying and masons' work to John Bronde, a mason of Bury St Edmunds. The contract of 1505 for the foundations of one range seems to have been successful, for in the following year Bronde was given a further contract for completing that range and building another. By 1508, however, the standard of his work was giving cause for concern and various parts of it were given to other craftsmen to complete. Lucas seems to have been reluctant to dispense with Bronde, possibly because of a shortage of masons in the area, but, significantly, the fresh contracts that he negotiated with him in 1508 and 1509 for further parts of the work were to be overseen by Thomas Loveday, the principal carpenter on the site. This attempt at increased supervision failed to have the desired effect, and in June 1510 Bronde was dismissed with 'moch of his said werk . . . not yet fynyshed'. Lucas then had to send to Cambridge to get workmen who were sufficiently competent to complete the work, and four years later parts of the building erected by Bronde were already being strengthened.[20]

The third method of working mentioned by Wren, payment by measure, overcame many of the problems associated with contract work. Instead of agreeing a lump sum for the whole, the work was broken down into all the separate operations which could be measured, and payment was made to individual craftsmen on the basis of a fixed price for each completed unit. This method was highly sensitive to the unequal degrees of skill and complexity involved in the different tasks carried out by the workmen. For example, the masons' work on the bay windows at Longleat in 1572 was paid for at the rate of 5s. for each of the capitals, 3s. for the base of each pilaster, 2s. the foot for the cornice, frieze, and architrave, 1s. a foot for window-heads and sills, 10d. the foot for jambs, 6d. a foot for the base of the pedestals, and 11s.6d. for every hundred feet of plain ashlar work.[21] Even the price for more straightforward work could be varied according to the stage that the building had reached. At Chantmarle in Dorset, the masons were paid 1s.8d. a perch for the walling of the ground storey, and 2s. a perch for the two upper storeys; the increased rate being due to the greater difficulties of working at a height above the ground.[22]

Although some work had been undertaken on a piece rate basis earlier in the century – for example, at Chevet Hall, Yorkshire in 1516[23] – it was only in the latter part of the sixteenth and the early part of the seventeenth century that it became the predominant method of working for most country house builders. By using piece rates, a much more acceptable pricing of the proposed work could be achieved, but it presupposed fairly sophisticated skills in calculating realistic rates. Consequently the acceptance of the system was accompanied by the emergence of specialized building surveyors, generally from craft backgrounds, who began to play an increasingly important role in the administration of building projects. Such a development corresponded to the more professional approach characteristic of the later country house builders.

The advantages of the piece rate system were not confined to financial considerations, or to the more specialized administration that it required. The craftsmen could be left to carry out their work as instructed with the minimum of supervision, and it was to their own advantage to do it as speedily as possible, for they were not being paid on a time basis. A close check could be made on their workmanship at the measuring stage, and as each workman's responsibility tended to be smaller than the collective responsibility of a contractor, the consequences of incompetence on the part of any one man could be effectively minimized. Similarly, the sudden departure of a craftsman was less likely to disrupt the work than if he were the sole contractor. The system also retained to the builder some of the personal control of the work that would have been sacrificed had he placed substantial parts of it in the hands of a contractor.

In practice it was rare for all the workmanship on a country house to be undertaken at piece rates. Some tasks, such as labouring and the routine craftsmanship, were more easily arranged on a direct labour basis, and as the numbers involved were smaller than if the whole enterprise had been carried out in this way, they could be easily administered. All the more skilled craft work, however, was invariably paid for at piece rates from the late sixteenth century onwards. The method by which the building of Trentham Hall, Staffordshire, was undertaken in the 1630s can be taken as a typical illustration of the situation by the end of the period.[24] All the labouring, apart from such easily measured work as trenching, was paid for by the day. All the joinery, glazing and smiths' work were at piece rates. The masonry and carpentry were predominantly carried out at piece rates between 1630 and 1635, although a small group of masons also worked at day rates during the same period. By 1636, the shell of the house had been largely completed, and the three masons and a similar number of carpenters who remained on the site for the final three years of the account were employed at day rates. Clearly during the early years of the enterprise all the specialized work had been executed at piece rates, while a nucleus of direct labour had been employed on the more routine tasks.

Sir Christopher Wren, in advising the Bishop of Oxford on the three ways of working, suggested that 'the best way in this business is to worke by measure'.[25] Twenty years earlier, two other prominent practitioners in the building world had pointed to the same conclusion. In 1663, Sir Balthazar Gerbier wrote

It is best for the builder to . . . have his works done by the Rod or square,[26]

and in 1665, Sir Roger Pratt offered similar advice at greater length when he commented:

If workmen be employed by the day, they will make but small haste to finish the building. If agreed with all by the great as to all particulars; which can judiciously be done by none, but those who understand the difference of work, which is very great; the difficulty is very much in making the bargain, which they still will be trying to break either in the matter or manner of their working, finding out all evasions which if prevented by Articles, as they should, and our near inspection their next slight is then to surprise you in the measure, and if this take not, then at last in casting up the several particulars.

All which are to be avoided by making them work by the great, distinguishing fully as to their materials and work, bargaining for all sorts that can any ways be done, though some of it probably never to be used, making the most comprehensive articles that may be to oblige to a certain time the avoiding of all unexpected and lurking demands, the terminating the manner of the measure, and to be perfectly versed in the ways and frauds of it.[27]

During the previous hundred years many country house builders had discarded the traditional direct labour and contract systems and had adopted this way of working. However, its acceptance had been dependent upon the emergence of a new type of building worker who was sufficiently literate to be able to understand and administer the sophisticated techniques of quantity surveying.

CHAPTER 5

The Administrative and Executive Labour Force

One of the most crucial steps in the building operation was the assembling of an adequate administrative and executive labour force. The efficient conclusion of the operation depended on the competence of the officials appointed to oversee the everyday details and to co-ordinate labour and materials so that the most economical use was made of the available resources. On most houses of any size it was physically impossible for one person to discharge all the administrative duties alone, and in practice the responsibility was usually divided up between a number of officials. When the house was relatively small and the builder was not active in national affairs which might take him away from the site for months at a time, he often administered the building himself, with the assistance of his relatives or his household steward. Francis Farrar, who built Harrold House in Bedfordshire between 1608 and 1610, was helped at various periods during the course of the building by his son-in-law, Thomas Boteler, and his brother-in-law, Humphrey Layton. Farrar acted as his own clerk and accountant, and supervised the administration on the site, but the purchase of materials and the arrangements for their carriage from distant sources such as King's Lynn and Northamptonshire was carried out as the occasion required by Boteler or Layton.[1] Farrar's administrative task was eased by employing his craftsmen by contract, and consequently the only part of his labour force which required close daily supervision was his labourers, and they never numbered more than fourteen in any one week. At Carreglwyd, Anglesey, in 1636, the total daily labour force never exceeded twenty-four, and was administered by the unnamed brother of the builder, Dr William Griffith, with the assistance of the principal mason. Griffith, a distinguished lawyer and Chancellor of the Dioceses of Bangor and St Asaph, was presumably too busy to concern himself directly with the management of his own affairs, for the same brother who drew up the building accounts was also responsible for the running of his household and his estate.[2]

It was only possible for the builder to administer his own building operation personally when the scale of that operation was relatively small, and when he was free from other commitments. Sir Edward Pytts, who in June 1611 began to make additions to his house at Kyre Wyard under his own supervision, was made Sheriff

Harrold House, Bedfordshire (now demolished) (RCHME © Crown Copyright).

of Worcestershire for the following year, and consequently in November he was forced to lay off part of his weekly labour force 'till my Sheriff work ended'. He then appointed a Staffordshire mason as 'Survey'r of the work & workmen', leaving his bailiff, Richard Turvill, free to undertake the remaining administrative duties.[3] This was a practical and common solution to the problem of organizing the building operation on many of the smaller sites. The principal officer of the gentleman's household was, after all, trained in the administering of his master's estates and in the handling of his finances, while a leading craftsman could usually be trusted to supervise other workmen and to ensure adequate standards of craftsmanship. It was an administrative system that was adopted for many of the documented buildings throughout the period, and can probably be considered the most common method of organization used by those men who only engaged in building once in their lifetime. The houses that they built were governed more by considerations of domestic comfort than by a desire for ostentatious architectural display, and consequently it was the simplest and most effective method available to them. It was not necessary to look further than their own household for a

Kyre Park, Worcestershire, as remodelled in the eighteenth century.

general administrator and clerk of the works. The work that they would be called upon to do could be seen as little more than an extension of their normal duties. If a competent craftsman was known, or could be found, he could be expected to be capable of dealing with the more specialized and technical side of the operation and would be able to advise on sources of labour and materials.

Documentation for the early part of the sixteenth century is relatively sparse, but the system was employed by Thomas Lucas, Henry VIII's Solicitor-General, for his house at Little Saxham, Suffolk, in 1505–14[4] and by Sir Thomas Kytson for the early years of his work at Hengrave, *c.* 1525–9.[5] It had been used in the medieval period, and was employed by Lord Hastings for Kirby Muxloe Castle in 1480–4.[6] Nicholas Bacon used it in a modified form for the modest house that he built at Redgrave in 1545–54. Instead of a household servant, he used a distant relative, John Bacon, to oversee his work with the assistance of the London mason John Gybbon.[7] Sir John Petre's work on Old Thorndon Hall, Essex, between 1575 and 1595, was organized by his steward, John Bentley, and a carpenter called Walter Madison.[8] Neither Madison nor Gybbon worked as craftsmen on the buildings that they supervised, but normally the supervising craftsmen were expected to execute work associated with their craft in addition to their other duties.

Generally the principal craftsman was subservient to the administrative officer, and usually was only concerned with matters confined to the technical side of the work. He was responsible to him for his actions, and seldom deputized for him when he was absent. Sir Thomas Tresham's building operations, for example, were administered by his steward, George Levens. He was away from the site for the week ending 22 June 1595, but his duties were temporarily carried out by another official of Tresham's household, John Androweson, and not by any of the principal craftsmen.[9]

The administrative combination of household servant and craftsman was occasionally employed on some of the more extensive building projects. The construction of Hill Hall, Essex, was organized for Sir Thomas Smith by John Dighton, the 'steward of his house', who was assisted by Richard Kirby, a bricklayer, as 'his chief architect'.[10] The work carried out at Syon House, Middlesex, for the 9th Earl of Northumberland, was supervised by a gentleman officer of his household, Christopher Ingram, assisted by John Dee, Northumberland's estate carpenter.[11] The organization for the early years at Longleat was administered in a similar fashion, with the main burden falling on Sir John Thynne's stewards, John Dodd in the 1540s and 1550s, George Walker in the early 1560s, and Thomas Vyttery.[12]

However, it was usual to employ a more diverse and sophisticated method of administration for buildings of this size. The necessity for a greater division among the administrative staff is well illustrated by the situation at Hengrave, Suffolk, between 1525 and 1540. In the early years the work was carried out by a small local labour force employed on a daily basis, and mainly using local material. The annual expenditure was modest, only exceeding £200 in 1527 and 1528, and the work was effectively administered by one man, Thomas Shethe, who seems to have been a member of Sir Thomas Kytson's household. In 1530 Kytson's plans for his house seem to have undergone a radical revision, and the scale of his building works was considerably increased. Only in 1532 did the annual expenditure again fall below £200, and by 1535 it was running at the level

Hill Hall, Essex.

of £350 a year. Although the local labour force continued to be employed, the majority of the work was now being executed by outside contractors who were responsible for providing their own workmen. A new administrative officer, Robert Watson, was appointed to be 'ruler of bylding', Shethe's duties now being confined to the boarding arrangements for the outside workmen and supervising the carriage of materials. Watson made all the contracts, both with the craftsmen and for materials. He travelled extensively to Brandon, Cambridge, and even as far as London seeking materials and craftsmen. He made regular trips to London to consult Kytson, and also supervised those workmen who were working away from the site cutting timber and digging stone. On the regular occasions when he was absent from Hengrave, Shethe deputized for him. In addition to Watson and Shethe, and the principal contractors responsible for their own men, a separate clerk of the works was also employed to check the workmen and draw up the accounts. This position was filled up to March 1535 by Myllis Mason, the parson of the neighbouring village of Flempton, and subsequently by Thomas Aldaye.[13] Mason was presumably employed on the clerical work because of his literacy, in the same way that the accounts for Chatsworth and Hardwick Old Hall in Derbyshire were kept by Bess of Hardwick's chaplain, the Revd Henry Jenkins.[14]

Some powerful magnates, such as Somerset in the middle of the sixteenth century and Robert Cecil at the end of the century, built several houses and were occasionally engaged in work simultaneously on more than one site. It was necessary for them to have separate administrative staffs at each of their sites, but these were generally subordinate to a central group of officials who co-ordinated the works as a whole and ensured that there was no unnecessary duplication of resources at a local level. In this respect their organizations were analogous to the Royal Works, and, on occasion, the officials that they used for their private purposes were employees of the Works. Between 1548 and 1551, Somerset employed separate supervisors, comptrollers and clerks at Somerset House in the Strand, Syon House, Odiham and Reading, in addition to the agents and bailiffs in charge of the preparations for his projected house at Great Bedwyn in Wiltshire. But all these officials reported to, and took instructions from, a few of Somerset's principal stewards, in particular Sir John Thynne, and the financing of all works was centrally controlled by John Pickarell, the duke's cofferer.[15] Only in this way was it possible for the work on the various scattered sites to proceed unhindered by the absence of a key official who might be attending another site, yet by having a centralized administration ensure that materials, money, and men were directed to the place where they were most needed.

Robert Cecil, who in the opening decade of the seventeenth century was building Salisbury House and the New Exchange in the Strand, Hatfield House in Hertfordshire, and Cranborne Manor in Dorset, was faced with similar problems of organization, and he solved them in a fashion that was broadly the same as that employed by the Duke of Somerset fifty years earlier. His three sites in or near London were under the financial control of Thomas Wilson, one of the leading officers in Cecil's household. Wilson was resident in Salisbury House, where he was able to supervise closely both operations being carried on in the Strand, and he rode down to Hatfield at frequent intervals to arrange for the financing of the work there. He also dealt with the carriage of material, much of which was shipped through London. For the early work at Salisbury House between 1599 and 1602, Cecil engaged the comptroller of the Royal Works, Simon Basil, as the site administrator. Basil was subsequently employed as general administrator and technical adviser for the New Exchange and Hatfield House. The everyday supervision on these sites was carried out by men with craft backgrounds who, in addition to their organizing ability, were capable of dealing with technical problems arising on the site. Cecil filled this post for the New Exchange with another employee of the Office of Works, William Southes, who was later to be appointed Master Mason at Windsor Castle. At Hatfield he employed a relatively unknown carpenter, Robert Liming, whose administrative and designing talents were subsequently patronized by Sir Henry Hobart for his house at Blickling in Norfolk. Wilson and Basil formed the nucleus of the centralized co-ordinating administration, playing an active role on all three sites but leaving the close supervision in the hands of Southes and Liming and their subordinates.[16] Cranborne was a considerable distance from London, and consequently it was impractical for Wilson and Basil to pay close attention to the work there in person. They were able to arrange for the shipment of materials through London and to send money and men where necessary to Dorset, but for all practical purposes, the building was administered by William Arnold, a west-country mason whose reputation was such that he was known to Sir Edward Hext as 'the absolutest & honestest workeman in Ingland'.[17]

Cranborne Manor, Dorset (RCHME © Crown Copyright).

Although on the majority of major building works in the sixteenth century the supervisors with craft backgrounds were generally subordinate to the household and financial administrators, the latter part of the century saw the emergence of a small group of professional surveyors capable of directing the whole operation, and frequently employed as the principal administrative officer to whom all the other officials were responsible. Almost without exception these surveyors had originally been practising craftsmen or were descended from craftsmen. Their emergence, and the consolidation of their position in the seventeenth century, can be seen as a process of acceptance of the qualified building specialist, which was similar to that which took place with regard to the architect over the same period. They were men who were capable of mastering the more specialized administrative techniques demanded by the growing predominance of piece-work as the method of working, and who were knowledgeable about such diverse things as the current prices of materials and the sharp practices that could be perpetrated by deceitful workmen. Occasionally they were responsible for the preparation of the design in addition to their administrative duties, but in general they never achieved the status that was accorded to the gentleman-architect of the type epitomized by Sir Roger Pratt. They remained basically artisans and, with a few notable exceptions, their relationship with the builder was that of employee rather than adviser. During the period when their roles were evolving, the distinction between architect and surveyor was often very confused, but by the later seventeenth century it was possible to define more precisely their separate functions. To Sir Roger Pratt, the surveyor organized the everyday administration of the building in response to the instructions that he received from the architect who had designed it.[18] The surveyor was the agent who enabled the architect's intentions to be satisfactorily fulfilled. In essence it was the crucial intellectual and social distinction between the liberal and mechanical arts which had accompanied the development of the Renaissance in architecture throughout Europe.

In the absence of any information about the background of Robert Watson, the 'ruler of bylding' at Hengrave, William Spicer, the Somerset mason who had been employed at Longleat between 1554 and 1563, seems to have been one of the earliest examples of a craftsman employed to direct a building operation in the period with which we are concerned. He was clearly a man with exceptional organizing ability, for, within five years of beginning work at Longleat as a junior craftsman, he had been given a contract worth £300 to build all the new work begun in 1559, and in addition was appointed bailiff and rent collector of Thynne's manor of Lullington in Somerset.[19] His building contract was not a success, and in 1563 he left Longleat with much of the work unfinished. Whatever his shortcomings as a building contractor, however, his administrative ability continued to be recognized. A letter preserved in the archives at Longleat shows that by 1571 he was being employed by the Earl of Leicester in charge of the works at Kenilworth Castle where he was directly responsible for the provision of materials, the hiring of the workmen and the negotiating of contracts.[20] The tone of the letter suggests that his position was of more consequence than merely that of craft supervisor. He seems to have had direction of the whole enterprise, and his role was probably similar to that of the professional surveyors found later in the century. Spicer was to achieve even greater administrative distinction in subsequent years, being appointed Surveyor of the Queen's Works at Berwick in 1584 and Surveyor of the Royal Works in 1596.

Another craftsman, who had spent part of his early career as a working mason at Longleat, also became in later life a professional surveyor of building operations. Robert Smythson worked for Thynne for twelve years starting in 1568. He was employed as one of the two principal masons, and there are no indications in the very full documentation for the building that he took any part in the administration other than supervising the other masons in his own gang. He was, however, a workman of considerable experience and reputation. Before working at Longleat he had been employed by Sir Francis Knollys, the Vice-Chamberlain, and he was personally recommended to Thynne by Humphrey Lovell, the Queen's Master Mason. In 1575, while still at Longleat, he carried out work for Sir Matthew Arundell at Wardour Castle. On the death of Thynne in 1580, Smythson moved to the Midlands to work for Sir Francis Willoughby, where, as his tombstone records, he was employed as 'Architector and Survayor unto yee most worthy house of Wollaton'. The amount of mason's work actually carried out by Smythson was minimal. His principal job was to direct the building operation, and to prepare the designs in consultation with Willoughby. The status of his position is marked by the appellation of 'Mr' accorded him in the building accounts.[21] Smythson remained at Wollaton for the rest of his life, and after the house had been completed he seems to have been employed by the Willoughby family in a general administrative capacity connected with their coal-mining enterprises. During the same period, he continued to prepare architectural designs for other patrons, and to supervise some of the building operations of the Cavendish family. An entry in the Hardwick Hall accounts for 1597 refers to him as 'Mr Smythson the Surveyour' although the actual building works were supervised by John Balechouse, a painter of Dutch origin. By this date, Smythson was being assisted in his building activities by his son John who had initially been trained as a mason in the final years of the work at Wollaton.

In 1612, Sir Charles Cavendish began to build at Bolsover Castle, Derbyshire, and John Smythson was engaged to direct the work and supply the design. By 1615 he had become a permanent employee of Cavendish with the title of bailiff, and was concerned with the general administration of part of his estates. His son, Huntingdon, who succeeded him as bailiff to the Cavendish estates, also seems to have been responsible for the direction of the works at Bolsover in 1629–30. Unlike his father, there is no evidence that he was ever trained as a working mason. His marriage into a gentry family is probably a fair indication of the status that the Smythson family had achieved within two generations of their craft origins.

Craftsmen who had achieved positions of responsibility in the Royal Works were especially experienced in the directing of building operations. The Surveyor of the Works and the various master craftsmen were more concerned with the administration of the Works than with the actual practice of their trade. Despite the lack of any major building projects under Elizabeth, the Royal Works was the only body organized to provide a structured training in the specialized job of supervising a large building operation. It is therefore not surprising that the administrative experience of men trained in the Works was sought by private patrons for employment on their own projects. As has already been noted, Robert Cecil made extensive use of Simon Basil to supervise three important building operations early in the seventeenth century. His father, Lord Burghley, had used the services of Henry Hawthorne, Purveyor to the Royal Works, at Theobalds, and later extensively patronized John Symonds, another leading Works craftsman, employing him as surveyor in charge of all his London houses.[22]

Robert Stickells, who had been employed in the Works since the 1580s, was appointed by the London Grocers Company in 1591 to direct the work of wainscoting their hall,[23] and John Thorpe, whose early training had been as a clerk in the Office of Works, was paid £5 as 'surveir of ye contractinge' for supervising the erection of a gallery at Belvoir for the Earl of Rutland in 1625–7.[24] Nicholas Stone was another employee of the Works whose expertise was sought by private patrons. In addition to his flourishing private practice as a monumental mason, he was employed by the Earl of Danby in 1631 'to desine a new hous for him at Corenbury in Oxfordsheer and to dereckt the workmen', and later in the decade he was appointed surveyor of the building of the new Goldsmith's Hall, and superintended the additions to Tart Hall, St James's Park, for the Countess of Arundel.[25]

The majority of building surveyors who had been connected with the Works were based in London, but the provincial surveyors who were increasingly coming into prominence in the early seventeenth century invariably emerged from a similar craft background. William Arnold, for example, who had directed the works for Cecil at Cranborne in Dorset, and was employed in a similar capacity at Wadham College, Oxford, in 1610, and for George Luttrell at Dunster Castle, Somerset, in 1617, was a Somerset mason,[26] as was Gabriel Moore, who was employed by John Strode 'to survey & direct the building' of Chantmarle House, Dorset, in 1612.[27] Lawrence Shipway, who 'sett forward the worke' at Condover Hall, Shropshire, in the 1590s, had previously been employed as contractor for the Church of St Wilfrid, Standish, Lancashire, in 1582 and as the master mason working on the Shire Hall at Stafford.[28] Robert Liming, the carpenter who had been employed by Cecil at Hatfield, in 1588, acted as one of the principal contractors for Sir Henry Hobart on his new house at Blickling, Norfolk, between 1618 and his death in 1629, but he was also given the official title of 'his lordship's surveyor of the said worke' and received a daily wage of 2s. 6d. for his duties over and above his contract payments.[29] Insufficient biographical details survive for the majority of early seventeenth-century craftsmen, but what is known about men such as the masons John Chaunce and Ralph Symons[30] suggests that they, too, were often principally employed as administrators.

Once the builder had decided on the form of administration that he was going to adopt for his work, he was faced with the problem of assembling sufficient labourers and craftsmen to carry it out. The size of his executive labour force obviously depended largely on the size of the project and the speed with which it needed to be completed. Sir William More employed little more than a total of fifty workmen between 1560 and 1569 to build his house at Loseley, near Guildford. Although it was not a large house, it was sufficient to receive the queen on three of her progresses.[31] The accounts only survive for the last six years for Trentham Hall, Staffordshire, built for Sir Richard Leveson between 1630 and 1639; but during the period for which we have documentation, he employed a total of 156 workmen, and it was only during the last three years of the enterprise that his annual labour force fell below 100. It is difficult to know how many of these men were working on the site at the same time because much of the work was carried out at piece rates. However, the maximum number of workmen paid at day rates rarely exceeded thirty in any one week and it is reasonable to assume that the total weekly labour force was somewhere in the region of fifty men.[32] At the other end of the scale, Harrold House, Bedfordshire, was built between 1608 and 1610 with a weekly labour force of under twenty,[33] and the average weekly labour force employed at Carreglwyd, Anglesey, in 1636 was approximately twenty-four.[34] In general, few private building operations seem to have employed a weekly labour force much in excess of sixty men. A maximum of fifty to sixty workmen can be traced in the fortnightly accounts for the work at Bolsover Castle, Derbyshire, between 1612 and 1624,[35] while no more than sixty men were ever employed at one time by Sir Roger Townshend on Raynham Hall, Norfolk, in 1619–25.[36] Sir Thomas Tresham's weekly labour force working on the much smaller Triangular Lodge in Northamptonshire was usually fewer than forty workmen in 1594 and 1595, and had dwindled to well below twenty in 1597 when the building was nearing completion.[37]

In contrast, royal projects, especially those built during the reign of Henry VIII, were often constructed on a vastly larger scale and usually at a speed that was beyond the resources of the private builder. The number of workmen employed in September 1538 on the palace of Nonsuch was 516,[38] and we are told that over 2,000 craftsmen and labourers were engaged on erecting temporary buildings at Guisnes in 1520 for the meeting of Francis I and Henry VIII.[39] The labour force used to build the palaces of St James's, Whitehall and Hampton Court must have been of considerable proportions. Defensive works, naturally, had to be built with the greatest possible speed, and consequently they necessitated the employment of large numbers of workmen. Sandgate Castle, Kent, one of a number of south coast forts built in 1539 and 1540 in response to the invasion scare, took only eighteen

Loseley House, Surrey.

months to complete. At the height of the work, in May 1540, over 900 workmen were engaged on the site.[40] The employment of so many men on royal works was not confined to the reign of Henry VIII. There was a work force of 428 men at Berwick in June 1557, for example.[41] Such voracious demands put an intolerable strain on the supply of building labour over the country as a whole, and the only way the Royal Works was able to maintain a labour force of the required size was by exercising its right of impressment.[42]

The only private builders who built on a scale and at a speed comparable with the Royal Works were a few figures prominent in government and at the Court. Holders of the most influential public offices, they often had access to some of the resources of the Royal Works. They built vast private palaces, far in excess of their personal needs. Many of them still survive, symbols of their builders' power and positions and, later in the period, symptoms of their dependence on the monarch. Most of these were built late in the sixteenth and early in the seventeenth centuries when the establishment of the royal progress under Elizabeth and James I gave those with sufficient resources the opportunity to seek favour at Court, and to acquire the rewards that accompanied it, by providing what were virtually occasional residences for the monarch. But the pattern had been set earlier in the century by the principal ministers of state. The labour force employed by Wolsey on his several buildings must at times have rivalled that employed by his sovereign, while Somerset in the following reign had almost 300 workmen engaged on the preliminary preparations for the house that he proposed to build at Great Bedwyn, Wiltshire.[43] The expenditure on labour for that house between 1548 and 1551, as recorded by his paymaster, was under £20. This, clearly, is a very incomplete figure, but in comparison with the sums of over £6,500 that are recorded as being spent on labour for Somerset House and £4,000 for Syon, it suggests that the number of workmen employed on his two major works was remarkably high.[44]

Sufficient evidence exists to suggest that many builders experienced considerable difficulty in assembling enough skilled craftsmen for their works. The building craftsmen released from the permanent staffs of the larger ecclesiastical establishments by the dissolution of the monasteries were probably insufficient to meet the increased demands for labour created by the expansion of the activities of the Royal Works during the later years of Henry VIII. Masons for the Royal Works at Nonsuch were sought in Gloucestershire, Wiltshire, Herefordshire, Worcestershire, Northamptonshire and Bedfordshire as well as in Surrey and Sussex.[45] At least three separate tours into the West Country were necessary in 1539 and 1540 to impress sufficient masons for Sandgate Castle, Kent,[46] and on another of the Royal Works, at Berwick in 1557, masons were impressed from as far away as Kent.[47] The impressment of workmen was a royal prerogative which continued to be used well into the seventeenth century, and which enabled the Crown to overcome temporary shortages and to assemble a sufficient labour force as and when needed. Occasionally commissions of impressment were granted to collegiate bodies, such as that for Christ's College, Cambridge, in 1510,[48] and those for Trinity College, Cambridge, in 1554 and 1560,[49] but they were not generally available for private builders. By taking workmen away to work on royal sites, they must have considerably increased the labour problems of the private builder. Sir

John Thynne was prepared to use his influence at Court to frustrate the commissioners should they threaten his labour force at Longleat,[50] but other builders were not so fortunate. We are told that William Jackson, a freemason, was unable to complete his contract of 1529 for work at Orby Church, Lincolnshire, because he had been pressed for the King's Works.[51] Understandably, such peremptory conscription was not always welcomed by the craftsmen themselves. The disciplining of Robert Short, a London carpenter, was recorded in 1504, 'for he would not goo to the Kynges workes',[52] and no doubt there were other cases of evasion which have not been recorded because they were more successful.

The impressment of labour for major royal works produced only temporary shortages in the private sector, but there are indications of a more permanent shortage of skilled building labour, and especially masons, throughout much of the sixteenth century. It has already been noted that masons were invariably the subject of royal commissions of impressment. A dearth of good masons in north Berkshire and Oxfordshire has been postulated for the period from 1530 onwards,[53] and in other parts of the country there is reason to suppose that builders experienced some difficulty in getting the masons they required. Robert Cecil recruited masons from Oxfordshire, Gloucestershire, Worcestershire, Warwickshire, Berkshire and Northamptonshire for his New Exchange in 1608. Even so he found it difficult to get enough, and was forced to advance money 'to som of the masones which were stubburn'.[54] In 1590 a mason for the Shire Hall, Stafford, was summoned from Bridgnorth, Shropshire, twenty-three miles away,[55] and many of the masons employed at Kyre Park, Worcestershire, between 1588 and 1618, came from distances of over twenty-five miles.[56] One of the masons working at Loseley House, Surrey, in 1562, had been brought from Oxford,[57] and thirteen masons and their labourers employed by Sir Nicholas Bacon at Redgrave, Suffolk, in 1551, came from London. There are several other examples in the building accounts of the period of masons being sought at a considerable distance, even on sites which were fairly close to areas of building stone, and consequently areas which can be assumed to have had a higher number of resident masons. In 1561, for example, a mason living at Ruscombe, near Reading, Berkshire, was engaged to work at Burghley House, Northamptonshire.[58] No doubt some of the examples were the result of builders seeking the services of specific craftsmen of skill and repute, as when Sir John Thynne requested the carver, John Chapman, from Sir William Sharington of Lacock Abbey, Wiltshire, only to be told that Chapman was first 'going to Dudley, to be sent thither by my Lord of Northumberland, to do things there of like effect'.[59] But there are too many examples for them all to be explicable in this way.

In addition there is evidence from the Longleat archives of some builders attempting to entice masons away from the service of other builders. In the summer of 1547 Andrew Baynton, son of Sir Edward Baynton, seems to have temporarily persuaded Sir John Thynne's principal mason, Berryman, to work for him before he had completed the work that he had agreed to do at Longleat. Baynton owned the lease on Berryman's house, and used this to force him to transfer his allegiance. Thynne rapidly made Baynton fully aware of his wrath, and assured Berryman that Baynton would 'do him no wrong nor yet put him to any troble' over his lease 'for though he threten him never so muche I am suer he wol take better advisement or ever he do anything', and Berryman was soon back at Longleat.[60] It is clear from Thynne's letter to his steward that he was prepared to use the full force of the law to secure the return of his mason. It is possible to explain the vigour of Thynne's reaction by the slight on his power and position, but in combination with the examples of masons being sought from a distance it does seem to indicate that there were insufficient masons with the required skills to easily meet the needs of all the builders in the sixteenth century.

This shortage also applied to a certain extent to the other trades connected with building. At Redgrave in 1552, Nicholas Bacon paid the expenses of his joiner while 'seeking for woorkmen to help hym', and his glazier and several of his other joiners came from London.[61] In 1576 he sent his son, Nathaniel, two pairs of sawyers from London to work at Stiffkey in Norfolk.[62] Edward Batten, the joiner employed on fitting out John Strode's new chapel at Chantmarle, Dorset, in 1617, came from Salisbury, a distance of forty-five miles.[63] The plumbers used by Sir Richard Leveson for his house at Trentham, Staffordshire, in 1633 and 1635, came from Bridgnorth, thirty-six miles away,[64] while the plumbers working at Petworth, Sussex, in 1595–6, came almost fifty miles from London.[65] This evidence must be seen against the background of the itinerant nature of the specialized building crafts, but it does seem to indicate a continual difficulty in finding a sufficient skilled labour force close at hand.

Labour was recruited in several ways. Some of the craftsmen and most of the labourers were invariably local men and their recruitment was presumably by word of mouth. Craftsmen from a distance were sometimes summoned by messenger. In 1594 a boy was sent to Witham to fetch a plumber to work at Old Thorndon Hall, Essex,[66] and the Oxford mason who was employed at Loseley in 1562 had been recruited by the master mason's boy who travelled to Oxford for the purpose.[67] The masons who had been temporarily laid off work on Sir Thomas Tresham's Triangular Lodge in 1595 were recalled by the despatch of a labourer to their homes at Weldon.[68] When the craftsman being sought was sufficiently important, sometimes the supervisor of the works would personally go and negotiate with him. The supervisor at Old Thorndon Hall, which was built largely of brick, travelled up to London by boat in August 1581 to arrange for a mason to carry out some work at the site[69] and his counterpart at Trinity College, Cambridge, rode to Thaxted in Essex, 'to bargen with the glasier for the wyndowes yet to glass' in the chapel.[70]

Sometimes workmen were summoned by letter, as when Sir Richard Leveson paid one of his building officials 3s. 'for money he laid out to send a letter to the masons the first journey' in June 1635. In the previous month Leveson had sent the local cobbler to Burton-on-Trent with a letter 'to stay a dutch masons journey'.[71] No doubt those craftsmen who were literate replied in a similar fashion. Thomas Accres, a skilled mason who had worked at Chatsworth in the 1570s and Wollaton in the 1580s, sent a letter to the supervisor at Hardwick in August 1594, and by the following spring he was working at the site.[72]

The builders themselves seem frequently to have solicited craftsmen of exceptional reputation from each other. Sir John Thynne's request for a carver from Sir William Sharington has already been noted. An unnamed plasterer

employed by Thynne was the subject of a similar request from Sir William
Cavendish, who wrote, probably in 1555,

> Sr I understand that you have A connyng plaisterer at Longlete wch hath in yor
> hall and in other places of yor house made Dyvse pendaunts and other ptye
> thyngs. Yf yor busynes be at An ende or wilbe by the next somer after this that
> comyth in I woold pray you that I myght have hym in to Darbyshere ffor my
> hall is yet onmade And therefore nowe myght he devyse wt my carpenter howe
> he shuld frame the same that it myght s[er]ve for his worke.[73]

Thynne presumably was unwilling to part with him at that date, for five years
later the widow of Cavendish, then married to Sir William St Loe, and more
familiar as Bess of Hardwick, wrote

> Thies are even to desire you to spare me your plaistere that flowered your halle
> whom I wold gladly have furthwith to be sent either to my howse at Chattesworthe
> . . . Or elles to London that I may sende him downe with all spede myselfe.

She added that if he was unavailable she would be grateful if Thynne would send
her another plasterer.[74]

    Conversely, craftsmen were often engaged on the direct recommendation of
builders for whom they had previously worked. Robert Smythson was almost
certainly brought to the notice of Sir Francis Willoughby of Wollaton by his brother-
in-law, Sir Matthew Arundell, for whom Smythson had executed some work at
Wardour Castle, Wiltshire, in or before 1576.[75] William Arnold, the mason, had been
commended to Dorothy Wadham by her 'good frend and lovinge neighboure Sr
Edward Phelipps', the builder of Montacute House, Somerset, and she, in turn,
requested Lord Petre to employ him on the building of Wadham College, Oxford.[76]
Sir Francis Newport, the builder of High Ercall and Eyton-on-Severn, wrote in
1595 to the Bailiffs of Shrewsbury, who were proposing to build a market hall,

> I pray you let mee comende a Mason of approved Skyll and honestye, one
> Walter Hancock, unto yo for the doing thereof. I think it is not unknowne to
> you that I have great cause to make tryall of workmen, and therefore can well
> write unto you of myne owne knowledge and experience that you cannott
> match the man in these parts (with any of that occupacon),

adding that if Mr Justice Owen, the builder of Condover Hall, Shropshire, 'were
in the country he would say as much on Hancock's behalf as I have done'.[77] A
mason working at Chatsworth in 1560 had been recommended by 'Sur James' and
two of the plasterers there in 1579 had been sent from Kenilworth by the Earl of
Leicester.[78] Sir Thomas Gresham provided Lord Burghley in 1567 with the
highly experienced Flemish mason, Henryk, who had previously been in charge
of the building of Gresham's Exchange in London,[79] and Edmund Withypoll, the
builder of Christ Church Mansion, Ipswich, sent Nicholas Bacon a number of
freemasons to work at his house at Redgrave in Suffolk.[80]

Craftsmen were also recruited on the recommendation of other craftsmen. It seems to have been common practice for the builder to consult with his surveyor or principal craftsman over the appointment of workmen. John Strode, for example, let the building of his house at Chantmarle to John, Joseph and Daniel Rowe, masons from Ham Hill, Somerset, who were 'prferred to me by Gabriell Moore my Surveyor'. Moore, who was also a mason by trade, came from Chinnock which was only a few miles from Ham Hill.[81] Inigo Jones, who designed a garden gateway for Beaufort House, Chelsea, wrote to Lionel Cranfield on 4 April 1620,

> According to yor honours desire I have sent you a Mason for your worke at Chelsea; his name is John Medhurst, hee is a yard stone man, and will fytt yor turne well.[82]

A number of the leading craftsmen at Wollaton in the 1580s had previously worked at Longleat and clearly owed their positions to the influence of Robert Smythson, surveyor at Wollaton and formerly one of the principal masons at Longleat. Similarly, some of the craftsmen from Wollaton later worked at Hardwick where Smythson was also involved in an executive capacity.[83]

Some of the more influential builders were able to approach officers of the Royal Works to find competent craftsmen for their own works. Humphrey Lovell, the Queen's Master Mason, sent Robert Smythson and his men to Longleat in 1568 'accordenge to his promes' to Sir John Thynne.[84] Somerset and the Cecils undoubtedly recruited part of their labour force in this way, as well as using leading personalities from the Works as administrators.

Once a builder began to make preparations, news of the impending work must have spread fairly rapidly and no doubt some of the labour force was made up of workmen arriving unannounced at the site in search of work. By its nature, this form of recruitment has left very little documentary evidence and often it can only be traced in its most extreme form to casual workmen employed for short periods of a few days. However, the accounts of Kyre Park, where preliminary work began in the autumn of 1588, contains an entry for December of 12s. given 'to two masons that came to seek work from Richmond',[85] and a letter of 1618 survives from Bernard Dinninghof, a glazier and building contractor, to Thomas Lumsden, offering to rebuild Sheriff Hutton Castle, Yorkshire, which begins

> Sir, – if it may please your worship, my being with you in York in Sir Arthur Ingram's garden at that time having some compliment concerning the building the which your worship would have done at the gatehouse at Sherif Hutton Castell . . . .[86]

In addition to offering to undertake all the work, Dinninghof also submitted architectural designs for the building. His letter was more of an attempt to solicit a commission for the whole project than an enquiry for work, but it is an interesting illustration of how craftsmen must sometimes have taken the initiative in seeking employment.

CHAPTER 6

Preparation of the Work

The preparation of the site and the accumulation of materials were frequently put in hand before the builder had considered the design of the projected building or begun to recruit the bulk of the labour force. Sir Edward Pytts, who paid 40s. in December 1588 'To John Symons of London for drawing my first platt for my house' and who had only begun to recruit workmen in the autumn of that year, recorded in his notebook that he 'Began to provide Stone, Brick, Timber, Wainscott, and other necessaries . . . anno Domini 1586 . . . mense Augusti', the same year that he had purchased the property. For the two years from 1586 the only building workmen that he employed were a mason and a labourer, engaged on opening up a quarry in the park and roughly dressing stone.[1] Similarly, Sir William More of Loseley, Surrey, spent the fourteen months from Michaelmas 1560 to Christmas 1561 accumulating stone and timber, digging sawpits, and burning bricks and lime. During that period, his labour force consisted of a few stone-diggers, masons, carpenters and labourers engaged on preparatory work

> for such buildnge as I made, viz a bruehowse & ye stone wall goynge from the same to my mylkehowse, and the stone wale goyng ffrom my stable to the garden, as also my pricons [preparations] then had for my buldyng to cum.[2]

The documents relating to many other building projects of the period show a similar pattern of initial preparation. The accounts for Gawthorpe Hall, Lancashire, commence on 1 February 1600 with the opening up of stone pits, felling of timber, and purchase of tools and materials. It was early August before workmen began levelling the ground for the hall, and the 16th of that month before the first stone was laid.[3] The preparations for Harrold House, Bedfordshire, were begun in May 1608, but it was February 1610 before the labourers started the foundation work,[4] and in Shropshire Thomas Owen began accumulating large quantities of building materials as soon as he acquired the manor of Condover in 1586, some twelve months before the 'trencheinge of the plott' was recorded in the accounts.[5]

A more detailed idea of the nature of the preparations carried out by the builder can be derived from the Bacon papers relating to Stiffkey Hall, Norfolk. Sir Nicholas Bacon bought the manor in 1571 for his son Nathaniel, who was to be married the following year. In the autumn of 1573, Nathaniel and his bride moved from Norwich to the neighbouring manor of Cockthorpe, and

Gawthorpe Hall, where preparations began in February and the first stone was laid in August 1600 (John Ashdown).

preparations were made for building. Already in March 1573 he had begun negotiating with the Dean and Chapter of Norwich for the purchase of timber from Hindolveston Wood, near Melton Constable. In September the following year he obtained a twenty-one year lease of the oaks in the wood. In November 1575 one of his servants 'bowght for my lord and honor a gret bargenye of tymbere of Mr Gorge Thembetthorpe of Fellshme' which was already sawn into lengths and had been seasoned. In the following year Bacon bought more timber from his father-in-law, Sir Thomas Gresham. Thus by the time that he was ready to commence the actual building, he had probably made arrangements for the provision of most of the timber that he would require. He had also been accumulating other basic materials from an early date. The house is largely constructed of brick, but he had initially determined to use stone for the dressings, and had accordingly sought to buy monastic stone from his neighbour, Edward Paston of Binham Priory. Meeting with a refusal from this source he bought a small amount of stone from Sir Henry Clinton and Christopher Wray. But the quantities that he was able to acquire were insufficient for his purpose so, inspired by the example of Clement Paston, the uncle of his neighbour, he altered his plans and used brick rendered with plaster for his dressings.

At the same time as he was accumulating materials, work was going ahead with the preparation of designs for the house. In April 1574, Sir Nicholas Bacon had written to his son asking for the exact measurements of the proposed site. The Lord Keeper had designs based on these measurements drawn up in London. In August of the following year he sent 'the plat that I drewe for Styfkey to the end that you showlde set out theise thinges followyng wch I cannot do by the instruccons I have alredy receyved'.

The remains of Stiffkey Hall begun in August 1576 five years after the purchase of the site (RCHME © Crown Copyright).

By April of 1576 the plans were sufficiently corrected for Nicholas to return them to his son 'to thentent that they and the grownd may be compared together'. This was clearly the preliminary step to the laying out of the foundations, and in August the construction of the house was finally begun, some five years after the original purchase of the site.[6]

House building, of course, represented a large capital investment, and it was in the interest of the prospective builder to spend a considerable period of time in his preparatory arrangements to ensure that he got the best return on his outlay and avoided any serious delays during the course of construction. The absence of any documentary reference in particular building accounts to a period of preparation cannot be taken to imply a lack of preparation, but should rather be interpreted as an indication that separate accounts were only begun when the actual building work commenced. It is impossible to imagine any country house being built without preliminary accumulation of material or preparation of the site. Most of the major decisions concerning the general design, type of materials, and method of undertaking the work, must have been considered at length before the first sod was cut. A good deal of thought, too, must have been given to the costing of the work, although it is difficult to see how this could have been achieved with any precision where the building was to be carried out by direct labour.

As Gerbier advised in 1662, 'Builders ought to calculate the charge of their designed building, and especially with what sum of money they are willing to part'.[7] There is very little extant evidence from the sixteenth century to show how builders estimated the costs of their intended work. When in September 1578 Sir Nicholas Bacon expressed his intention to provide sufficient money to build a new chapel for Corpus Christi College, Cambridge, a rough plan was prepared, and on the basis of its dimensions estimates of the cost of the work were drawn up by working craftsmen. 'The charges of ye chappell as they were estemed by the artificers' came to £202.12s., but the basis of their estimation was thoroughly inadequate, excluding as it did such essential items as the wages of the labourers and the cost of making the foundations. In addition, the plans were subsequently altered but the original estimate for the work continued to be adhered to. Needless to say, it was grossly exceeded.[8] Peculiar considerations applied to the Oxford and Cambridge colleges, for potential benefactors wished to know fairly precisely the extent of their financial liability, as when Fulke Greville wrote to the Master of Jesus College, Cambridge, in 1617, confirming his intention to finance the provision of new lodgings:

> Let me therfore entreat you, with all speed, fullie and particularly to enforme your selfe by some honest and skilfull workman what the charge will be of convertinge the west end of your Chappell into lodginge chambers. And I pray you send me a bill of all particulars, viz. of the precise height, length, and breadth of the platt; of the certayne number, cizes, and prices of the Sommers, Juistes, and Bordes . . . for the floores; of the transomes and studdes for the partitions; of the lights with theyr irons, casements, and glasse; of bricke for chimneyes, and all other materialles, with the severall charges of the workmanshippe.[9]

Domestic builders seem to have been less concerned with a precise costing of their work. It is probable that this was partly due to their method of financing their building out of current revenue over an indeterminate period of time, the overall cost being subordinate to the amount of money readily available at any given moment. In addition, for some builders, such as the builders of the 'prodigy' houses, considerations of costs were clearly secondary to the powerful motives that inspired them to build in the way that they did.[10] Estimates were certainly made for the purpose of calculating the amount of materials necessary in subsequent years, such as that for bricks at Hatfield[11] and for lead at Redgrave,[12] but there is very little evidence for the preliminary costing of the total work. There are occasional examples of specific jobs being costed while the work was in progress, as at Burghley in 1564 when the mason was instructed to

> Make a profe of v foote square, what the chardges wilbe, to take ye grounde out of yor garden to the loones [lowness] of the flower in yor lower gallerie, so as you may have an estimate of the rest . . .[13]

However, by the seventeenth century there seems to have been a growing awareness of the benefits of adequate costing, which can possibly be related to the emergence of specialized building surveyors who must invariably have been expected to have been capable of preparing estimates with a reasonable degree of accuracy. This is certainly the implication behind Chancery proceedings instituted by George Luttrell against the surveyor and mason William Arnold in 1619. Luttrell was claiming against Arnold for the unsatisfactory way in which he had fulfilled an agreement made in 1617 to oversee the work at Dunster Castle, Somerset, and part of the indictment was that work originally estimated at £462

Condover Hall, Shropshire (RCHME © Crown Copyright).

was now likely to amount to £1,200.[14] A contributory factor must have been the growing acceptance of piece-work as a desirable method of working, which enabled preliminary estimates based on quantities to be made. The only document of any length relating to the costing of a proposed building enterprise that survives from the period was only able to achieve its remarkably precise calculations by assuming that the materials were to be worked on a piece rate basis. It was drawn up in 1615 by the principal carpenter and a leading household official of the Earl of Northumberland when the earl was contemplating building a palatial new house at Petworth, a project which he subsequently abandoned in favour of extensions to the existing house. Their calculations, based 'according to a Plotte thereof and directions therunto given by the said Earle', cover some eleven pages of detailed analysis before they arrive at the exact sum of £25,572.18*s*.4*d*. for the total work. Significantly, they emphasize that

> Whereas wee make computacon as the rates of all matterialls may be now bought, hearafter may be risen and therfore to trust at all tymes to nothing but quantitie which wee thinck to be true.

It is a most impressive document, of which a sample entry relating to the ashlar work for the gatehouse towers must suffice to give an indication of the thoroughness with which they carried out their task:

> The working of 4736 foote of Ashler at iiii*d*. the foote beinge the six inches surface of those towres with the Battlements at iiii*d*. the foote, lxxviii *li*. vi*s*.
> The stones for the rough wale of 325 rodd 486 loades, the digginge and caringe at x*d*. ye Loade. xx *li*. v *s*.

The sixe inches Ashelere wille take 95 loades digginge and caryinge at xviii *d.* the loade, vii *li.* ii *s.* vi *d.*
Both which will require 116 loade of Lyme at ix *s.* iiii *d.* a Loade, liiii *li.* ii *s.* viii *d.*
And of sande for the same lyme 500 at vi *d.* the loade digginge and caryinge xii *li.* x *s.*[15]

Northumberland is known to have taken great care over the preparations for his building work. The letter that he wrote to Cecil in 1603 expressing his intention, 'now that I am a builder', to visit 'Copthall . . . Tibballs . . . and every place of mark where curiosities are used' was not just a gratuitous compliment to Cecil's own building. In the same year his carpenter was indeed sent to look at Theobalds, and bound together with the Petworth estimates of 1615 are a collection of notes on the sizes of the main rooms of ten important contemporary buildings and a memorandum on 'materialls for buildinge'.[16] For his work at Syon earlier in the century, Northumberland had been among the first English builders to have used architectural models, and his correspondence with his officials and friends throughout the country regarding the right choice of materials still survives.[17] Among his papers preserved at Syon are some undated calculations in his own hand for rebuilding the wine cellar at Petworth at a cost of £97.17*s.* 6*d.*, using 50,000 bricks.[18]

From the evidence that is available, it is clear that Northumberland was an exceptionally well-prepared builder but it is highly improbable that he was alone among his contemporaries in taking adequate precautions before he actually started to build. However, there must still have been builders in the seventeenth century who embarked on their work rashly without sufficient preparations, for as late as 1672 Sir Roger Pratt was able to write:

How though it cannot well be supposed that any rational man should put himself upon building without having first made in his purse some competent provision, yet are the examples but too many of the sufferings of those who have not first laboured to make of their expenses some near calculation . . .[19]

Although the preliminary planning must have been of paramount importance, it was still necessary to exercise a considerable degree of forethought in the advance preparation of material throughout the course of the work. A lack of sufficient materials at any particular point could lead to an under-employment of parts of the labour force and consequently added expense. It was specifically written into the contract of 1547 between Sir Richard Edgecumbe and Roger Palmer for the building of Mount Edgcumbe, Cornwall, that Sir Richard was

by the warnyng of xii dayes to have in redynes all maner of stuff necessary or for lake of suche preparation the seyd Roger and hys company shall have from tyme to tyme their Jorney Wages as they use to take of other men.[20]

At St John's College, Cambridge, in 1598, where it was the contractors' responsibility to provide materials, they were bound to have accumulated sufficient material on the site by the beginning of August each year for the whole of the following year's work,[21] and the two masons who were making windows for Thorpe Hall, Northamptonshire, in 1653, were bound by a clause in their contract to deliver them from time to time at the site so that building 'shall not at any time be hindered for want of ye sd: windowes'.[22]

The instructions that Sir Thomas Tresham issued to his steward in the autumn of 1597 make explicit some of the reasons for stockpiling materials in advance. He ordered as much stone as possible to be got from the quarries while the weather held, so that in the following spring, building could begin four to six weeks before the state of the ground would allow carts to be used, and he also instructed his steward to ensure that there were always sufficient jambs and other works of freestone in store for eight weeks use, otherwise the freemasons would in summer 'loyter and linger out ther worke to needless charge and encumbrance many ways'.[23] As a result of the weather, construction work usually came to a halt during the worst of the winter months, but with the sort of planning shown by Tresham the effects of this could be minimized. However, if building was to make a prompt start as soon as the weather improved, and if craftsmen were to be able to prepare their materials under cover while the weather was still bad, it was essential that sufficient quantities of material had been accumulated before the winter had set in. Consequently, Bernard Dinninghof, in his letter of October 1618 to Thomas Lumsden offering to rebuild Sheriff Hutton Castle, Yorkshire, advised that

> if you be aminded to build I would set on in the quarry to get stone for window stones and hew the same this winter against the spring[24]

and at Old Thorndon Hall, Essex, sand was being dug in October 1580 'in redynes agaynste the next yeare'.[25] In October 1547, Sir John Thynne wrote at length to his steward with instructions to prepare for the winter. They included a request for him to enlist the aid of Thynne's friends during the present fine weather to carry stone to Longleat from the quarries in readiness for the next year, and to ensure that sufficient laths were made during the winter so that a plasterer could be employed at the beginning of the following year.[26]

In the early weeks of the new building season, there was not always sufficient construction work to occupy the assembled labour force, especially if the weather was poor. The situation could be alleviated by putting the craftsmen to work on preparing materials only if there were sufficient materials already in store on site. Thus William Cecil's steward at Burghley was able to write to him on 16 May 1562, 'yor masons sence they came have ben yet hetherto onestlye occupied in making reyde of suche stone as is nedfull furste to be ocupied'.[27]

Where work on a particular building was continuously in progress over a number of years, much of the material was probably accumulated well in advance of its use, being acquired as the availability of the material and the finance allowed. Sir John Petre, who had begun to remodel Old Thorndon Hall, Essex, in 1573, bought the slate for the roof of his banqueting house in 1587 although he did not actually use it until 1594,[28] and Sir Thomas Smith who began rebuilding Hill Hall, Essex, in 1568, refers in his will of 1576 to 'all the brick, timber, chalk, sand and all other stuff I have prepared' for the house.[29]

CHAPTER 7

The Realization of the Design

Although this study is not primarily concerned with the technology of the building industry, there are important aspects connected with the construction work that have to be examined. In particular, it is necessary to consider how the detailed technical information about the design of the house was communicated to the ordinary workmen who were entrusted with its execution. In their various writings, Sir Henry Wotton, Sir Roger Pratt and Sir Balthazar Gerbier all laid particular emphasis on the necessity of making a wooden or pasteboard model of the building before the work should begin, but there is little consistent evidence for any widespread use of architectural models in England during the sixteenth and early seventeenth centuries.

The earliest documentary mention of the construction of a model was by a French joiner for Longleat in 1568. It seems probable that this was in conscious imitation of current continental practice.[1] Robert Adams, later to become Surveyor of the Royal Works, possibly made a model for the Earl of Southampton's house at Dogmersfield, Hampshire, sometime before 1581, but there are no other examples known from the sixteenth century.[2] Models for details, such as staircases and roofs, became more frequent in the following century, but there are still very few known for complete buildings.[3] Ralph Symons probably made one for the hall of Trinity College, Cambridge, in 1604, and in Oxford the model for University College still miraculously survives. Constructed shortly before 1634, it consists of drawings of the various elevations stuck on to pasteboard and sewn together at the corners. Its flimsy and ephemeral nature is a sufficient explanation as to why it is the only surviving example of an architectural model from the period. Wooden models must have been sturdier but even so they do not seem to have been considered worth retaining once their primary function had been achieved. Thus the wooden model made for £3 by the joiner for Canterbury Quadrangle at St John's College, Oxford, during the building campaign of 1631–6, was not preserved in the College archives.[4] The value of models was promoted by Renaissance theorists from Alberti onwards and it is not surprising that Inigo Jones was paid for making two models for the Queen's House at Greenwich during the accounting period 1616–18, and for the Banqueting House in 1619.[5] The only documented model made for a complete

The pasteboard model made for University College, Oxford, c. 1634 (Howard Colvin).

country house was in 1622 when a mason and a joiner made one for Sir Roger Townshend's house at Raynham, Norfolk.[6]

The few models that are known to have been made in England were primarily intended to solve details of planning and to show the clients what their completed work would look like, and would not have been of any real value in communicating precise technical information to the stonecutters and masons. Detailed written specifications, such as were incorporated in a number of building contracts of the period, would have been more useful in providing the contractor with a general conception of the work that was to be carried out. However, although the contract with John Atkinson for the Legge Building at Gonville and Caius College, Cambridge, in 1618, for example, contains sufficient instructions for the erection of the shell of the building,[7] it omits any mention of such essential details as the form of the mouldings and precise measurements for features like the sills and the jambs. A similar criticism can be made against all the other written specifications that survive. Where these specifications were combined with plans and drawings, as in the contract of 1586 for Woollavington, Sussex,[8] their usefulness was increased considerably, but they still failed to provide the necessary detailed technical information. None of the surviving plans and elevations could have been used as blueprints for construction, for they rarely show more than the most general overall dimensions and omit entirely the detailed measurements and such important information as the jointings of the stones and precise details of the mouldings. The function of many of the drawings was clearly similar to that of the architectural models; they were made to give some indication of how the building would look. But it must be remembered that these were the drawings that were most likely to survive, for generally they were the presentation copies intended for show and not subject to continual handling

Ground and first floor plans attached to the building contract for Woollavington annotated with the overall dimensions of the rooms (Sussex Archaeological Society).

PLAN OF FIRST FLOOR.

on the site. On the other hand, there is no evidence from those that survive to suggest that the working drawings differed appreciably in the amount of information that they contained.

Despite the objections that have been made about their usefulness as complete blueprints, however, it is evident that they fulfilled a practical function in the building process. They were used, for example, in costing the proposed work and calculating the necessary quantities of materials, as John Smythson's annotated drawings for the marble room at Bolsover graphically illustrate.[9] They were also used on the site for the laying out of the foundations. Sir Nicholas Bacon sent the plans for Stiffkey Hall to Norfolk in April 1576 'to thentent that they and the grownd may be compared together',[10] and in 1549 one of the Duke of Somerset's agents at Wulfhall in Wiltshire wrote to Sir John Thynne that he would

trace and set forth my lords grace's house according to the plat which my lord's grace resolved upon the last time, and so be ready to lay the foundation.[11]

Furthermore, drawings were made of separate features such as windows and panelling and, although few of these have survived, there are sufficient documentary references to show that they were used as working guides by the craftsmen. This is evident from the references to 'plattes' for battlements, pinnacles and vaults in the masons' contracts for King's College Chapel,

John Smythson's annotated drawing for the Marble Room at Bolsover Castle (British Architectural Library, RIBA, London).

Cambridge, in 1512 and 1513,[12] and from a contract whereby the joiner at Chatsworth, Derbyshire, was 'to seall the . . . parloure . . . according to a patterne drawne for the same'.[13] Similar examples could be cited for masons making windows, carpenters framing roofs, and even painters concerned with interior decoration. The important part played by drawings in the execution of the work is emphasized by a letter that Sir Thomas Gresham wrote to Lord Burghley in February 1568 informing him that

> Henricke hath lost the patrone of the pillors for your galerie in the country, so, he can procede no further in the workinge thereof, untill he have another.[14]

So despite the apparent deficiencies of contemporary drawings, they clearly were used in connection with construction work, and it follows that the details they lack were provided in other ways. Mouldings were made by providing the craftsmen with full-size templates from which to work, a practice which had been in use throughout the medieval period, and which was to continue well after the end of the period under consideration. The templates, or 'moulds', were usually drawn out by the surveyor or master craftsmen, or whoever had been appointed to oversee the technical details of the design. When Nicholas Stone contracted to build Cornbury Park, Oxfordshire, in 1631, it was stipulated that he was to direct the workmen and to make all their moulds,[15] and at Raynham Hall, Norfolk, William Edge, the principal mason, was engaged in July 1621 on drawing

Full-size mouldings drawn by John Thorpe (by courtesy of the Trustees of Sir John Soane's Museum).

Working drawings for the apex of a roof truss (lower right) and an oriel window (upper left) set out on a plastered wall at Acton Court.

'patterns for mowld'.[16] A number of sheets of drawings of moulds for both timber and stone details survive in the Thorpe collection and the production of these patterns must have been common practice on most building sites.[17] They were not always drawn on paper. At Acton Court, Somerset, probably in the 1550s, the full-size details of the base for an oriel window were drawn directly on to the recently plastered wall of a ground floor corridor, apparently in an attempt to judge the effect of alternative mouldings and to work out the precise jointing of the individual stones. Other constructional graffiti on the same wall include calculations for the setting out of the pitch of a roof.

The next stage in the process was to turn the drawings into templates that could be actually used on site. These were usually made by the joiner but they were sometimes made by workmen employed in the other crafts. The templates at Raynham were made of oak, but it was more common for them to be made of deal. A few more were made from pasteboard[18] or paper.[19] They were employed by masons, carpenters, plasterers, bricklayers, and even, on occasion, by plumbers. Once a set of moulds for a particular feature had been made, they could be used for similar features in other parts of the building, and there is even evidence that they were used on other buildings. When a plasterer was hired to work at Old Thorndon Hall, Essex, in 1577, the carriage of his moulds to the site was paid for,[20] and in 1575 Nathaniel Bacon expressed his intention of borrowing the moulds that Clement Paston had used for the windows of his house in Norfolk to use as models for the work at Stiffkey.[21]

Additional technical information would have been supplied to the workmen by verbal instructions from the surveyor or the leading craftsmen. Consequently the realization of the design of a building was basically achieved through the supervisor of the work, who received his instructions from consultations with the client and from written specifications and drawings, and passed these on to the relevant workmen through working drawings, full-size templates, and by word of mouth. It was a method which relied for its success on close and continuous site supervision. This partly explains the importance attached to the position of surveyor, and was one of the factors responsible for the emergence towards the end of the sixteenth century of specialized building supervisors.

Given this method of working, it is apparent that work was begun on many buildings with only a very general conception of the finished design. This has already been suggested from some of the evidence relating to the process of design, and can be inferred in other cases from documentary examples. One of the inherent dangers of working in this way was that insufficient initial planning could result in mistakes in the design of the building that would only become apparent when the construction was at an advanced stage, and the alterations necessary to rectify the fault could lead to considerable extra expense. Work on the Triangular Lodge for Sir Thomas Tresham was disrupted in October 1594 when the top floor had to be removed and set higher to allow for the 'convenient coveyance' of the stairs,[22] a basic mistake of planning that suggests that not enough care had been taken in the preparation of the initial design. In the following year it was decided that twelve decorative letters which had already been carved were too small, and they had to be discarded.[23]

Alterations while the work was in progress are frequently met with in the building accounts. Sometimes this was the result of a revision of the requirements of the builder caused by factors such as over-expenditure, but more commonly they resulted from the imprecision of the initial planning procedures and the practice of improvising solutions to questions of detail as they arose. The design for Hatfield House, where work had commenced in August 1607, was altered in 1609 because of the Earl of Salisbury's mounting debts, but major revisions had already been made in 1608 and further alterations were carried out in 1610 as a result of the particular consideration of details of the plan and design. It appears that the detailed designs of the principal front at Hatfield were not commenced until as late as October 1609, when work had already been in progress on the house for over two years.[24] Alterations to the original design of Little Saxham Hall, Suffolk, for Thomas Lucas, took place in almost every year that the work was in progress, and ranged from raising the foundations by an extra foot in 1501, to enlarging the chapel in 1509 and 1510.[25]

The recent application of archaeological techniques to the study of the surviving fabric of standing structures has reinforced the documentary evidence for the erratic progress of most building campaigns which resulted from imperfect detailed planning. At Audley End and Hill Hall, for example, Paul Drury has demonstrated how the work on these two houses was punctuated by pauses in construction, changes in the details of the design, faulty workmanship and improvised corrections to prefabricated elements when they came to be put into their final position on the building. The eccentric form of the arrangements at the upper end of the hall at Chastleton House, Oxfordshire, where the east wall has been radically chamfered at its north end to allow sufficient space for the doorway into the remainder of the house can only be explained, as Nicholas Cooper has suggested, by the incorrect setting out of the courtyard, the consequence of which would only have become apparent when the construction of the fabric was well advanced.[26]

In addition to the inconvenience and delays caused by alterations to the fabric while the work was in progress, the builder was also likely to incur additional expenditure. When Sir Richard Leveson decided to raise the height of three chimneys at Trentham Hall, Staffordshire, in 1635, he had to pay for the re-slating of part of the roof as well as for the actual work on the chimneys, and the fellows of St John's College, Cambridge, paid an extra £205 to their contractors in 1599 for altering the height of the buildings that they had commenced the previous year.[27] An endorsement on the contract of 1547 between Sir Richard Edgecumbe and Roger Palmer for the building of Mount Edgecumbe specifically bound the former to pay for any extra work resulting from changes made to the initial plan,[28] but sometimes alterations seem to have been initiated by the building contractor or surveyor without authorization from the person for whom the building was being constructed.[29]

Although some examples of alterations carried out after the work had been started can be attributed to the changing circumstances or the growing pretensions of the builder, such as those at Theobalds which, as Cecil wrote 'was begun by me with a mean measure but encrease by occasion of her Majesty's often coming',[30] many of the examples resulted directly from the method of working whereby the details of the design were only fully resolved on the site while the building was actually under construction. The architectural theorists of the seventeenth century were largely paraphrasing Italian and French practice in their advocacy of the construction of models, but they were also suggesting a solution to what must have been a common problem; that of working out in three-dimensional terms the details of the design before commencing to build. It was a problem that was eventually to be solved by improvements in draughtsmanship and in the technical expertise of the building industry, but even as late as 1660, the advice of Sir Roger Pratt must have remained appropriate:

> get a model of wood to be most exactly framed . . . and as you shall then like it, so go on with your building, or change it till it please you, but resolve after you have once laid one stone never to alter your design, except it may be done without pulling down anything; for if you be once irresolute in that, your alterations may chance to cost you half as much as your whole building . . .[31]

CHAPTER 8

Financing and Expenditure

It is necessary to exercise the greatest caution in drawing conclusions about comparative expenditure on building during the period under discussion. Because of the erratic methods of accounting, it is never possible to be certain that the total outlay on a particular building had been recorded in the accounts that survive. Even when the documentation is apparently complete there is always the possibility that substantial items, especially materials, had been entered under a separate account. Occasionally, where the account for the last year of building survives, the accountant would make a general statement about the total cost of the work, such as that for Trentham Hall, Staffordshire, that:

> The whole charge of all the worke for the building of the mannor house at Trentham with stables, barnes, in the feilds and others neere the house & all other houses of office with gardens, orchards & panns thereunto belonging with conveyanse of water to all the houses of office, wch said workes began the twelfte day of june 1630 & ended the second of march 1638 as more at large may appeare by 3 severall bookes of Accompt subscribed with Sr Richard Levesons owne hand now at this pr'sent delivered unto him – £6165.17s.4d.[1]

More frequently, however, the account abruptly stops with no clear indication that the fitting-out of the building had been fully completed. Consequently there are very few country houses for which the total building cost is definitely known. Even where summary accounts exist, it is inadvisable to accept them uncritically, as is shown by an examination of the entries relating to the Duke of Somerset's house at Wulfhall, near Great Bedwyn, Wiltshire, in the account roll of his paymaster of the works. During the period from 1548 to 1551 the account records that only £45.6s.8¼d. was spent on work at the house, of which sum almost a quarter was devoted to the purchase of nails and ironwork, while less than £8 was paid in wages to the labourers.[2] However, the fragments of correspondence that survive for 1549 from the duke's agents and bailiffs in Wiltshire to Sir John Thynne reveal that in that year alone over 585 acres for the estate were surveyed, enclosed and ditched; quarries were opened up, brick earth dug and brick-making begun; a conduit house and a brick conduit some 1,600 feet in length and 15 feet in depth were constructed; the foundations of the house were laid, and the craftsmen working on the site included masons and bricklayers as well as brickmakers and lime-burners. The total labour force in May was in excess of 280 men, and twenty carts were in use solely to serve the bricklayers.[3] Clearly a large part of the expenditure on Wulfhall failed to get recorded on the central paymaster's summary account.

Given the unreliability of the available figures and the incompleteness of the majority of accounts, it is difficult to make any meaningful comparisons between individual expenditure on building at specific points during the period. It is clear that the court nobility spent a greater proportion of their resources in the late sixteenth and early seventeenth centuries on ostentatious building than their predecessors, but even at this level of society it is difficult to substantiate this assertion with precise figures. In 1610 Robert Cecil, Earl of Salisbury, was in debt to the sum of £42,395, and a large part of this must have been due to the building work that he was engaged upon in the first decade of the seventeenth century.[4] Hatfield House alone cost him nearly £39,000 between 1607 and 1612, and during the same period he made extensive additions to Cranborne House in Dorset and built the New Exchange in London, as well as continuing the work on Salisbury House, London, begun in 1599. Professor Stone has similarly attributed a large part of the responsibility for the debts of £46,000 left by the Earl of Winchester to his ambitious building at Basing and Chelsea.[5] The £200,000 that the Earl of Suffolk is reputed to have told King James I that he spent on building Audley End[6] was possibly an exaggeration, but nevertheless the cost was greatly in excess of that spent by Salisbury on Hatfield, and when Suffolk died in 1626 his estate was heavily encumbered with debt. Such excessive expenditure, however, was not universal among the aristocracy. The Earl of Northumberland, for example, abandoned his plans for building a new house at Petworth in 1615 on receipt of an estimate for the project in excess of £25,000. His landed income at the time was in the region of £11,000 per annum and the building could have been financed without much difficulty out of current revenue, but as his obligations included the composition of £11,000 on his fine in Star Chamber and dowries for two daughters, he contented himself with making less expensive additions to the existing house.[7] Northumberland's sympathy for the Catholic cause denied him any political ambition and consequently he seems to have had little incentive to build on a scale ruinous to his financial stability. In general it was established political figures and those seeking preferment who built the prodigy houses.

Few houses of the nobility built before the reign of Elizabeth were conceived on such an excessive scale, and it is unlikely that their cost, as a proportion of the builder's estate, bore any comparative relation to that expended by later builders such as Burghley, Salisbury and Suffolk. Precise details of expenditure are lacking, but the £994 spent between 1480 and 1484 by Lord Hastings on Kirby Muxloe Castle, Leicestershire, was well within his income over the same period.[8] He proclaimed his noble status by building in brick, a material almost unknown in the Midlands at the time, and not by a conspicuous display of size and costly

Audley End, Essex.

decoration. In the first half of the sixteenth century the initiative in ostentatious building was taken by Henry VIII and few of his subjects were willing to compete. Lord Marney's grand mansion at Layer Marney in Essex got no further than the eight-storeyed gatehouse before work stopped with his death in 1523, and the inadvisability of building on a princely scale seems to have been one of the lessons drawn from the fall of both Wolsey and Buckingham. Thomas Cromwell, significantly, built nothing comparable with Wolsey's palaces in Whitehall and at Hampton.

The death of Henry VIII heralded the end of royal leadership in palatial building. The Duke of Somerset, principal minister during the minority of Edward VI, was responsible for the most impressive buildings of the middle of the century. During the period between 1548 and 1551 he spent at least £10,000 on Somerset House in the Strand and £5,500 on his country house at Syon in Middlesex, while a further £2,000 was recorded as being spent on building at his other houses in Oxfordshire, Hampshire, Wiltshire and Berkshire.[9]

The unfinished remains of Kirby Muxloe Castle, Leicestershire.

Elizabeth I, preoccupied with restricting royal expenditure, built very little and positively encouraged the initiative in palatial building to remain with her leading ministers of state. William Cecil led the way with Burghley House and Theobalds, and some of his fellow peers were not slow to follow. At one stage his annual expenditure on Theobalds was well in excess of £2,000.[10] By the time his son came to build Hatfield House under James I this figure was comfortably exceeded in every year that building was in progress. As has already been suggested, the building of noble palaces fit to entertain the monarch on summer progresses often left the builder deeply in debt. A growing awareness of the disastrous financial effects of ostentatious building, combined with a decline in the practice of royal progresses under Charles I, resulted in a greater restraint in the scale and opulence of noble building after the first quarter of the seventeenth century. The reduction of crown patronage and the increasing isolation of the Court in the decade before the Civil War were further factors that tended to diminish the necessity for building in a way that was designed, in part at least, to secure preferment.

The general pattern of aristocratic expenditure on building during the period under consideration is fairly clear, even if the precise figures remain largely obscured. There was little ostentatious expenditure while the crown was sensitive to anything that could be construed as personal rivalry in a field where it had consciously chosen to demonstrate its primacy; but once the dominant figure of Henry VIII had been succeeded by the minority of Edward VI and the parsimony

Somerset House as drawn by John Thorpe (by courtesy of the Trustees of Sir John Soane's Museum).

of Elizabeth, the impetus, and ultimately the necessity, for lavish building passed to the leading courtiers and ministers of state. Noble expenditure on architecture reached its height in the early years of James I, but after about 1620 dramatically declined.

This pattern of expenditure was largely confined to the nobility and the politically ambitious courtiers, whom, it must be emphasized, formed only a small proportion of the country house builders of the period. For the remainder, there are few indications of a general rise in expenditure on building. The picture is necessarily incomplete. There are few figures available for the period up to the middle of the sixteenth century, and it must be remembered that there are too many variables involved for any precise parallels to be drawn between the expenditure on particular houses. Few of the houses for which accounts survive are strictly comparable in size, and this reservation is further complicated by the fact that only some accounts include payments for such things as food and drink for the work force, or estimated costs of material deriving from the builder's own estate, or the value of materials and carriage given by friends. In addition, many of the accounts are incomplete and only a few of them contain entries relating to landscaping and the general clearing up of the site after the actual construction work had been completed. In the latter part of the sixteenth century and the early part of the seventeenth century, the prevailing architectural fashion was for a wealth of applied decoration particularly on interiors, and this must have necessarily increased expenditure on building during that period. Individual expenditure also varied according to the availability of the chosen material. Should a material be sought that was not available locally, its expensive carriage to the site would have considerably increased the cost of the building. However, on the whole, the smaller country houses seem to have been largely built of local materials with only the small quantities used for special effects being brought great distances. This was the policy adopted by Sir John Petre when he rebuilt Old Thorndon Hall. He used local brick for the main shell of the house, but he bought small quantities of Purbeck stone from Dorset and Beer stone from Devon for special dressings, and he roofed his tiny banqueting house with Devon slate.[11]

Despite the almost infinite number of variables, the conclusions that can be drawn with caution from the figures that remain are difficult to reconcile with the assertion of Professor Stone that there was a startling rise in building costs in the early seventeenth century that appears to have far outstripped the 'price revolution'.[12] The expenditure of a small minority of country house builders increased in that period, but there were particular social and political reasons for this which were unrelated to any rise in costs. Given the lack of reliable statistics it is only possible to comment on expenditure on building and not comparative costs. Nevertheless, it is probable that there was an approximate relationship between the two. If the figures of the large prodigy houses are excluded, the general picture that is presented is of a fairly stable level of expenditure throughout the sixteenth century, with a noticeable but by no means startling rise beginning around the second decade of the seventeenth century.

Little Saxham Hall, Suffolk, built between 1505 and 1514 by Sir Thomas Lucas, secretary to Jasper, Duke of Bedford, and subsequently Solicitor-General to Henry VIII, cost £1,425.[13] Sir Thomas Kytson, the London merchant, spent something over £3,500 between 1525 and 1539 on building his larger and more ambitious house at Hengrave in the same county,[14] while Redgrave Hall, also in Suffolk, built by Sir Nicholas Bacon when he was Solicitor to the Court of Augmentations, cost just over £1,250 between 1545 and 1554.[15] Bacon's rise in political prominence was reflected in his expenditure of £3,177.11s.9¼d., on building Gorhambury House, Hertfordshire, in 1563–1568.[16] However, during the same decade, Sir William More, a highly experienced parliamentarian, Deputy Lieutenant and twice Sheriff of the county of Surrey, built Loseley House near Guildford for a recorded cost of only £1,600.19s.7½d. Little credence can be attached to the enormous sum of £40,000 said to have been spent by Sir Henry Cheney on his house at Toddington, Bedfordshire in the 1560s.[17] It was a very large house of three courtyards but, even so, it is unlikely to have cost such an exceptional sum. No comparable figures are extant for country houses built in the 1570s and '80s, but it is instructive that when William Dickenson, bailiff to the Earl of Shrewsbury, built himself a house in Sheffield between 1575 and 1576 it cost him less than £50,[18] and in the 1590s Sir Thomas Tresham spent less than £1,000 on his extensive minor building works in Northamptonshire.[19] In the seventeenth century it was still possible to build a country house of moderate size for a comparatively small sum, as the incomplete accounts for Harrold House, Bedfordshire, show. During the two years between 1608 and 1610 when the shell of the house was erected, Francis Farrar spent little over £160 on the work. On the other side of the country in Herefordshire John Coke spent just over £300 on the carcass of his timber-framed house at Hall Court, Much Marcle, during the same two years.[20] The cost of larger houses, however, had almost certainly risen. The accounts for 1619–22 show the expenditure of £3,500 on part of the fabric of Raynham Hall, Norfolk, for Sir Roger Townshend,[21] while a contemporary estimate of the cost of building Fountains Hall, Yorkshire, in the second decade of the century, was £3,000.[22] Between 1602 and 1607, a similar sum was spent on building Ashley Park, Surrey,[23] and Irmingland Hall, Norfolk, built at about the same time, was said to have cost Sir Nathaniel Bacon £3,991.[24] Sir John Strode built himself a house at Chantmarle in Dorset for £1,142, but this sum excluded 'much stone, many timber trees, and a very great number of carriages of stones'.[25] These were all items that would have added considerably to the cost. Trentham Hall, Staffordshire, built between 1630 and 1639, cost Sir Richard Leveson just over £6,000,[26] and Sir Basil Dixwell spent £8,000 by his own account on building Broome Park, Kent, between 1635 and 1638.[27] In 1638–40 the addition of a new wing and the building of a splendidly decorated coach-house and stable block at Holland House, Kensington, cost £6,584.9s.4d.[28] These figures suggest an appreciable rise in expenditure in the 1630s, but even so they are only approximately twice the sum spent by Sir Thomas Kytson a century earlier, and as late as 1669 Sir Roger Pratt was able to build a handsome if modest house for himself for £2,800.[29] There clearly was a rise in building expenditure in the seventeenth century, but it is equally clear that it was by no means as steep as the general rise in food prices.

The money expended on building was one of the largest capital sums laid out by the majority of country house builders. The estates of a few noble families were plunged into debt as a result of building, but for the builder of the smaller country house the consequences were rarely disastrous. The heaviest expenditure on building usually took place in the first few years of the work when large quantities of material were assembled, the executive labour force set up, and the shell of the building begun. At Trentham Hall, Staffordshire, for example, where the total expenditure between 1630 and 1639 was £6,165.17s.4d., the sum laid out in the first three years was £2,817.8s.2d., or nearly half the total.[30] With foresight, it was possible to mitigate the difficulty of raising sufficient funds for the initial expenditure. If materials had been stockpiled for some years prior to starting work, or if surplus profits had been accumulated for the purpose, then the estate of the builder would not have been subject to undue strain when building began. Such advance planning, however, was probably rarely thorough enough to obviate the need for a certain amount of short-term manipulation of the resources of the builder. Leases would have to be granted for low rents and large entry fines, woodlands farmed, and rent charges sold to raise extra capital, while the prospective builder would call in any money that he might have out on loan. In 1668, when Sir Roger Pratt was considering rebuilding his house at Ryston, Norfolk, he wrote a memorandum to himself,

> To see what moneys I have out & to consider well in what hands, & to adjust all interest due to mee, & to speedily call in what moneys I shall think fitt for my intended building.[31]

Fountains Hall, Yorkshire.

Broome Park, Kent.

Following the accumulation of sufficient funds to meet the initial expenditure, many builders seem to have been largely successful in financing the bulk of their works out of current revenue. Special conditions, again, apply to the ostentatious courtier houses where excessive expenditure made deep inroads into capital, but the majority of builders appear to have allocated certain items from their annual income for building expenses and the amount of work executed in that year would be fairly loosely related to the product of those items. Sir Thomas Tresham largely organized the financing of his building work in this fashion. In 1594, for example, he set aside £112.18s.10d. made up of certain rents and the proceeds of selling timber and livestock to pay for his work on the Triangular Lodge.[32] His expenditure over the same period was £114.6s.10½d., leaving a deficit of only £1.8s.0½d. to be made up from other sources.[33] The pattern of his expenditure seems to have varied little in subsequent years, with much of the finance for his various building works being provided by rent money supplemented by the occasional sale of superfluous materials, horses, sheep, and on one occasion a cottage.[34] Sir Francis Willoughby used his resources in a similar way in the 1580s when he largely financed the building of Wollaton Hall, Nottinghamshire, out of the income from his rents and coalmines.[35] In the building accounts for 1586 for example, receipts, including over £600 for 'collmoney' were in excess of £1,700 while the recorded disbursements totalled just over £990.

Few of the builders of smaller country houses had a surplus income as large as that of Sir Francis Willoughby, and the amount of money that they would have been able to put into their building every year must have been comparatively small. It was probably as a result of limited investment capital that many of the buildings that they erected took so long to complete. Chantmarle in Dorset was begun in April 1612, but it was 1623 before the work was finished. The modest Redgrave Hall, built at the outset of Sir Nicholas Bacon's career, took nearly ten years to complete, and Sir Thomas Tresham spent four years building the minute Triangular Lodge at Rushton. It usually took something like ten years to build a small country house, whereas, by way of contrast, the Earl of Salisbury's mansion at Hatfield was built and the gardens laid out within five years of the work commencing. It was certainly technically feasible to build at a faster rate and, given the domestic inconvenience while building was in progress, it was probably highly desirable to do so. Several factors could have been responsible for the slow pace of construction. The shortage of skilled building craftsmen has already been mentioned, and this clearly would have been reflected in the speed with which the less influential builders were able to build. However, a more important limitation was probably that imposed by the amount of money available from year to year. The annual income of the builder was liable to fluctuate and, where the building was being financed out of current revenue, the effects of this would be apparent in the accounts. At Loseley, Sir William More spent approximately £180 and £220 respectively on the first two years of building, but for the next three years between 1563 and 1566 his annual expenditure dropped to an average of £65. In 1567 his expenditure rose to £292 and it remained around that higher level for the final two years of the work.[36] In the absence of any other evidence, it is reasonable to explain the dramatic fall in expenditure at such a crucial stage of the work by a reduction in his income over the same period. A similar explanation can be suggested at Redgrave where Sir Nicholas Bacon's expenditure in 1548 dropped to £101 following the outlay of £268 in the previous year, but rose again to £170 in 1550 and £200 in 1551.[37] Although many of the accounts are uninformative on the method by which the work was financed, it would seem a reasonable assumption that where progress was slow and the annual expenditure was subject to otherwise inexplicable fluctuations, the building was being financed largely out of current revenue.

Throughout the period, few builders seem to have made use of commercial loans to help finance their work. There are no examples of money borrowed at interest being employed on any of the surviving sixteenth-century accounts, and the very few examples from the seventeenth century are for comparatively small amounts and date from well into the century. In the early years of his work at Trentham, Staffordshire, when his expenditure was at its highest, Sir Richard Leveson was using two separate loans of £200 to help finance the building. He paid the interest on the loans at six-monthly intervals, at the statutory rate of 8 per cent per annum. By the summer of 1633 he had paid off one of the loans, but the remaining loan was continued until January 1635.[38] The £400 that he was borrowing in 1633 was equal to a third of his total expenditure in that year, and it seems likely that he was using it in an attempt to finish the building at a faster rate than his ordinary resources would allow. By the end of 1635, when he was no longer borrowing extra capital, he had paid off the majority of his masons and carpenters, and the fitting out of the building over the next four years proceeded at a more leisurely pace. Sir Roger Pratt also borrowed money to assist him in the rebuilding of Ryston Hall, Norfolk. The exact details of the transaction are unknown, but in 1670 he owed £20 in 'Interest money to Piggot & Grene'.[39] It is uncertain what period this interest covered, but as the total cost of the house was only £2,900, it is unlikely that the capital borrowed was very large. Pratt himself had lent £1,300 at interest in 1650 to his relative Sir George Pratt, to enable him to build Coleshill House in Berkshire.[40]

The difficulties of raising sufficient capital were solved for a few builders by generous gifts from their relatives. Stiffkey Hall, Norfolk, built to provide a suitable home for the newly married Nathaniel Bacon, was largely paid for by his father, Sir Nicholas Bacon. At the time of its construction, Nathaniel was clearly incapable of financing such a project. In a letter of 1576 he wrote to his father that 'ye charg is too great for my present estat'. Sir Nicholas bought the manor, paid for the building materials, supplied some of the skilled labour force, and in his will he bequeathed the estate to his son together with £200 towards the cost of finishing the house.[41] Bess of Hardwick gave £300 in 1593 to her son, William Cavendish, when he was building Oldcotes in Derbyshire, and in 1599 she contributed a further £100 to the building expenses. Another of her sons, Charles Cavendish, similarly received £300 from his mother in 1597 and another £100 in 1599 to help pay for the house that he was building at Kirkby-in-Ashfield, Nottinghamshire.[42] Harrold House, Bedfordshire, was partly financed by Sir Thomas Boteler, the son-in-law of the builder, Francis Farrar. The accounts for 1608–10 show the expenditure of £162.8s.4d., of which £65 had been contributed by Boteler. This was probably more in the nature of an investment than a gift, for in 1614 Farrar settled the property on the heirs of Sir Thomas and Dame Alice, his wife.[43]

Part III

MATERIALS

Longleat

The end is to build well.

SIR HENRY WOTTON, 1624

CHAPTER 9

The Principal Materials

Whether of timber, brick or stone, the majority of country houses were built of local materials. The difficulty, and above all the expense, of transporting bulky materials meant that all but the most extravagant builders were restricted to the materials close at hand. It was only those builders for whom costs were secondary to considerations of magnificence who were able to use distant sources for their basic materials.

Although choice of materials was to a large extent governed by the ease with which they were available, great care was often taken before selecting those which were most suitable. In December 1575, when Nathaniel Bacon had decided to use moulded brick dressings for his house at Stiffkey, Norfolk, he wrote to his father:

> in ye beginning of ye spring [I will] cause tryall to be mad how ye [ground] in Styfkey [will serve] for yt purpose.[1]

At Rushton, Northamptonshire, when a new quarry of ironstone for Sir Thomas Tresham's Triangular Lodge was opened up in 1595, one of the masons spent a full working week making 'ashelers and a coyne of redstone wrought only for trial of the stone'.[2]

Experimentation was not confined to the basic materials of the fabric, and a similar care was exercised over the choice of the materials for the more important fittings. The joiner at Gawthorpe Hall, Lancashire, for example, spent part of March 1605 in 'tryeinge of tymber' for the great table in the dining chamber.[3] The builders of the larger houses were equally selective in choosing their materials. In 1609, when the Earl of Northumberland was about to battlement Syon House, Middlesex, he sought the advice of his officers up and down the country and had tests made on various samples of stone from Northumberland before deciding to use Purbeck stone,[4] and the surviving correspondence concerning the preparations for the Duke of Somerset's house at Great Bedwyn, Wiltshire, in 1548 and 1549, is largely devoted to a discussion of the merits of various quarries. To help choose the most suitable quarry one of his agents in Wiltshire sent 'a wallet of stone to London, whereon I have written upon every stone where he grew'.[5] A proposal to add a colonnade to the river side of Salisbury House, London, in 1610, uncertain as to whether Caen stone or Beer stone would be the more suitable for the project, suggested that:

all stones both for pillers and frontispice may lye roughe hewed at theyr quarryes two winters at the leaste and then a man shall assuredly see which be the stones will hold and he shall see a nomber that at the first he would have thought serviceable breake and moulder away.[6]

However, it is doubtful whether many builders went to such expensive and time-consuming lengths before selecting their building stone. For most of them it was simply a choice between what they possessed on their own estates and what was available from outside sources in the surrounding area.

STONE

Although brick was used to build a number of prestigious buildings in the sixteenth and seventeenth centuries, the time-honoured popularity of stone was unaffected. For the majority of country house builders, brick provided an alternative building material only in those areas where stone was not easily available. Even in these areas, brick-built houses were often embellished with stone dressings, for finely dressed stone was still a material that was indicative of social status. If a builder was unable to obtain sufficient stone he was sometimes prepared to imitate its appearance in other materials. Clement Paston used moulded brick

Eastbury House with brick windows disguised to 'shewe as freestone'.

for the window dressings at Oxnead Hall in Norfolk in 1570, and 'yei shewe as freestone'. Nathaniel Bacon followed his example at Stiffkey Hall in the same county and treated several of his brick windows with plaster in an attempt to achieve the same effect.[7] Other examples of a similar practice in eastern England include the gatehouse at Giffords Hall, Stoke-by-Nayland, Suffolk, Ingatestone Hall and Eastbury House, both in Essex. In London, Paul D'Ewes even specified that the wooden windows on the three houses that he was building at Charing Cross in 1626 were to be finished 'wth collour of whight lead like stone worke'.[8]

This imitation of stone was not just a stylistic conceit. There was clearly a very strong desire on the part of many builders for a prominent display of stone to adorn the principal elevations of their houses, but it was a desire that was limited by practical considerations. If they were not able to acquire stone on reasonable terms, they were prepared to use other materials that provided the form if not the substance. Mainly because of the difficulties and the heavy costs of transportation, it was only the influential and the wealthy who were able to bring stone from distant quarries to use on their buildings. The majority of builders chose to build in other materials if there was no building stone available in the vicinity of their proposed house, or easily accessible by water. They would, if it were possible, use small quantities of stone for decorative effect, but they were not prepared to go to excessive lengths to acquire it. Thus the distribution of stone-built country houses largely reflects the geological distribution of suitable building stone, and the exceptions to this pattern can usually be explained by good communications by water.

The majority of houses were built of local stone. Gawthorpe Hall, Lancashire, was largely constructed of red sandstone from quarries opened up on the site,[9] while the stone for the fabric of Loseley House, Surrey, came from Guildford, just over three miles away.[10] Sir Thomas Tresham's various building works of the late sixteenth and early seventeenth centuries mainly used stone from the local quarries at Rushton, Pipewell and Pilton, although small quantities were brought from the highly regarded quarries at Weldon and King's Cliffe, both of which were within fifteen miles of the site.[11] The large quantities of stone required for Sir Richard Leveson's Trentham Hall, Staffordshire, in the 1630s, were all dug in the neighbourhood of the house.[12]

The use of local stone was not confined to the smaller country houses. Some of the most ostentatious houses of the period exhibit a similar preference. Burghley House, the mansion of William Cecil, was built mostly of stone from Barnack, where the quarries were almost within sight of the house, although stone for some of the more exotic fittings was shipped from Antwerp by Sir Thomas Gresham.[13] Hardwick Hall, Derbyshire, the climax of Elizabeth of Shrewsbury's building career, is largely of local sandstone, and Sir Christopher Hatton's Kirby Hall, Northamptonshire, was built of stone from his quarries at Weldon, three miles away.

Some builders did use stone from more distant sources. Much of the stone for the early work at Longleat, Wiltshire, was quarried locally although it had been supplemented with Bath stone from Haselbury, twenty-five miles away. By 1567, however, when the design of the house entered its third phase, Sir John Thynne was getting the bulk of his stone from the quarries near Bath. By this date considerations of architectural effect were probably of more importance to him

William Cecil's Burghley House, built of Barnack stone.

than convenience of supply, but even so none of his stone was brought from a greater distance than the twenty-seven miles to his own quarries at Cheddar.[14] John Strode used stone from Ham and Whatley, respectively nineteen and twenty-six miles from the site of his house at Chantmarle in Dorset, but the expense was not great for 'a very great number of carriages of stones . . . were freely given me by me neighbours'.[15] There were very few builders indeed who sought stone from such diverse sources as those employed by Robert Cecil, Earl of Salisbury. During the first decade of the seventeenth century, for his buildings at Hatfield and London, he was using stone from Kent, Oxfordshire, Derbyshire, Yorkshire, Devon, Dorset, Lincolnshire, Northumberland and Normandy, in addition to a small quantity of marble from Italy.[16] His father, Lord Burghley, has already been noted as using stone brought over from Holland, and he also imported stone from Spain in 1584 'to helpe finishe a device in the grete chambr at tebolts'.[17] These, however, were for fittings, and the fabric of both his principal houses was of local materials. Caen stone from northern France was highly prized by powerful builders in southern England and, where convenient sea transport was available, it was a practical choice for those who could afford it. Warblington House for the Countess of Salisbury and the converted Titchfield Abbey for Sir Thomas Wriothesley, both in Hampshire, used quantities of Caen stone for decorative effects shipped through Southampton in the 1520s and '30s. Lord Cobham employed substantial quantities of Caen stone on Cobham Hall, Kent, in the 1580s and '90s, as well as black touchstone from Derbyshire given to him by Bess of Hardwick.[18]

However, there were usually special circumstances involved when builders used stone that had to be transported by land for any distance. Although some of the stone for Wollaton Hall, Nottinghamshire, was quarried locally, most of it was brought thirty-five miles from Ancaster in Lincolnshire, and there is a persistent legend that Sir Francis Willoughby's pack-horses carried coal from his mines at Wollaton to the quarries and returned laden with stone.[19] Unfortunately, the books relating to materials and carriage are missing from the surviving building accounts for Wollaton and it is not possible to verify the story, but the arrangement would not seem to have been inherently improbable.

Sometimes the special reason for bringing stone from a distance was the opportunity of a good bargain, or the influence of an acquaintance at the source. Thus in 1594, Sir Edward Pytts paid the very reasonable sum of £6.15s.

> for 10 tun of Hoscum hedd stone being so great that 10 stones conteyned the 10 tun hadd from my cosen Pytts chamberleyn of Brystowe [Bristol] of the executors of one that hadd provided them for some great purpose.

Although the stone was some eighty-five miles away from the house that Pytts was building in Worcestershire, the carriage was a relatively simple matter using the River Severn.[20]

Indeed, the availability of water transport seems to have been the crucial factor in considering the use of quarries further than a few miles from the site. Old Thorndon Hall in Essex, for example, was a brick-built house which incorporated small quantities of stone for decorative effect. For his gatehouse and terrace, Sir John Petre bought stone in Devon in 1594.[21] The quarries at Beer were conveniently situated close to the sea, as were those on the Isle of Purbeck from which he bought stone in 1581, and the only land transport involved was for the ten miles to the site from Grays Thurrock where the stone was landed. Similarly, the Merstham stone and Kentish Rag used in 1586 and 1594 were brought down the River Medway and then carried by sea to Grays. At Kyre Park, the principal sources of stone were from quarries opened up in the park and Madeley Quarry in Shropshire, some thirty-six miles away. The stone from the latter was carried down the Severn to Bewdley, and thence by land to Kyre, the overland stage of the journey costing only 5s. the load.[22]

The great limestone quarries of the east Midlands were all accessible to the comparatively stoneless counties of East Anglia via the River Ouse, the River Nene and the River Welland. Stone from Clipsham and Weldon, brought up the Little Ouse to Brandon, was used at Little Saxham Hall, Suffolk, between 1505 and 1514.[23] The upper storey of Hengrave Hall, Suffolk, was built of King's Cliffe stone in the 1530s, and again Brandon provided the collecting point.[24] In the early seventeenth century, the stone for Raynham Hall, Norfolk, came from Ketton and Clipsham and was carried by water to King's Lynn, where it was transferred to carts for the eighteen-mile journey to the site.[25] The problems of transportation will be considered in more general terms elsewhere. As a factor in the distribution of stone away from the quarries, they were of the highest importance. Transport by land of such a heavy and bulky material was generally difficult and consequently added greatly to the cost of stone delivered at the site. Water carriage was considerably easier and less expensive. As a result it was the quarries that were near water that produced the most sought-after stone and which created the distribution pattern for those country houses of the sixteenth and seventeenth centuries that were not built of local stone.

Transport costs were only one factor in the price of stone; albeit a factor which disproportionately increased in importance the further the quarry was situated from the building site. But, as has already been emphasized, most houses were built of local stone, often from quarries opened up on the estate. These quarries, of course, belonged to the builder, and the only expense that was involved was in digging the stone and moving it the short distance to where the house was being built. Some builders who used their own stone for the fabric of the building also bought small quantities of better stone for special effects. Thus Harrold House, Bedfordshire, was built of stone dug in Francis Farrar's own pits on the site, but the string-courses and some of the windows were of stone from the quarries at Olney and Warrington, six miles away, and the remaining windows and the porch were of Weldon stone.[26] The proposals for the new house at Petworth for the Earl of Northumberland in 1615 show that the house was largely to be built of stone quarried in two places in the park, but that Purbeck and Beer stone were to be bought for paving and lining the ovens.[27]

If the stone on the builder's own land was of insufficient quality, or if there was no stone at all, he sometimes bought a quarry to provide him with the necessary material. Sir John Thynne bought a quarry at Haselbury, near Box, in 1573,[28] although this was only one of several sources of supply. When Sir Christopher Hatton bought the unfinished Kirby Hall from the executors of Sir Humphrey Stafford in 1575, he also bought the neighbouring quarry land at Weldon. After completing the house, he leased the quarries out to various local masons.[29] The agent for Robert Cecil even went to the length of buying a quarry at Caen in Normandy in the early seventeenth century to expedite the supply of that stone for the earl's various building projects.[30]

However, most builders only required stone for a single building operation of limited duration, and their needs could be met by renting a quarry. Sir William More rented a quarry at Guildford for seven years between 1563 and 1569, and it provided almost all the stone that he required to build Loseley House.[31] William Dickenson, bailiff to the Earl of Shrewsbury, rented a quarry from his employer to provide the stone for the house that he built for himself in Sheffield in 1575,[32] and Sir John Thynne had been renting quarries from the Duchess of Somerset and a farmer at Slaughterford for seven years before he bought his quarry at Haselbury.[33]

Both the purchase and the renting of a quarry meant that the builder had to arrange and supervise the extraction of the stone. This meant setting up a separate administrative organization away from the building site, and many builders preferred to buy direct from quarry owners and stone suppliers instead. The Weldon stone for Harrold House was bought from the Grumbold family, who leased some of the quarry land in the village from Lord Hatton.[34] From the late sixteenth century, stone from the quarries at Little Barrington in Gloucestershire and Taynton in Oxfordshire was supplied by Timothy Strong, who

> had several apprentices, and kept several masons and labourers employed in those quarries, to serve the Country with what they wanted in his way of trade.[35]

The business was continued with great success by his sons and grandsons in the following century. Both the Grumbolds and the Strongs were masons, as were many of the other stone suppliers, such as Arnold Goversonne who provided the Ketton stone for Raynham Hall, Norfolk, in 1621,[36] and Gabriel Caldam who owned quarries in Kent and supplied stone for the Royal Works in the 1530s and '40s.[37] Quarrying must have provided alternative employment for masons resident in stone areas when they were not engaged on building work. The quarries that they worked often seem to have been small,[38] and they were probably only capable of supplying stone for dressings and not for the complete fabric of a large house. Rented quarries, or quarries owned by the builder, provided the bulk of the stone for the country houses.

Where a large amount of stone was required it was often quarried by the builder's own work force. Usually one of the principal masons on the site would be sent to the quarry to examine and select the stone which would be most suitable for the building, and then the extraction would be undertaken by labourers and less skilled workmen. Thus the stone from King's Cliffe used at Hengrave Hall, Suffolk, in 1537, was chosen by two of Sir Thomas Kytson's masons in April and by the end of the month his labourers were working at the quarry.[39] When the stone was quarried within the estate, the total work force was usually provided by the builder himself, as at Trentham Hall, Staffordshire, in the 1630s,[40] and at Harrold House, Bedfordshire, in 1608–10,[41] but when the stone came from some distance away from the site the builder's workmen were used to supplement the quarryman's labour force. When Sir Edward Pytts was about to start the rebuilding of Kyre Park, Worcestershire, in 1588, he gave the quarryman of Madeley Quarry, Shropshire, 5s. 'toward hiring of workmen to uncover the quarry', and in addition sent two of his own labourers to the quarry to help extract the stone.[42] This must have been inconvenient for the builder, for arrangements would have to have been made for the boarding of the workmen while they were away from the site, but few quarries were capable of the independent production of large quantities of stone to satisfy an irregular demand. The organization maintained by Timothy Strong at Little Barrington and Taynton was probably unusual.

Occasionally the quarrying was carried out by masons but usually it was a job reserved for unskilled labour. Where masons were employed at the quarry they were generally engaged on more skilled tasks, such as squaring and dressing the blocks of stone as they were quarried. The principal mason at Longleat in 1546 was occupied in working 'stone square at the quarrie'[43] and most of the stone for Trentham Hall, Staffordshire, was dressed by the masons at the quarry.[44] One very good reason for roughly squaring stone at the quarry was that a certain amount of surplus weight was thereby removed, and thus the problems and the cost of transport were not quite so great. Another reason, possibly of even more importance, was that freestones are more easily worked when first quarried, as they are comparatively soft. On exposure to the atmosphere they gradually harden, and as transport was slow, advantage could only be taken of their initial softness at the quarry face.

Usually it was only the blocks of stone for walling that were worked upon by the masons at the quarry, but there are a few examples of more finely carved work being executed. In 1563, the mason William Spicer contracted to make a number of windows for Longleat at the quarry at Oldford, Somerset,[45] and in 1570 another of Thynne's masons, Thomas Gregory, made sixteen chimney-shafts at Haselbury quarry.[46] The scutcheons for Sir Thomas Tresham's Triangular Lodge were made in the quarry at Pipewell in 1596,[47] and much of the masons' work for his lodge at Lyveden was executed in the quarry at Weldon.[48] Where the quarry was close to the site of the building, as at Bolsover Castle, Derbyshire, in 1613, the masons mainly worked at the quarry, but on the whole, detailed carving of stone from distant quarries was executed at the site.

In the seventeenth century, there is some evidence to suggest a growing practice of commissioning independent masons who were not employed directly as wage-earners by the builder, to provide finished stone-work at the site. There was, of course, a long-standing medieval tradition of monumental masons carving figures and tombs in their own workshops for erection wherever they were required,[49] and this trade continued to flourish in the sixteenth and seventeenth centuries. In 1569, Sir William More bought three 'figures' in London to set over the porch at Loseley House, Surrey,[50] and the 8th Earl of Northumberland bought a fountain in London in the 1580s for erection at Petworth House, Sussex.[51] Chimney-pieces were also delivered ready-made at the site. The Duke of Northumberland ordered a chimney-piece for Dudley Castle, Staffordshire, in 1552 from John Chapman, who made it at Lacock Abbey in Wiltshire where he was working for Sir William Sharington, and sent it up by cart the following year.[52] In the seventeenth century, Nicholas Stone made chimney-pieces and other interior fittings in his London workshop for clients as far away as Yorkshire and Norfolk,[53] and he was also able to provide craftsmen if necessary to arrange for their erection on site. All these masons, however, were skilled carvers who specialized in decorative work; but there were other masons towards the end of the period who were providing ready-made structural stonework. In 1608 Francis Farrar bought 'wyndowe stuffe & corbell table' from a mason at Olney, and in 1610 the Grumbolds of Weldon provided him with 'stone reddy wrought' including 'toppstones' for his house at Harrold, Bedfordshire.[54] A similar service was provided by John Ashley and Sampson Frisbey, Ketton freemasons, who agreed to supply thirty-eight ready-made windows to the site at Thorpe Hall, Northamptonshire, in 1653.[55] There are even examples of finished stonework being sent overseas to Ireland, as when Sir Richard Boyle, 1st Earl of Cork, was preparing to build a house for his son at Gill Abbey, near Cork, in 1637, and 'employed Robert Belcher, into England, to supplie me with ffree stone chymneis, doores, and lightes, readie made at the free stone quarries at Donderry Hill, near Bristoll'.[56]

BRICK

The early part of the sixteenth century has been called with some justification the first great age of English brickwork.[57] As a material, brick was of considerable status throughout the century. The decorative properties inherent in the material were exploited to the full during the reign of Henry VIII, especially in the use of elaborately moulded and rubbed bricks for such prominent features as chimney-stacks and gable ends. It is clear that by the sixteenth century, the craft of bricklaying had reached a high level of technical perfection, although the most virtuoso effects were still largely confined to the eastern counties. By the end of the century, it had become an important building material in Hampshire and Berkshire, as well as in the counties surrounding London and in the south-east and eastern parts of the country, but brick was still rarely used in the Midlands and apart from the isolated example of Stevenstone, near Torrington, in Devon, rebuilt in the early sixteenth century by George Rolle, a London lawyer, it does not seem to have been adopted in the south-west until well into the seventeenth century.[58] The pattern of its distribution was largely imposed by geological factors, for in areas where building stone was easily obtainable the local material was generally preferred.

Although the use of brick in areas where suitable clay was available was no longer a novelty by the sixteenth century, it was still a material that was almost solely confined to important buildings. Very few houses of a social level below that of the country house were built wholly of brick during the period. This meant that there must have been a very erratic demand for the material, and that the making of bricks was almost always closely associated with the construction of the building that was to use them. This generalization is less valid, of course, for the eastern counties, particularly Norfolk, Suffolk and Essex, where there was a longer tradition of brick-making and where building in brick had passed further down the social scale; but even in this part of England there is little evidence for the independent manufacture of bricks on any scale. The large quantities of bricks required to build a country house were almost invariably made on the site or within a very short distance of it. Besides enabling the builder or his agents to closely supervise the process, this had the added advantage of reducing to a minimum the costs of transporting the heavy finished material.

In the sixteenth century brick-making was largely a seasonal activity with all the stages of manufacture being spread over twelve months. The accounts for Sir Nicholas Bacon's house at Redgrave, Suffolk, give a full description of how the process was carried out at the middle of the century. The clay was dug in the autumn or early winter and then spread out in an open field to be broken up by the moisture and frost. In the spring it was watered and trampled under foot. Any pebbles which would be liable to cause the clay to split in the course of firing were removed at this stage. The clay was then cut to size using wooden moulds, and left to dry in stacks for a period of about a month. The bricks were fired in kilns or clamps and by the time the process had been completed it was time to start digging the clay for the following year.[59] The bricks used for the building of Kyre Park, Worcestershire, between 1588 and 1594, were made in a similar way, with an annual firing in the late summer extending over a fortnight.[60]

Weather conditions were important to the success of the operation. It was, for example, crucial that there should be little rain during the time that the unburnt bricks were drying. The comments made by Sir Edward Pytts at the end of each years' brick-making at Kyre Park clearly illustrate the effects of the weather on production. In 1588 his brickmaker had contracted to make 200,000 bricks, but in the event produced only 57,000 'for no more colde be made this yeare because the continuall rayne letted', and again in 1592 only 100,800 bricks were made because 'the beginning of sommer proved very wett and unseasonable for making thereof'.

The clamps, which often seem to have been very temporary affairs and were rebuilt each year, were generally wood-fired. Brush wood and 'gren', or unseasoned, wood were used at Little Saxham, Suffolk, in 1507,[61] although coal was in use on the site for burning lime. It appears that there was a definite preference in the sixteenth century for wood-fired brick, for Sir Edward Pytts also made use of substantial amounts of coal at Kyre Park but only burnt wood at his brick-kilns. By the seventeenth century, however, there is evidence of an increasing use of coal. The Earl of Salisbury initially had the bricks for Hatfield House made in wood-fired kilns, but towards the end of the enterprise coal was being used,[62] and the brick-kilns at Raynham Hall, Norfolk, used both coal and wood for fuel between 1619 and 1622.[63] It is unlikely that the change was wholly due to a shortage of timber. Possibly it was being realized that the predictable burning qualities of coal could take some of the uncertainty out of the firing process.

Complaints about insufficiently burnt bricks are frequently met with. The contract with a brickmaker for 200,000 bricks at Little Saxham Hall in 1505 specifically excluded any bricks from the total that were not thoroughly burnt,[64] and bricks from 'the evill burned clampe' at Redgrave Hall, Suffolk, were only fit for use as rubble.[65] At Loseley House, Surrey, in 1561 a clamp of over 120,000 bricks had to be fired again because the bricks had been insufficiently burnt.[66] It was more usual for only part of the bricks in any particular batch to be unsatisfactory, as with the clamp burnt by Sir Edward Pytts at Kyre Park in 1594, where

> the side toward the meddowe is worst burnt because the winde lay allwaies in that end: the other side is throwlie burnt.[67]

Although the bricks measuring $9\frac{1}{2} \times 4\frac{1}{2} \times 2\frac{1}{4}$ inches in use at Eton College in 1543–4 were said to be 'of a lawfull scantlyng'[68] there was, in fact, little uniformity in the size of bricks in use during the period. Given the way that they were made to order as required, this is hardly surprising. Those at Little Saxham Hall in 1505 were 'to be x inch in length, v inch in brede, and ij inch & di in thiknesse when it is wele and sufficiently brent',[69] while the bricks used at Redgrave Hall measured $9 \times 4 \times 2$ inches.[70] Eastbury House, Essex, was built in the 1560s with $10 \times 4\frac{1}{2} \times 2\frac{1}{2}$ inch bricks.[71] In the early seventeenth century Ince Castle, Cornwall, used bricks with the comparatively small dimensions of $8 \times 4 \times 2$ inches,[72] and later in the century Sir Balthazar Gerbier advocated an ideal size of $9\frac{1}{2} \times 4\frac{5}{8} \times 2\frac{3}{4}$ inches.[73]

The overall picture that emerges of brick-making in the sixteenth and early seventeenth centuries is of a largely localized activity. There were specialized brick-makers who travelled some distance for employment, such as the two brick-makers from Essex working at Raynham Hall, Norfolk, in 1619,[74] but on the whole brick-makers tended to be local men who could be called upon during the fairly short periods of the year when their services were necessary. It is unlikely that the manufacture of bricks provided them with a full-time occupation, but in the eastern counties at least there was probably enough building taking place to provide them with some work during most years. For over twenty years from 1573 to about 1595, the requirements of Old Thorndon Hall, Essex, provided annual work for Walter Guy of Great Warley and George Bowes of East Horndon.[75] It is significant that neither of these men had their own kilns. They were employed only to make bricks at the various kilns set up around the site of the house. This was the usual arrangement for most of the brick-built houses of the period. The builder supplied the equipment, including the moulds, and the brick-maker provided only his labour and his skill.[76] There are a few examples of ready-made bricks being bought, but they are generally of insignificant amounts, such as the 2,200 bricks bought in May 1635 for the stone-built Trentham Hall, Staffordshire, and used 'for the topping of a chymney in ye evidence house'.[77]

As most of the bricks were made on the site it was possible for many of the stages in the manufacturing process to be carried out by unskilled labour. The expertise of the brick-maker was only really necessary to select the clay and to supervise the moulding and firing of the bricks. Consequently brick-makers tended either to be employed on a part-time basis, working only in the autumn and the spring, in which case they could only be regularly available if they were local men, or they were capable of carrying out other tasks on the site during the periods when they were not making bricks. Thus, Hugh Hether, the brick-maker at Longleat between 1568 and 1576, was also employed as a labourer,[78] while the bricks for Kyre Park, Worcestershire, were made by Thomas Lem, who also acted as the principal mason.[79]

Terracotta was a specialized form of brick made from fine-textured clays and it demanded great care and skill in its manufacture. The firing was particularly crucial but, like brick, it seems to have been produced to order on site rather than imported from abroad as was once thought. It was capable of being moulded with very fine surface decoration and is usually associated with precocious early Renaissance details at houses such as Hampton Court, Sutton Place and Layer Marney, but it was also used as a facing material. Its popularity was confined to a short period in the early sixteenth century and its distribution was restricted to southern and eastern England, especially East Anglia and the Thames Valley.[80]

TIMBER

Although country houses in many counties were built of timber, the only extant documentary information for timber-framed houses of any size are contracts of 1551 for an extension to Sir Thomas Bromley's house at Eyton-on-Severn, Shropshire, and of 1617 for alterations to a house in Lancashire.[81] The building accounts of 1608–10 for John Coke's modest house of Hall Court at Much Marcle, Herefordshire, are something of an exception, and consequently timber will largely be considered here in its secondary role as a material for the framework of roofs and floors and as a medium for applied decoration.

The most common variety of wood used for structural purposes was oak. It seems to have been generally preferred, both for its qualities of strength and durability, and for its natural abundance. There are, however, a few examples of other types of wood being used. A.W. Clapham found that almost all the woodwork of the Court House at Barking in Essex was of chestnut, including the frame, the roof, the stairs, and the windows.[82] It is no longer possible to test this

A terracotta medallion on Cardinal Wolsey's Hampton Court.

assertion as the building has been demolished and the accounts for its construction do not specify what sort of timber was used.[83] It should be noted, however, that oak and chestnut became visually almost indistinguishable with age. The Court House was built in 1567, and at about the same time Clement Sysley was building Eastbury House, just over a mile away, where he is said to have similarly employed chestnut for a staircase and some of the floor joists.[84] Elm was another timber sometimes used instead of oak. Francis Farrar employed it at Harrold House, Bedfordshire, in 1609,[85] and it was also used at Raynham Hall,

Terracotta decoration at Sutton Place.

Norfolk, in 1619 and 1621.[86] In addition, Sir Roger Townshend used a small quantity of maple at Raynham, as did Sir Nicholas Bacon at Redgrave Hall, Suffolk, in the mid-sixteenth century.[87] These are isolated examples, however, and generally oak was the preferred wood.

Oak was also used for interior fittings such as floorboards and panelling, but owing to its tendency to warp and crack it was necessary to season it carefully. Deal, which was easier to work and which seasoned more quickly, was growing in popularity. Walnut was used on occasion, generally for furniture as at Wollaton in 1587[88] where tables were made from it; but at Kyre Park, Worcestershire, in 1595, a quantity of 8 ft planks were possibly used for floorboards.[89] Ash and alder were used for scaffolding poles, and at Loseley House, Surrey, in 1566, ash boards were used for flooring.[90]

Much of the structural timberwork seems to have been used unseasoned. It has been estimated that a trunk of oak requires a year's seasoning for each inch of thickness plus an additional year for every three inches of the total thickness[91] and few builders would have been able to plan their complete timber supply that far in advance. In addition, unseasoned oak was much easier to work, and as it dried out it became harder, so that the strength of the work was not necessarily compromised by the wood's tendency to warp. Carpenters were generally conservative in their estimates of stresses and tolerances, although weaknesses in the design of the timberwork for the early seventeenth-century Schools Quadrangle, at Oxford, were aggravated by the use of unseasoned timber.[92]

It was crucial, however, that the finer woodwork such as floors, doors, and panelling, should not warp. There was little margin for error in this sort of work, and generally it was specifically stated that the timber used should be properly seasoned. In the contract for the Perse Building at Gonville and Caius College,

Cambridge, in 1617, the floorboards and the doors were to be of 'seasoned board of oake', but there were no instructions for the seasoning of the structural timbers.[93] Contracts for the Legge Building at the same college in 1618, for St John's College in 1598, and for St Catharine's Hall in 1611, were similarly selective in their instructions.[94] In June 1547, Sir John Thynne wrote from France to his steward at Longleat to ensure that he would

> not forget that there be plancks sawen for my dores so that they may be seasoned in tyme,[95]

and the only wood specifically stated to be seasoned at Trentham Hall, Staffordshire, in the 1630s, was used by the joiners for panelling and flooring.[96] At Rushton Hall, Northamptonshire, in 1595, insufficient seasoning caused the gallery floor to warp in several places and in consequence it had to be replaced shortly after it had been laid.[97]

Sir John Thynne placed the responsibility for ensuring that the wood had been correctly treated on his joiners,

> for if I shall finde any faut with the workmanship or the seasoning of their stuf they shall make it agayn.[98]

He recommended that when the wood had been sawn into planks they should be 'laid up drye with stikks betweene it so that it may season the better'.[99] Another method for seasoning panelling, similar to the modern technique, was that suggested by William Spicer to the Earl of Leicester in 1571. The trees at Kenilworth were to be cut to size and the pieces then immersed in water to remove the acid and the sap. The process was to be completed by the use of a drying kiln or oven.[100] It was a method that was far more sophisticated and quicker than that in use at Longleat twenty-four years earlier.

The sources of timber supply were generally local, although a number of builders seem to have experienced difficulty in accumulating sufficient quantities. Most builders possessed some woodland of their own but sometimes it was insufficient to meet the heavy demands of a building programme, and there are a number of documented buildings where timber had to be brought from a source well away from the site. There is evidence of difficulties of supply in certain parts of the country as early as the first decade of the sixteenth century. Timber, like stone, was a difficult material to transport, and the costs of carrying it were considerable; consequently it is not unreasonable to deduce that a builder who brought quantities of timber, other than softwood for internal work, from outside the neighbourhood of his building, was unable to find enough local timber for his works. Although much of the timber used in the first few years for Little Saxham Hall came from within a radius of six miles of the site, by 1508, trees from Winfarthing Park in Norfolk, thirty-three miles away, were being used, and other sources of supply were being sought at Hundon Park, eleven miles away and Rattlesden, thirteen miles away.[101] When Sir Thomas Kytson built Hengrave Hall, a few miles distant, he seems to have had similar difficulties over his timber supply. Some was brought the fifteen miles from Woolpit Wood, near Stowmarket, and in 1527 and 1528 he bought and dismantled two timber-framed houses and a barn and had the timber transported to the site where, presumably, it was re-used in an inconspicuous place in the new building.[102]

Most of the evidence for a shortage of building timber in the first half of the sixteenth century is confined to East Anglia, and particularly to Suffolk, but by June 1567 Sir John Thynne was writing from Longleat in Wiltshire to the Earl of Hertford thanking him for fifty trees and hoping for a similar number in the following year, 'timber being my only lack'.[103] In 1587, timber for Wollaton Hall, Nottinghamshire, was brought nearly forty miles from Kingsbury in Warwickshire,[104] and among Sir Francis Willoughby's other sources of supply were Middleton, Derbyshire,[105] twenty-five miles away, and West Hallam, seven miles away.[106] The difficulty of finding sufficient timber was as acute in Norfolk as it was in Suffolk. Sir Nathaniel Bacon began negotiating for timber for his house at Stiffkey early in 1573, although work on the building did not commence until 1576. In 1574 he secured a lease on the oaks in Hindolveston Wood, eleven miles from the site, and in the following year one of his agents bought 'a gret bargenye of tymbere of Mr George Thembetthorpe' of Foulsham, fourteen miles away, which was 'redye brocon so that it lake but the framyn'. Further timber was purchased in 1576 from Sir Thomas Gresham's wood at Mileham, eighteen miles from Stiffkey.[107]

Other areas where there is documentary evidence of a shortage of timber include Plymouth in the early seventeenth century, where the demands of the shipbuilding industry led the overseers for the building of the new Guildhall to import timber from Ireland,[108] and parts of Lancashire where the timber for Gawthorpe Hall was brought from eight miles away, and laths and boards had to be purchased in Halifax, twenty-seven miles distant.[109] Clearly there was a scarcity of good building timber but it only seems to have been a major problem in certain parts of the country, and was not faced by all the builders of whom we have record. A large number of country houses, particularly in the south and in parts of the Midlands, were predominantly built of local timber. The builders of such houses as Hardwick Hall and Bolsover Castle in Derbyshire, Harrold House in Bedfordshire, Loseley House, Surrey, and Old Thorndon Hall, Essex, seem to have had little trouble in getting sufficient structural timber in the immediate neighbourhood of their building sites. When the estimates were drawn up in 1615 for the Earl of Northumberland's proposed new building at Petworth, Sussex, it was envisaged that the estate would be able to provide all the required timber apart from the soft wood for the panelling which was to be supplied by the joiner.[110]

It seems that the generally accepted thesis of a growing shortage of timber in the late sixteenth and early seventeenth centuries must be modified to a certain extent in its application to the building industry. In the first place, there is evidence that it was affecting builders in Suffolk from the very beginning of the sixteenth century, and on the other hand it seems that a large number of country house builders, particularly in the south-east and in the north Midlands, completely escaped the effects of any shortage. It is instructive to note that much of the contemporary evidence for a shortage of timber was concerned with its use as a fuel.[111] There were few complaints of a scarcity of building wood before the seventeenth century. In the first edition of William Harrison's *Description of England* in 1577, 'lacke of wood' for building was noted 'in the fennie countries', but in the second edition of 1586, the reference was extended to include the 'northern parts'.[112] John Norden expressed concern in 1607 about the depletion in Wealden timber that had taken place during the previous thirty years,[113] and Robert Reyce wrote in 1618, significantly with reference to Suffolk, of

> the carelesse wast of this age of our wonted plenty of timber, and other building stuffe . . . .[114]

In certain areas good building timber was in short supply, but this shortage was far from universal throughout the country.[115]

The timber to be used in the building was generally selected by the principal carpenter who examined the standing trees in the wood. At Stafford in 1589, the carpenter responsible for the roof of the new Shire Hall was given a dinner 'at choosing the Trees',[116] and two carpenters at Condover Hall, Shropshire, were paid 1s. each in February 1587 'for the veweinge of Timber in Longenoes-woodde'.[117] Saw pits, a recent innovation in the sixteenth century, were often constructed in the woods, and the trees were invariably sawn and roughly shaped on the spot as they were felled, both for convenience of transport and because they were easier to work in a 'green' state. The contract with the Shrewsbury carpenter John Sandford for a five-bay extension to Sir Thomas Bromley's house at Eyton-on-Severn, in 1551, specified that the complete frame was to be made at the wood in Acton Burnell before being transported and re-erected on the site.[118] But it was more common for the felled and sawn trees to be carried directly to the building site, where the carpenters could work on them at the 'framing yard', or 'framing place'.[119] Here the joints were made and the framework of features such as the roof assembled to check that the work was true. Adjustments could be more easily made at this stage than when the framework was in position on the building. The positions of all the main members were marked by roman numerals, and the framework was then dismantled ready for re-erecting on the building.

The placing of the frame in position was a particularly difficult job, and often extra labour was employed on a casual basis to assist the regular carpenters. At Trentham Hall, Staffordshire, ten extra men were taken on for two days in July 1633, to help the carpenters erect the stable.[120] Gloves were provided for the men involved, as at the Shire Hall, Stafford, in 1590, 'to hale ropes with',[121] and there were occasionally accidents. At Stafford 3s. 4d. was spent 'ffor spices and fitt meates and other necessaries ministered to Tusle sore bruised with a fall in rearing', and at Trentham in 1637 one of the casual labourers was given 5s., 'being hurt with a fall of the barne' that he was helping to erect.[122] The placing of the roof in position, marking as it did almost the final stage in the erection of the shell of the building, was often an occasion for celebration. Usually ale was provided for the workmen, but at William Dickenson's house in Sheffield in 1576, the substantial sum of £2.6s.9d. was spent on 'meat and drinck that Day that the howse was Reared,'[123] and at Gawthorpe Hall, Lancashire, the placing of the roof in June 1602 was celebrated with music when 6d. was 'gyven to a pypper upon the rearing day'.[124]

ROOFING MATERIALS

Tiles, which were one of the most popular roof coverings, were invariably made on the site or within the locality of the building. Their process of manufacture differed little from the methods used for making bricks. They were generally made by the same craftsmen using the same brick earth, and were fired in the same kilns, often together with the bricks, although specially decorated tiles which required more skill to manufacture were sometimes bought ready-made.

Recent research has produced a substantial body of documentary and archaeological evidence for the use of blue slate for roofing over a wide area of southern England in the Middle Ages.[125] The main sources of this slate were Devon and Cornwall, and it was sometimes even carried into areas where other local slates, such as the sandstone 'slates' of Horsham, were more readily available. One of the probable reasons for their extraordinary popularity was that they could usually be split much thinner than stone slates and consequently their use produced a much lighter roof covering. The advantages of this presumably outweighed the necessity of transporting them over considerable distances. Much of the transport, in any case, was by sea and river which was comparatively less expensive and difficult than land carriage.

Despite some evidence for a decline in the trade of West Country slates to Sussex after the middle of the fifteenth century, which can possibly be accounted for by a more vigorous exploitation of the local slates, they were employed on a number of important country houses in southern England in the sixteenth and seventeenth centuries. In 1529 the abbot of the monastery of Tavistock in Devon was instructed by Royal Commission to supply blue slate for use at Hampton Court,[126] and in 1574 Sir John Thynne bought 13,000 Cornish slates for Longleat.[127] Devonshire slate for Sir John Petre's banqueting house at Old Thorndon Hall, Essex, was carried by sea from Salcombe to Grays Thurrock in 1587.[128] In the seventeenth century, Lord Salisbury used small quantities of slate shipped from Plymouth on Hatfield House,[129] and Sir Francis Bacon roofed his curious banqueting house at Verulam with Cornish slate.[130] The Earl of Northumberland's intention in 1615 to use 667,000 pieces 'of blew slate to cover all the rooffes of them galleries' at Petworth suggests that the material continued to be used in Sussex for larger houses.[131] At Ashley Park, Surrey, 'blue slate' was used to cover the entrance porch and three dormer windows, presumably to contrast with the colour of the other roofing materials.[132]

There are few references to blue slates from Wales being employed on English country houses during the period, but no doubt they were used on occasion for houses in the west Midlands, and in 1564 Welsh slate was sent to Dublin for work on the cathedral.[133]

Fissile limestones and sandstones were also used as roofing materials, although their distribution tended to be fairly local and there is no evidence for a widespread trade similar to that for blue slates. Where suitable deposits were close to the sea, as at Purbeck, there were difficulties in extraction,[134] and as the technique of frost splitting was not discovered until the end of the sixteenth century, the slates had to be laboriously split by hand along the natural bedding planes.[135] The considerable weight of a stone roof which necessitated a much heavier timber framework was possibly a further inhibition to any extensive use of the material away from its area of origin. It was necessary to mine the limestone slates of the Cotswolds around Burford, and of Northamptonshire at Collyweston, but existing buildings in the locality show that they were extensively used, especially in the seventeenth century, and the proximity of the universities of Oxford and Cambridge provided them with further outlets. The sandstone slates quarried near Horsham were used in Surrey and Sussex, and to some extent in Kent. Loseley House, Surrey, was one of the larger houses on which they were employed[136] and it was intended to cover the main part of the Earl of Northumberland's house at Petworth in 1615 with them in contrast to the blue slate roofed galleries.[137] Sandstone slates were also used for roofing in parts of the west and north of England, and Bess of Hardwick employed them for Hardwick Old Hall, Derbyshire.[138]

Lead was used for a variety of purposes on the building site. Its malleable qualities and freedom from rust meant that it was extensively used for glazing and for rainwater systems. It was a highly expensive material. Between 1635 and 1638 £500, out of a total expenditure of £8,000, was spent on lead for Broome Park, Kent.[139] High costs, together with its general unsuitability for the purpose, meant that lead was rarely used for steeply-pitched roofs, although it was often employed to cover the curved and ogee-shaped turrets so characteristic of many of the buildings of the period. Lead, however, was virtually the only material capable of providing a watertight covering for roofs of a gentle or flat pitch, and its use for this purpose increased with the introduction of classical architectural motifs and the growing use of the roof as an important social space. Somerset House in London built between 1547 and 1552 was among the first houses to use lead extensively in this way, and it was subsequently used for such great houses as Longleat, Hardwick Hall and Hatfield.

The most important sources for lead were the mines of Derbyshire in the north, and of the Mendips in the south-west, but in view of the high basic cost of the material together with its transportation costs, considerable amounts of lead seem to have been re-used, especially in the south and the east of the country. At Hengrave Hall, Suffolk, in 1526, 112 lb of lead were bought from the vicar of nearby Cavenham, and in 1537 sixty loads of lead were brought from the abbey at Bury St Edmunds.[140] In 1509, long before the dissolution, the abbot of Bury had sold lead to Sir Thomas Lucas for Little Saxham Hall, Suffolk,[141] and after the dissolution of the monasteries increased quantities of lead suitable for re-using came on to the market. Much of this was used by the Royal Works, as at Canterbury in 1542,[142] but, like other monastic materials, a large amount was available for the private sector. Sir John Thynne got some lead in 1547 from Amesbury Abbey, Wiltshire, which had been granted at the dissolution to his patron, the Earl of Somerset,[143] and in 1573 William Cecil paid £42 for lead from the dissolved college at Fotheringhay, Northamptonshire, for use at Burghley House.[144]

OTHER MATERIALS

The main structural materials have been considered in the preceding sections, and it remains to say something about the other materials which went to make up the finished house. The mortar for binding together the stones or bricks was generally composed of lime and sand. It was made by a method similar to that in use in the building industry in recent times, whereby the lime is mixed, or 'slaked', with water and then thoroughly beaten before being covered with sand and left to stand for a period, sometimes for as long as several months. It was unskilled work and at Dartford in 1543 the mortarmen were paid at the same rate as the common labourers,

> Wurking in carrying of watr to slaike lyme wt & in slaikyng of the saide lyme wt sande. And moreover in seiftyng the said lyme & sande for to make mortr wt . . .[145]

A similar process was carried out at Sir Thomas Tresham's works at Rushton in 1596, where the labourers prepared a place for making mortar towards the end of July, spent most of the following two months burning lime and slaking it, and in October began to beat and temper it. In the first week of November they finished beating it and covered it with sand ready for use the following year.[146]

The lime for the mortar was made by burning chalk or limestone and it was frequently manufactured on the site. At Little Saxham Hall in 1505 the lime-kiln was constructed by the limeburner himself.[147] The limeburner also helped to make his own kiln at Loseley House, Surrey, in 1562, where he was assisted by three masons, two bricklayers and two labourers. The kiln took almost two weeks to build and 10,000 bricks were used in its construction.[148] It must have been a fairly large structure, and it was used for burning bricks as well as lime. Some builders, unlike Sir William More, seem to have underestimated initially the amount of mortar required for their works, and were forced to take remedial measures at a later stage to meet the increased demands. Sir Roger Townshend's lime-kiln at Raynham, Norfolk, which was set up in April 1619, was demolished and rebuilt with a larger capacity in 1622,[149] and Sir Thomas Tresham had to enlarge his lime-kiln considerably in 1596.[150]

The chalk or limestone used in the kilns was often found locally, although sometimes not without difficulty. At Trentham Hall, Staffordshire, in the 1630s, the first few weeks in each building season were spent seeking out new sources of supply, and in April 1634, twenty tons of lime were bought at Clayton, two miles away, 'to supply ye workemens wants when my quarrey was wrought out'.[151]

Where the raw materials were not easily available it was necessary to buy lime ready-burnt. Sir William Petre bought lime in Woodham Ferrers for repairs at East Thorndon in Essex in 1550,[152] and his son, Sir John Petre, crossed the Thames to Northfleet in Kent to find the necessary lime for his work at Old Thorndon Hall later in the century.[153] Lime was also used as an agricultural fertilizer, and when only small quantities were required for building purposes they were, no doubt, supplied by men such as George Feltwell and John Nybgrave, limeburners of Little Hadham, Hertfordshire, who in 1548 rented 'a parcel of chalk ground with two lym kylles' for twenty-one years from Sir Gyles Capell, the lord of the manor.[154]

The sand for the mortar was usually dug locally, although Sir Basil Dixwell, if the notes of Henry Oxinden are to be believed, spent the enormous sum of £500 on sand for Broome Park, Kent, between 1635 and 1638.[155] Black mortar was sometimes required for special effects, and this was achieved by introducing coal dust into the mixture, as at Old Thorndon Hall, Essex, in 1594, where it was used by the slaters working on the roof of the banqueting house which was being covered with West Country slates.[156]

A cement made of wax and resin had been used instead of mortar in the medieval period for masonry that was particularly exposed to the influence of wet,[157] and the practice continued throughout the sixteenth century. At Little Saxham Hall in 1507, wax and resin were bought 'for my masons',[158] and at Loseley House in 1569 'oyle and rosen to syment wtall' were provided in connection with the glazing of the house.[159] Some of the purposes to which cement of this nature was put are made explicit in the accounts for Old Thorndon Hall. In March and April 1587, wax and resin were bought at Brentwood 'to make syment for the hall porche', and in August of the same year 'yellow wax' was provided to make cement for the great chimney.[160] Two pounds of resin and two pounds of wax were bought for Condover Hall, Shropshire, in 1592, 'to symmen the broken stones togaether',[161] and the builder of Grafton Manor, Worcestershire, in 1569, used a mixture of linseed oil, resin and chalk 'for to symende the glase wyndowes from the wether beatinge into the Chambr'.[162] Another method used by builders to make their mortar resistant to damp was by the insertion of oyster shells,[163] and quantities of these were purchased by the Protector Somerset for his various works between 1548 and 1551.[164]

Iron was used for a large variety of purposes, both functional and decorative, in building. Clamps for stonework, glazing bars, the workmen's tools, and, of course, vast quantities of nails were all made of iron, as were the more artistic fittings such as hinges and fire-backs. A moderately sized country house, such as Trentham Hall in Staffordshire, provided sufficient work to keep two smiths in almost full-time employment throughout the most active years of the building,[165] but few builders seem to have been prepared to set up a forge on the site. At Kirby Muxloe Castle, Leicestershire, a timber-framed forge with a slate roof was constructed in 1481,[166] and at Kyre Park, Worcestershire, in 1589, a timber 'Hovell for . . . a Smith to work in' was made.[167] It is not altogether clear whether the latter was actually a forge, but at Raynham Hall, Norfolk, in 1622, a lock was bought 'for ye Dore of ye Smithes fforge',[168] and at Trentham Hall in August 1635 a carpenter and some labourers were engaged on 'taking downe the forge'.[169]

Lawrence Shuttleworth rented an anvil and other equipment from a smith of Burnley in 1601 when he was building Gawthorpe Hall, Lancashire,[170] but many builders seem to have employed local smiths who worked in their own workshops and were paid at piece rates both for the materials and for their workmanship. Hence at Bolsover Castle, Derbyshire, in 1613, the bulk of the metalwork was executed at piece rates by a smith from Bolsover, and the door hooks, grates and glazing bars were made on the same terms by a more skilled smith from Norton Cuckney, just over six miles away.[171]

Often the smith provided his own iron, but on those occasions when it was bought by the builder, the craftsman was usually entrusted with the choice, as at

Rushton in 1594 when the two local smiths working on the Triangular Lodge were sent to Wellingborough to purchase iron,[172] or at Raynham Hall, Norfolk, in 1622, when the smith travelled as far as London to choose iron.[173] The original source of most of the iron used was rarely stated in the documents, except where it was of foreign origin. As in the medieval period, quantities of iron were imported from Spain,[174] and that chosen by the smith of Raynham at London was Spanish, as was the iron imported into Bristol by Sir John Thynne and used at Longleat.[175] Sir Nicholas Bacon provided his smith at Redgrave Hall, Suffolk, with iron from Amiens as well as from Spain,[176] and no doubt some of the iron used by other builders was also imported.

By the sixteenth century, glazed windows were to be found in even the most minor rooms of the country house. The manufacture of glass is known to have been carried on in England on a small scale from at least as early as the thirteenth century,[177] but glass from the readily accessible centres in Burgundy, Lorraine and Normandy seems to have been generally preferred for its higher quality. In 1557, Thomas Charnock in his *Breviary of Natural Philosophy* lamented that 'as for glassmakers, they be scant in the land', but the English glassmaking industry underwent a considerable expansion after 1567 when the French merchant Jean Carré obtained a patent to manufacture window glass in the Weald and brought over glassmakers from Lorraine and Normandy. By 1579 there were sufficient French workmen at Wisborough Green, Sussex, to hold their own religious services, and this influx of foreign skill led to a great improvement in the quality of native window glass. The forests of the Weald probably provided most of the native glass used in the south-east of the country, while the Midlands seem to have been largely supplied from Staffordshire.[178] Other glass furnace sites dating from the sixteenth century have been located in Hampshire and around the Bristol Channel, and further north in Lancashire, Cheshire and Yorkshire. Early in the seventeenth century, the growing use of coal for firing the furnaces meant that the glass industry moved to new sites on the coalfields, particularly at Newcastle and Stourbridge, and by 1649 it was claimed that the glasshouses at Newcastle served most of the kingdom with broad glass for windows.[179]

Where there was sufficient fuel, the manufacture of glass was a relatively simple if skilled process, but there is little evidence to suggest that temporary furnaces were set up solely to glaze a single house. Not unexpectedly, a notable exception was at Hardwick Hall where the Countess of Shrewsbury set up a glasshouse for three years during the course of the building works.[180] However, most glass was bought ready-made from the glassmakers themselves or from middlemen, and sometimes carried vast distances to the site. The builders of an orphanage in Plymouth, for example, sent all the way to London for their glass in 1618, but in other provincial centres working glaziers such as Nicholas Eyffeler of Warwick would have been able to supply both plain and painted glass to meet the local market.[181] The documentation relating to a failed attempt to set up a glass-making works at Wollaton by Sir Percival Willoughby in 1615 gives a very full account of the financial investment and the risks involved in the commercial production of glass. In order to be viable it was recommended that there should be

John Smythson's plan of the proposed glasshouse at Wollaton (Nottingham University Library).

either 8 fornes howses having butt 2 maister workmen a peice in them, or els 4 double workmen apeice, yf they do make the complement of 800 ton apece.

In addition there were to be three or four workmen in each glasshouse tending the fires and engaged on other labouring tasks. One of the proposed glasshouses is illustrated in a plan dated 30 July 1615 by John Smythson, which shows a substantial square building with a central furnace and two projecting ash boxes linked by a covered passage to a two-storeyed glassmakers' cottage. There was to be one warehouse on the site of the glassworks and another warehouse two miles away at Nottingham Bridges where the glass was to be loaded on to barges to make the difficult journey by river to Hull and then by sea to London. In the event only two glasshouses were built at Wollaton and the enterprise soon foundered as a result of the excessive transport costs to the all-important London market.[182]

Despite the expanding native industry, many builders continued to specify imported glass. The windows of the chapel at Trinity College, Cambridge, in 1564, were to be glazed with Burgundy glass, and the time limit of the contract was to be dependent on when 'passedge by sea' could be arranged.[183] Normandy, Burgundy and Rhenish glass were supplied by a Worcester glazier for Grafton Manor in 1576, and 'French glasse' was used at Trentham Hall in 1634.[184] Even as late as 1660 Sir Roger Pratt was able to write that

The best glass that we have here of our own, is that of Newcastle, but from abroad for windows, is that of Normandy.[185]

However, the source of the glass was rarely noted in the building accounts, and from the later sixteenth century onwards much of it was undoubtedly English glass.

Although glass was in common use for country houses, it continued to be a highly valued material which was treated with economy. In the 1620s the Earl of Middlesex paid his glazier an annual retainer of £4 simply to maintain the glass at Copthall, Essex.[186] Faulty pieces of glass were used in garret windows, and the re-use of old glass was a common practice, especially in the sixteenth century. When extensions were made to the Hall of the Carpenters' Company in London in 1572, the glazier used 41 feet of new glass and 36 feet of re-used glass, and one of the towers at Hengrave Hall, Suffolk, was glazed 'wt old glasse' in 1536.[187] Considerable amounts of re-used glass were employed by Henry VIII's Office of Works, and monastic glass was carefully salvaged after the dissolution, as at the demolition of the college of Fotheringhay, Northamptonshire, in 1573, when all the glass and iron in the windows were sold for £12.[188]

There is little information specifically about plaster to be derived from most of the building accounts. It must have been used in fairly large quantities for wall surfaces and ceilings, but few of the accountants mention its purchase or its manufacture on the site. This was presumably because much of the plaster was simply composed of lime and sand strengthened with chopped straw or hair and no distinction was made between the purchase of the basic materials for this purpose or for making mortar. Robert Caldwell, however, who drew up the accounts for Grafton Manor, Worcestershire, was more forthcoming. In July and October 1569 he recorded the purchase at Worcester of lime from Bristol specifically for the use of the plasterers, and in November 1568 he differentiated between plaster of 'the best sorte' at 6s. 8d. the load and plaster of 'the worser sorte' for which he only paid 3s. 4d. the load.[189]

The finest plaster was made of gypsum, which was to be found chiefly in parts of Dorset, Yorkshire and the Trent Valley. When it was used outside these areas it had to be transported, sometimes for great distances. Sir Robert Sheffield of Butterwick, Lincolnshire, gave Sir Thomas Lucas thirty-two tons of plaster in 1507 for Little Saxham Hall, Suffolk. It was almost certainly made from gypsum, and to reach its destination it had to be carried overland to Boston, shipped by sea to Kings Lynn, taken up the River Ouse to Brandon, and finally transferred to carts again for the journey to Little Saxham.[190] The organization of its carriage must have involved considerable administrative effort, and gives some indication that gypsum plaster was very highly regarded. Similar plaster for Hengrave Hall, a few miles away from Little Saxham, was bought by Sir Thomas Kytson in 1538 at Collyweston, Northamptonshire, although the price that he paid included transport as far as Brandon where his own carts were able to collect it for the final stage of the journey.[191]

The specialized and often exotic materials used by the decorative painters to make their colours were frequently supplied by the craftsmen themselves, the builders simply reimbursing the painters when they submitted their bills. Thus,

Sir Thomas Tresham received a bill from his painter early in the seventeenth century for work carried out over a period of sixteen weeks and three days, and for

> ooille thre gaullens and a haulfe ....23s.
> whit lead forti iiii pound ....23s. vid.
> haulfe a boucke off gould ....12d.
> bllu, black, yealou, read, grean, gouldsicse
> and all cind off coulles ....20s.[192]

The craftsmen bought their materials, apparently on credit, from tradesmen, an arrangement that could result in difficulties for the craftsmen if the builder was slow in settling his accounts, as Thomas Selby discovered when he executed a considerable amount of work for Lord Zouche at Bramshill House, Hampshire, between 1615 and 1617. By 1619 only part of the bill had been paid and Selby was forced to remind his former employer that

> The stuffe belonging to the worke cost 20 markes for which your petitioner is yet indebted to dyvers men who seeke daylie to arrest your said peticioner for the same, soe that for feare he cannot perform any busynes whereby to get his living beeing restrayned of libertie to his utter undoinge.

Similarly, James Mylton, a painter working at Copthall in the 1630s, in submitting his bill to the Earl of Middlesex for outstanding materials and workmanship added the plea

> . . . dessiring your Lordship to [pay] me at your Lordships plesur for I gooe in great dannger for want of monney.[193]

Some builders bought painting materials direct from the tradesmen in the larger market centres, but the distances that were sometimes involved make it clear why the majority preferred the craftsmen to supply their own materials. Much of the materials for the painter at Hardwick Hall, Derbyshire, were bought in London,[194] and although the builders of Little Saxham Hall and Hengrave Hall in Suffolk were able to obtain some of the materials from a 'grossor of bury', they also had to buy others in London.[195]

A large variety of other materials appear in the building accounts, such as coal for burning lime and bricks, ochre for enhancing the colouring of brickwork, and hair for mixing with plaster or cleaning tools. Candles were bought on a number of building sites, both to provide light for craftsmen working on the interior of the building during the winter months and to heat up solder for plumbers engaged on soldering lead pipes. Other materials included bracken for thatching unfinished walls to protect them from frost during the winter, moss for bedding stone roof slates, and a vast array of miscellaneous purchases such as ropes, glue, thread, charcoal, pitch and so on. The building of a country house must have acted as a considerable stimulus to the local economy during the period that it was under construction.

CHAPTER 10

The Supply of Materials

Some of the sources of supply for specific materials have already been mentioned. Much of their material generally came from the builder's own estates and from the most conveniently accessible quarries and forests, but sometimes it was necessary to supplement these sources from further afield. The interest which many builders displayed in the architecture of their friends and peers, and the freedom with which they exchanged ideas and even skilled craftsmen, often extended to the provision of quantities of materials which individual builders lacked. Sir Thomas Gresham and his agents in Antwerp were busy in the 1560s supplying building materials from the Netherlands to Sir William Cecil and the Earl of Ormond,[1] and in a more local context Sir John Strode noted that 'much stone [and] many Timber trees . . . were freely given me by my neighbours' for Chantmarle House, Dorset.[2] In 1589 Sir Edward Pytts gave 2,000 boards which were surplus to his requirements at Kyre Park to Ralph Sheldon 'toward the bourding of his newe house' at Weston in Warwickshire.[3] Sir John Thynne was given a number of trees for Longleat at various dates,[4] as was Sir William More at Loseley in the 1560s.[5] Although most of the recorded gifts of materials were of timber, a few builders were given quantities of stone. Lord Burghley sent stone to the Earl of Leicester in 1575 'toward the making a lytle banquett house' in his garden, and in 1601 Sir Robert Cecil was given some stone from Penshurst by Lady Sydney.[6]

The workmen engaged upon the building sometimes provided another source of supply although they, of course, charged the going rate. It was normal for masons and quarrymen to act as stone-suppliers and many of the other crafts occasionally furnished some of their own materials. Thus the carpenter's bill for the gallery at Copthall, Essex, in 1639, included £8 'for Drye Deale boards brought from London out of other folks yards & myne owne'.[7] It was common practice for joiners to supply wainscot and even the glue and nails to fix it. Tilers frequently provided their own laths and tile-pins, and plumbers sometimes used their own lead. Many craftsmen must have accumulated limited quantities of the materials that were relevant to their craft and which they were able to supply as the need arose. Some of the workmen employed on building the Guildhall at Plymouth in the early seventeenth century bought up the surplus material remaining at the completion of the work, presumably with the intention of using it on a subsequent job.[8] Similarly, at the sale of materials from the dissolved college at Fotheringhay, Northamptonshire, in 1573, the Weldon mason William Grumbold bought most of the stone from the foundations.[9] A few craftsmen were

Chantmarle House, Dorset (RCHME © Crown Copyright).

also able to supply materials for other crafts, although the amounts involved were generally insignificant, such as the 'greate peece of timber' bought from a mason working on the market house at Aylesbury in 1645 or the 510 bricks supplied by the plumber employed on the same work.[10] Some craftsmen undoubtedly acted as dealers in building material but their overall effect on country house building was small because such large quantities of materials were required that it was necessary for the builder to establish regular links with the primary sources to ensure the constant availability of supplies. In addition, although limited credit was available to workmen buying materials, it was only the builder who had sufficient reserves of capital to buy in bulk.

Small items of ready-made smiths' work such as nails and locks, and miscellaneous equipment like buckets and sieves, were occasionally bought at local markets and fairs. Sir Roger Townshend patronised more than a dozen fairs within a radius of forty miles of Raynham Hall, Norfolk, between 1619 and 1622,[11] but most builders only made an occasional purchase from this source. Sir John Petre of Thorndon Hall, for example, bought some pails for his mortar makers and a finishing saw at Brentwood fair in 1581 and a small quantity of lath nails at Ingatestone fair in 1589,[12] while Thomas Lucas bought lath nails, lead and coal at the famous Sturbridge fair in 1507 and 1508 for Little Saxham Hall.[13]

When the glazier and building contractor Bernard Dinninghof wrote to Thomas Lumsden in October 1618 offering to rebuild Sheriff Hutton Castle, Yorkshire, he observed,

> You are aminded to take down the Castell, wherein will be found much timbre for that purpose, also iron for window bars and bands for doors and casements and such like necessarys, and also lead for the gutters and wankes and cant windows.[14]

Raynham Hall, Norfolk (RCHME © Crown Copyright).

Many other builders re-used old materials to similar effect. Sir Nicholas Bacon used materials from the existing building on the site when he built Gorhambury House in the 1560s,[15] and Sir Charles Cavendish employed stone from his abandoned house at Kirkby-in-Ashfield and from the ruined castle on the site when he commenced work at Bolsover Castle in 1613.[16] Even builders of the very highest status used old material in their new works when the opportunity arose. The old royal palace at Hatfield provided Robert Cecil with bricks which he used for garden walls and for rubble filling to level the courtyards of his new house[17] and when James Needham, shortly to become Surveyor of the Royal Works, contracted to make a new gallery and summer house at Exeter House, London, in 1530, he took

to his owen use all the olde gallary as it now stondith holie and all the olde brik and stones as well in the fundaction as elles where towards the newe makyne of the other gallary.[18]

The dissolution of the monasteries made available a vast quantity of material which was capable of re-use by domestic builders, and many of the recipients of monastic property were quick to take advantage of this opportunity to realize an immediate return on their investment. Dunkeswell Abbey, Devon, which was dissolved on 14 February 1539, was granted to Lord John Russell who, by 27 November in the same year, had sold 'all manner of glass, iron, timber, stones,

Part of the roofscape and an inner courtyard at Longleat.

tomb-stones, tile stones, and paving tile, and all other stuff' to John Haydon who was about to start work on his new house at Cadhay.[19] Bells and lead were usually expressly excluded from the sale of monastic property into lay hands, but all the other easily portable materials, such as iron and glass, were probably soon removed and sold. Few builders could have lived very far away from a monastic site, and many of them must have acquired materials after the dissolution. Among the various purchasers of materials from the dissolved college at Fotheringhay, Northamptonshire, in 1573, were aristocratic builders such as Lord Burghley, craftsmen like William Grumbold, and a number of smaller buyers like the inhabitants of the neighbouring village of Woodnewton who paid 10*s*. for battlement stone 'for their church'.[20]

Former monastic stone continued to be available long after the dissolution. In the 1560s Sir William More obtained fourteen loads of stone from 'the friars in Guildford' and ninety-one loads from Waverley Abbey for his house at Loseley, Surrey.[21] Sir Nicholas Bacon's Gorhambury House, built between 1563 and 1568, incorporated stone from St Albans Abbey,[22] and in the seventeenth century, the Earl of Salisbury used stone from the former monastery of St Augustine at Canterbury for both Hatfield House and his New Exchange.[23] Fountains Hall in

Lacock Abbey, where the monastic cloister was retained in Sir William Sharington's unfinished conversion.

Yorkshire, built early in the century by Sir Stephen Proctor, contained 'stone gott at hand out of the abby walls',[24] and as late as 1621 Sir Roger Townshend was making the foundations of his house at Raynham out of stone taken from Coxford Abbey.[25] Generally, it was only possible to re-use stone for foundations and rubble walling, and the supply of monastic stone for this purpose seems to have exceeded the immediate demand in the years after the dissolution. In addition, some of the owners of former monastic property chose to reserve the materials for their own possible future use, as Nathaniel Bacon discovered in 1575 when he attempted unsuccessfully to buy stone from Edward Paston whose family had acquired Binham Priory, Norfolk, over thirty years earlier in 1541.[26] Moral scruples, too, possibly inhibited some of the new owners from fully exploiting their monastic possessions, and although they were prepared to farm the lands, it was left to later generations to demolish the buildings and utilize the materials that they contained. Some monastic buildings were never systematically dismantled and their substantial remains are still visible in many parts of the country. Many more, however, were incorporated so completely in domestic conversions that very little of the substantial amount of building material that they contributed to the fabric is immediately apparent. A house like Longleat betrays its monastic origins only in the eccentric form of its inner courtyards, whereas Lacock Abbey in the same county of Wiltshire brazenly displays the gothic tracery of the monastic cloister immediately below the inserted domestic windows and chimney-stacks of Sir William Sharington's unfinished conversion.[27]

CHAPTER 11

The Transport of Materials

The delivery of building materials to the site could be both expensive and difficult. For example, six chalders of coal which cost Thomas Lucas 1s. 8d. to purchase at Kings Lynn in 1505 cost a further 6s.8d. to carry to Little Saxham,[1] and Sir William More paid only 2s. a load for stone ready dug and dressed at Gatton quarry in the 1560s, but the carriage to the site at Loseley cost him more than six times that amount.[2] The state of the roads and the difficulties caused by bad weather added to the problems of land carriage. During the winter the average loads carried by the carters from London to Hatfield for Lord Salisbury's new house were little more than half those carried in the summer,[3] and even in the month of June, Sir John Thynne's steward complained to him from Longleat that

> the wether is and hathe bene Rayne every daye of a longe tyme here insomoche that there wilbe no caryinge hadd withoute double charges.[4]

The transportation of materials could be further disrupted by a temporary shortage of carts during the major events of the farming calendar. The delivery of stone to Longleat was again held up in March 1562 when Thynne's tenants at Upton Scudamore understandably refused to provide him with carriage 'before they have mayd an end of Sowynge',[5] and in August 1601 Lady Sydney was pessimistic about her ability to find carriage for the stone that she was providing for Salisbury from Penshurst, for 'in this country at harvest time [carriage] is somewhat scarce to come by'.[6]

Wherever possible, water transport was used for moving bulky materials, and the effects of this on the distribution of building stone has already been noted. The rivers of East Anglia, particularly the Ouse and the Nene, were of prime importance in moving materials to the documented houses of the area such as Little Saxham Hall, Hengrave Hall and Redgrave Hall, all in Suffolk. They made it possible for the builders of those houses to use the limestone from the Midland quarries and to benefit from the wide range of goods available at King's Lynn. When Sir Robert Sheffield of Butterwick in Lincolnshire made a gift of 32 tons of plaster in 1507 to Thomas Lucas for Little Saxham Hall, the journey

Redgrave Hall, Suffolk, from a painting of c. *1660* (RCHME © Crown Copyright).

of some eighty miles was largely accomplished by water, using the Wash from Boston to Lynn and then the River Ouse to Brandon.[7] Although the detailed cost is not recorded, it would probably have been prohibitive to have attempted the carriage by land for it cost 20s. to carry only part of the consignment overland to Boston. Imported materials, especially the softwoods of the Baltic, penetrated deep into the country via the rivers, so that even a builder of modest means, such as Francis Farrar of Harrold House, Bedfordshire, was able to buy deal boards at

Lynn and bring them by water to the site.[8] On the western side of the country, the proximity of the River Severn to Kyre Park enabled Sir Edward Pytts to get much of his stone from the quarries at Madeley in Shropshire, thirty-six miles away, and even to use small quantities from Bath and from Painswick in Gloucestershire, while Lawrence Shuttleworth was able to buy lead at Stockport and Manchester and to bring it to the site at Gawthorpe, Lancashire, by means of the River Calder.[9] It is interesting to note that the carriage of a ton of glass from the glassworks at Wollaton was calculated in 1615 as costing 4s.0d. for the two miles overland to the River Trent, whereas the eighty-five miles by water to Hull was estimated at 7s.6d. and the sea journey to London a further 8s.0d. Wharfage and fees increased the delivered cost at London to £1.2s.7d. a ton of which the initial short land carriage was responsible for a disproportionate amount.[10]

No matter how well placed a house was in relation to water transport some land carriage was necessary, if only to bring the materials from the waterside to the building site, and for those houses, like Longleat, which were situated far from any navigable waterways, the accumulation of the required materials was wholly dependent on a system of overland transport. The organization of transport varied from site to site. Some builders relied on local carriers, hiring them and their carts on a day-to-day basis when there were specific loads to be shifted. Although it was a policy followed by a number of builders, including Sir Thomas Kytson at Hengrave, the conflicting demands of the local community for the services of the carriers were capable of producing temporary shortages of carts which could disrupt the building programme. Consequently, most builders turned to local carriers for occasional help only when building activity was at its height and in general they relied on a more permanent organization for the transportation of their materials.

On most building sites there was usually a steady demand for a certain amount of carrying throughout the building season and a number of builders thought it worth their while to employ one or two carters on an annual basis. Lawrence Shuttleworth, who was engaged on building Gawthorpe Hall in the first decade of the seventeenth century, paid his regular carter £2 a year in quarterly instalments, and in July 1601, at the height of the building season, he hired an additional carter 'untell mychilmes for xvd. in the wicke, broken worke and holle', a phrase which implies that he was to be paid whether there was sufficient work for him to do or not.[11] Additional carts were hired for short periods when necessary, but the bulk of the work was executed by the permanent carters. Similarly, Sir Thomas Tresham employed the same carter for every week that he was building at Rushton, Northamptonshire, between 1593 and 1597. He paid him by the week rather than at a daily rate as was his practice with the other workmen on the site, and found him alternative work in the gardens when there was no carrying for him to do.[12] Clearly carters were seen by some employers as highly valued members of the building team.

Where substantial quantities of materials were being provided from the same source away from the neighbourhood of the buildings, some builders preferred to arrange for the necessary transport by negotiation with independent contractors. Much of the stone for Kyre Park, Worcestershire, for example, was quarried at

Madeley in Shropshire. The quarryman, as part of his contract, arranged for its carriage down the River Severn to Bewdley, and separate contracts were made with Richard Bishop of Stottesdon, Shropshire, and Robert Tyrry of Mornall, Worcestershire, to transport it overland from the riverside to the building site.[13] The stone from Thorney Abbey, Cambridgeshire, used to build the chapel at Corpus Christi College, Cambridge, in 1579, was similarly carried in stages by three separate contracts, being first carried from the abbey to Guyhirn by the River Nene, then to Jesus Green by the River Cam, and finally overland to the site.[14]

Sometimes a builder was able to call upon additional sources of carriage which, although by their nature were only available at irregular intervals, could be of considerable asssistance to the permanent labour force. Many builders, for example, still retained the obligation of boon-work from their tenants, and this was usually partly fulfilled while building work was in progress by the provision of carriage. Where the builder owned a large number of manors it was possible to get a substantial part of the local carrying done in this way. At Longleat, Sir John Thynne regularly used boon-labour for carriage from his tenants of Frome, Woodlands, Deverill, Marston, Longbridge Deverill, Crockerton, Cheddar and Haselbury, and occasionally from some of his other manors. The tenants provided their own carts and generally only worked for one day. They were not paid but were always given food and drink while they were working.[15] It appears that the tenants had a certain amount of choice as to when they would provide their labour and that their own needs took precedence over their lord's demands for their carts.[16]

The conditions of employment of boon-labour were similar on other building sites, but few builders were able to use it on such a large scale as Sir John Thynne, who in a short period in 1568 had as many as forty tenants carrying for him.[17] Most builders appear to have been in a similar position to Sir Thomas Tresham, who was able to call upon a few carts each year from his tenants in the manors of Rothwell, Orton and Rushton.[18] Although most builders only employed their tenants for a few days in the immediate vicinity of the work, there were occasions when they were sent further afield, as in 1587 when timber for Sir Francis Willoughby's house at Wollaton was brought almost forty miles from his newly acquired manor at Kingsbury in Warwickshire, a journey that necessitated several nights away from home for the carters.[19] Basically a relic of feudalism, the obligation to provide boon-labour survived on some manors well into the seventeenth century and, as late as 1634, Sir Richard Leveson's tenants were undertaking some of the carriage during the building of Trentham Hall, Staffordshire.[20]

Some builders were also helped to transport their materials by their friends. So much carriage was given free to Sir William More while he was building Loseley House, that he only had to hire a full-time team of his own for thirty-seven days in 1562,[21] and as previously noted, John Strode's costs in building Chantmarle House in Dorset between 1612 and 1623 had been considerably reduced because of the

> very great number of carriages of stones both from Hambden & Whatley quarrs freely given me by my neighbours, especially of Beauminster & Netherbury.[22]

Rushton Hall, Northamptonshire, from an engraving by William Winstanley of 1741.

Sir John Thynne must have sorely strained many of his friendships with his frequent requests for assistance in carrying materials to Longleat. In July 1547 he wrote to his steward telling him to call upon the Earl of Hertford, Vincent Mompesson, 'and other my friends' to get as much stone as possible to Longleat for the following year's work, adding 'in any wise hire nether carraige of timber nor stoone but when you must neds'.[23] When in October of the same year the weather turned unseasonably fine, he again solicited his friends' help in getting stone home,[24] and in November he turned to them for the carriage of a load of timber from Bristol.[25]

It is probable that the carriage provided by these friends of the builder was frequently undertaken by their tenants as boon-service. Thus Cecil was informed in June 1556 that 'mr barteleyes tenentes bryng to Burghley all yor plaster yt is at Sestern [Sewstern, Leicestershire]'[26] and Thynne's steward wrote to him in 1567 that

> Mr Bamfild hath pmysed to John Ryder that he will cause his tennants to helpe you with as mych carriage as ys possible from Mr Colthere.[27]

The equipment used by individual builders for land transport varied considerably. The stone for the final version of Longleat was carried from the quarries near Bath on wheel-less drags pulled by oxen,[28] a method also used by Sir Thomas Tresham in Northamptonshire[29] and Sir Edward Pytts in Worcestershire.[30] The Countess of Shrewsbury transported most of the materials for Hardwick Hall by pack-horse.[31] However, the most common form of transport to the building site was by carts drawn by horses or oxen. Most builders possessed some carts of their own and usually these sufficed for nearly all their building requirements. Apart from four days in July 1633 when he hired a carter and his team, and some assistance from his tenants in the spring of the following year, Sir Richard Leveson used only his own carts and workmen during the nine years that he was building Trentham Hall, Staffordshire.[32] Frequently, however, extra carts were necessary. Most builders, like Sir Thomas Kytson at Hengrave Hall, preferred to hire them as the occasion demanded, paying an inclusive daily or weekly sum for the carter and his cart. Other builders bought new carts and employed labour solely to operate them. Sir Roger Townshend, for example, who began work on Raynham Hall, Norfolk, in 1619, bought a cart at Newmarket in May for £7, and then in June spent a further £12 at Newmarket on another cart, some cart wheels and an axle-tree.[33]

Oxen as well as horses were extensively used for carrying purposes. Thomas Lucas bought 'a kyne' in December 1505 to carry earth for the levelling of the site of Little Saxham Hall, Suffolk,[34] and Sir John Thynne instructed his steward in June 1547 to purchase six to eight oxen for the carriage of materials.[35] The timber brought from Kingsbury to Wollaton Hall in 1587 was carried by 'cattle',[36] and the building account for Beaudesert Hall, Staffordshire, for Lord Paget in 1575 includes 3s. 'payed to the Smythe for showinge the oxen'.[37] Even as late as 1631, Sir Arthur Ingram was using oxen during the rebuilding of Temple Newsam in the West Riding of Yorkshire.[38] The animals were tended by the regular carters, who were also responsible for the routine maintenance of the carts and associated equipment. Local wheelrights were employed on a casual basis for more specialized repair work. Materials which were brought from a long distance away from the site, or which were carried in separate stages by different carriers, sometimes had to be stored in transit. 1s.6d. was spent on 'howse rome' in Bolton for sixty-nine loads of lead being brought from Stockport to Gawthorpe Hall,

Lancashire, in November 1602, and wainscot from Ireland for the same house was deposited in the tithe barn at Much Hoole near the coast in the summer of 1607 before being carried inland.[39] The iron railing for the tombs to the 3rd and 4th Earls of Rutland were stored in 'her layship's brewhouse at Newark' on their way from Gainsborough to Bottesford in Leicestershire in 1592.[40]

Sir Robert Cecil hired a yard and warehouse in Redcross Street, London, to store the materials coming into the capital before they were transported to the site at Hatfield,[41] but there were few other builders who required permanent storage accommodation on this scale. Sir John Petre, who made occasional purchases in London, was generally able to find sufficient space for his materials in the inns of Whitechapel and Aldgate. In March 1590, for example, he bought wainscot at an inn called The White Lion in Thames Street which he carried to The Swan in Whitechapel where he paid 4*d.* for a week's storage before carrying it down to Thorndon in Essex.[42]

Goods in transit were particularly vulnerable to pilfering and despite the precautions taken for their storage, loads of materials did not always arrive intact at the site. Sir Edward Pytts of Kyre Park, Worcestershire, bought a ton of lead in Bristol in 1614 and he very indignantly noted that one of the eighteen pigs in the load was 'by the way stollen', and although 'contrary to promise', he nevertheless had to pay for it.[43] Once on the site, stringent arrangements were made for the security of the building materials. At Kyre Park, timber was stored in the 'masons work-house',[44] and the scaffolding being used at Dublin Cathedral in 1564 and 1565 was kept in 'safety in the Mary chapel under lock'.[45] During the building of Whitehall Palace in 1531, stakes, thorns and bushes were bought to surround some of the materials and to safeguard them.[46] However, the more conventional form of protection on most domestic building sites was to keep the materials under lock and key wherever possible. Thus at Raynham Hall, a stock lock was bought in 1621 for 'ye Closett Dore on ye gardinge Chambr, to shett upp ther instrumts & necessaries'[47] and another lock was purchased in 1622 for the door where the 'wrought fresestone lyeth & An other stocke locke for ye Dore of ye Smithes fforge'.[48]

The last step in the transportation of materials came when they were placed in the final position on the building itself. The more portable materials, of course, could be carried by the craftsmen and their labourers, but heavier materials such as stone and timber required specialized lifting gear. This could be provided by a simple system of ropes and pulleys, and in 1568 Sir John Thynne bought two brass pulleys in London for Longleat.[49] However, most country house building sites seem to have been equipped with more sophisticated machinery. Wooden cranes were in use at Redgrave Hall in the 1540s[50] and Rushton Hall in the 1590s.[51] At Raynham Hall in 1621 the carpenter and the smith made 'a crane to drive downe pylles'.[52] These cranes were almost certainly operated by hand, but an iron crane used in the construction of the New Haven at Chester in 1567 was powered by a form of treadmill worked by female labourers, who were also employed in other tasks about the site.[53] No contemporary lifting machinery is known to survive from a domestic context but there are a number of windlasses, vertical capstans and jibs still visible in a few major ecclesiastical buildings which

The pulley devised by John Webb in 1637 to lift heavy stones at St Paul's Cathedral (Olive, Countess Fitzwilliam's Wentworth Settlement Trustees and the Director of Leisure Services, Sheffield City Council).

suggest that the treadmill principle was a common form of power for lifting heavy loads to a great height.[54] Sixteenth-century illustrations for building cranes, pile-drivers and devices for extracting water from foundation trenches survive in Italy and it is probable that the machinery available to the English country house builder was broadly similar.[55] Indeed, the drawing made by John Webb in 1637 for a pulley to be used in lifting stones for the remodelling of St Paul's Cathedral was based on an illustration in Cosimo Bartoli's edition of Alberti's *L'architettura*, a copy of which was owned by his mentor, Inigo Jones.[56]

THE WORKMEN

Burghley Lodge

he ys so wonderfully sought being in deede the
absolutest & honestest workeman in Ingland.

SIR EDWARD HEXT ON WILLIAM ARNOLD,
1610

CHAPTER 12

Craftsmen

The requirements of the country house building industry meant that many of the craftsmen employed in it were both wage-earners and itinerant, and that consequently their way of life differed radically from that of artisans in other occupations in the sixteenth and early seventeenth centuries. There were, of course, exceptions to this general pattern. A number of building artificers were small masters who hired out their own labour and who undertook works by contract, and in some urban areas there was sufficient building and maintenance work to support a permanently settled labour force. However, an analysis of the building accounts that survive for country houses makes it clear that many of the craftsmen engaged in this branch of the industry were undoubtedly itinerant wage-earners.

Insufficient accounts remain to give anything more than an outline picture of the mobility of most craftsmen. It is known, for instance, that William Cotes, mason, came from Gloucester in February 1615 to work for Sir Edward Pytts at Kyre Park, Worcestershire, but nothing is known about his subsequent movements after the completion of the house.[1] Other masons and bricklayers working on the same house came from Bromsgrove, twenty-five miles away, and Alvechurch, thirty miles away. Some of the chimney-pieces were executed on the site by Gerard Holleman, the Dutch carver resident in London, who moved on to make a monument to Richard Barneby and his wife at nearby Bockleton after he had finished at Kyre.[2] Six of the eleven masons known to have worked at the house definitely came from over twenty miles away, and of the remaining five, one probably came from outside the district. The carpenters were probably all local men, but this only reflects the less specialized nature of their craft which provided them with sufficient alternative employment opportunities in the neighbourhood.

Carpenters were in an advantageous position because they were not tied to the fluctuating demands of the local building industry, but other craftsmen were more restricted in their choice of work. Sometimes there was enough building activity within a fairly small radius to keep them occupied for much of their working life without having to move out of the district. Richard Wright, a glazier of Bury St Edmunds, worked at Little Saxham Hall, four miles outside the town, in 1509 and 1510.[3] He was still living in Bury three years later when he undertook a contract to glaze the hall, chapel and Master's Lodgings at St John's College, Cambridge, which was twenty-five miles away.[4] In the 1520s, he was back in the neighbourhood of Bury working for Sir Thomas Kytson at Hengrave Hall and he continued to be employed there at intervals until at least 1536.[5] Although little

The monument to Richard Barneby and his wife in Bockleton Church, Worcestershire, carved by Gerrard Holleman and erected in 1594 after he had finished working at Kyre Park.

else is known about him, it is clear that there was sufficient work in the area to enable him to live and practise close to Bury for over twenty-five years.

The proximity of the University of Cambridge, where a considerable amount of building activity took place throughout the period, acted as a stabilizing influence on the neighbouring building industry, providing alternative employment to supplement the irregular opportunities available locally. There is no evidence that the demands of the university caused a shortage of skilled building labour in the surrounding countryside. On the contrary, by encouraging craftsmen to remain in the area, it seems to have had the reverse effect. The case of Richard Wright has already been noted, and some of the other craftsmen who worked with him at Little Saxham Hall similarly found employment in Cambridge. William Burden and Thomas Butler, who originally came from Ely, were the principal freemasons at the house between 1505 and 1509. They then departed for Cambridge but in 1511, when the contractor employed by Sir Thomas Lucas had left with some of his work unfinished, they returned to the site.[6] Burden, at least, went back to Cambridge, for in 1513 he was working on the church of St Mary the Great.[7] The most important carpenter employed at Little Saxham was Thomas Loveday, who came from Sudbury in 1505. He finished working at the house in 1510 and six years later he undertook a contract for the fittings in the chapel, hall and library of St John's College where Richard Wright had been employed a few years previously.[8] Loveday continued to find employment in Cambridge, working on the gateway of Trinity College between 1528 and 1535.[9]

By any strict definition, these craftsmen were, of course, itinerant. Loveday, for example, had to travel almost twenty miles from Sudbury to work at Little Saxham and if, as seems likely, he came from Sudbury to Cambridge in 1516 that entailed another journey of over thirty-five miles. But, as far as can be traced, during the thirty years of his known working career he never had to leave an area more than two or three days away from his home town in search of work.

The movements of many other building craftsmen were similarly restricted. Conditions in the neighbourhood of Oxford and other large urban centres, particularly London, were similar to those near Cambridge and in certain areas enough country house building was being undertaken to provide almost continuous employment for a nucleus of craftsmen. In Suffolk, John Lynge, a mason and bricklayer, worked at Little Saxham Hall from 1507 to 1514 and at Hengrave Hall from 1525 to 1537.[10] Richard Wright glazed both houses. William Ponyard worked as a mason at Hengrave from 1536 to 1540, where he was responsible for the remarkably sophisticated oriel window over the main entrance.[11] His subsequent movements are unknown until 1553 but he presumably remained in the area, for in that year he was employed in a well-paid advisory capacity by Sir Nicholas Bacon at Redgrave Hall.[12] Of the other craftsmen working at Redgrave, the Brenning family of tilers from Bury and Simon Field, a plumber from Diss, are known subsequently to have been working in 1564 for Sir Thomas Cornwallis at Brome Hall in the same county.[13] These accounts only document a small number of the country houses that were built in the area in the first half of the sixteenth century and clearly the employment prospects for skilled craftsmen engaged on country house building in Suffolk were good at that period.

Similar patterns of employment can be seen elsewhere. In the north Midlands, the houses built by the related families of the Talbots and the Cavendishes kept large numbers of building craftsmen employed for over three generations. Chatsworth House, Derbyshire, was started in 1552 and continued into the 1570s. Worksop Manor, Nottinghamshire, dated from the 1580s, as did the remodelling of Old Hardwick Hall, Derbyshire. In the 1590s, Hardwick Hall and Oldcotes, Derbyshire, Kirkby-in-Ashfield, Nottinghamshire, and Pontefract Hall, Yorkshire, were built, and in the seventeenth century the building projects of the Cavendishes included Welbeck Abbey, Nottinghamshire, Bolsover Castle, Derbyshire, and Slingsby Castle in Yorkshire. The names of the craftsmen who worked on most of these buildings are unrecorded, but in many cases they must have been the same. This can be suggested on stylistic grounds, and partly confirmed by the records that survive for Chatsworth, Oldcotes and Hardwick.[14] At least sixteen of the craftsmen who were employed at Chatsworth also worked at Hardwick, and some of them exceeded twenty years' service on the two houses. John Hibard and John Rowarth, carpenters who were working at Chatsworth in 1560, were still working for the Countess of Shrewsbury at Hardwick Old Hall in 1587. George Hicket, another carpenter, was working at Chatsworth in 1576 and at Hardwick in 1597, while a mason, Thomas Outram, worked at Chatsworth from 1560 and at Hardwick from 1587. Other craftsmen who were employed at these houses are known to have

The oriel window at Hengrave Hall carved by William Ponyard in 1538.

found additional work elsewhere in the area. Thomas Beighton, a carpenter employed at Chatsworth from 1580 and Hardwick from 1588, had been working in 1575 for William Dickenson in Sheffield.[15] Dickenson was bailiff to the Earl of Shrewsbury and possibly Beighton was already in the employ of the Talbots at that date. Other important houses going up in the north Midlands at the same time provided further employment opportunities for craftsmen, and Thomas Accres, a highly skilled marble mason who worked at Chatsworth in 1576, travelled to Wollaton to work for Sir Francis Willoughby between 1584 and 1588, before returning into the service of Bess at Hardwick in 1595.[16] Robert Smythson, 'Architector and Surveyor unto yee most worthy house of Wollaton', was paid for unspecified work at Hardwick in 1597 probably relating to the design of the house,[17] and other craftsmen from Wollaton who later worked at Hardwick included the masons John and Christopher Rodes, and possibly Christopher Lovell.[18]

Fragmentary evidence for similar mobility within a restricted area is available for other parts of the country. In the south-west the sketch books of the Abbott family of plasterers show them to have found continuous employment in Devon over a period of more than 150 years.[19] The earliest designs date from about 1575 and were compiled by John Abbott of Frithelstock (1565–1635). They were continued by his son, Richard (born 1612) and the final designs were made by his son, John (1639–1727). As far as can be determined, none of the family was ever employed outside the south-west. Another plasterer, Robert Easton of Stogursey, Somerset, is known to have worked at Combe Florey in his native county in 1599 and at Chantmarle in neighbouring Dorset in 1615. The stylistic evidence from other houses suggests that he found sufficient work in the region to keep him employed for most of his working life.[20] In Staffordshire, John Greaves was the principal carpenter employed on the alterations to Lord Paget's Beaudesert Hall in 1575 and 1576,[21] and when in 1591 part of the roof of the newly built Shire Hall at Stafford, twelve miles away, collapsed, Greaves was called in to make the necessary repairs.[22] As fifteen years separate the two dates, it is probable that Greaves had not had to move far out of the county in search of employment during the intervening period. Henry Hobbes, alias Hunt, a freemason of Arundel, Sussex, seems to have been similarly occupied by the work available in his own county. In 1586 he undertook a contract for Giles Garton to build a kitchen wing for his house at East Lavington, about ten miles from Arundel,[23] and nine years later he was employed by the 9th Earl of Northumberland on 'the new building near the wine-cellar' at Petworth, fifteen miles from Arundel.[24]

Similarly, nearly all the craftsmen in the building accounts for the additions to Holland House in 1638–40 can be associated with other work in the London area.[25] William Dodson, the bricklayer, had probably been employed earlier in the century in the building of Ashley Park, near Kingston-upon-Thames.[26] William Mason, the principal mason, had been the main contractor for St Paul's Church, Covent Garden, in 1631 and in 1635 had taken a number of building leases on houses in the Piazza.[27] Among the other craftsmen who had also been involved in the Earl of Bedford's development in Covent Garden were the carpenter, Richard Vesey, Thomas Stephens, mason, Thomas Bagley, a glazier who had also worked on Whitehall Palace in 1614,[28] Erasmus Marsh, smith, and Thomas Charley, a plumber.[29] Hugh Justice, another of the Holland House plumbers, had previously worked for the Earl of Middlesex both on his London House in St Bartholomews and at Copthall, his country seat in Essex.[30] Undoubtedly, the most esteemed craftsman employed at Holland House was the painter, Matthew Goodrich, who had also worked for the Earl of Middlesex[31] and on St Paul's Church, Covent Garden,[32] as well as painting some of the mouldings at the Queen's House, Greenwich,[33] and the woodwork of the stairs at Ham House, Surrey.[34]

These craftsmen, whose movements were largely confined within an area of twenty or thirty miles, probably formed the nucleus of the labour force on most building sites. The reputation of the most skilled of them would be well known in the area and consequently they would be employed when work was available. However, although the mobility of most craftsmen was of limited extent, others undoubtedly travelled long distances during their working career. The limitations of the evidence make it almost impossible to trace all the movements of individual craftsmen but enough is known about some of them to demonstrate the remarkable range of their itinerancy. Research into the career and work of Robert Smythson has shown that he was possibly born in Westmorland and by the 1560s he was working for Sir Francis Knollys, presumably on his principal house at Caversham near Reading. In 1568 he travelled the seventy-five miles to Longleat, Wiltshire, to work for Sir John Thynne. He remained at Longleat until the building was halted by Thynne's death in 1580 and then moved to Wollaton in Nottinghamshire, some 170 miles away. Work on Sir Francis Willoughby's Wollaton Hall was completed in 1588, but Smythson remained in the village until his death in 1614, his subsequent architectural career being in an advisory capacity which did not require his continuous attendance at the various sites where he was employed. By the age of forty-three, Smythson had moved home three or four times and had travelled almost 250 miles to practise his craft, excluding the original journey south from his birthplace.[35]

Beaudesert Hall, Staffordshire, where the carpenter John Greaves was employed in 1575 and 1576.

Similar distances were travelled by other craftsmen. A group of Yorkshire building craftsmen, including the masons John and Martin Ackroyd and John Bentley, and the carpenter Thomas Holt, came south to Oxford in 1609 to work at Merton College. They were subsequently employed on the Schools Quadrangle of the Bodleian Library and in 1611 Bentley travelled briefly into Worcestershire to draw plans for Sir Edward Pytts at Kyre Park.[36] Pytts also brought the mason Thomas Sergianson fifty miles from Coventry for the same purpose. Ralph Symons, one of the leading masons working in Cambridge in the late sixteenth and early seventeenth centuries, had originally come from Berkhamstead in Hertfordshire.[37] He is first noted in Cambridge in 1585, but early in the 1590s he seems to have been working in London. He was back in Cambridge by 1596 where he continued to work until 1605. In that year he was described as 'late of Cambridge', and presumably he had moved on to find employment elsewhere.

One of the reasons for Symons' departure from Cambridge was a dispute over his workmanship for King's College, and a similar motive in 1563 led the Somerset mason William Spicer to leave Longleat, where he had been employed since 1554. Nunney, his home village, was only a few miles away from Longleat, but by 1571 he was working for the Earl of Leicester at Kenilworth Castle, 120 miles away. In 1584 he was made Surveyor of the Queen's Works at Berwick and in 1596 he was appointed Surveyor of the Royal Works in London.[38] Sir John Thynne's dissatisfaction with him clearly did not hinder his subsequent career. John Hills, another of Thynne's masons at Longleat, originally came from Kent. In 1550 he seems to have been working for the Duke of Somerset at Brentford and in 1568 he moved to Longleat. Twelve years later he accompanied Robert Smythson to Wollaton, where he worked until the house was completed in 1588. At the time of his death in 1592, he was living in Worksop, where it is possible that he had been employed on the building of the Manor Lodge for the Earl of Shrewsbury.[39]

It was not only masons who were prepared to travel great distances in order to practice their craft. John Scampion, a carpenter, was born in 1580 in the Hertfordshire parish of Great Hormead. At the time of his second marriage in March 1622 he was living in London, but shortly afterwards he moved to Montgomery in Wales where, together with his brother Samuel, he played a prominent role in the erection of a substantial new building for Lord Herbert at Montgomery Castle. The evidence from the parish registers suggests that the Scampions remained in the town until some time after 1625 and then moved on elsewhere.[40]

There were many different reasons why some craftsmen spent most of their working lives in the same area while others followed their employment across the country. When work on a particular house came to an end, it is very unlikely that there were ever enough building jobs available in the neighbourhood for all the craftsmen to obtain immediate alternative employment. Some, no doubt, did find building or maintenance work, while others probably left the building industry altogether until such time as another house was commenced in the locality. But some at least of the more enterprising craftsmen must have gone in search of work and the rumour of secure employment on a major country house probably spurred some of them to travel considerable distances, such as the two masons noted in the Kyre Park building accounts 'that came to seek work' from Weston in

Warwickshire,[41] or the blacksmith at Raynham Hall, Norfolk, in 1619 'whoe cam from Blicklinge', where he had been working on Sir Henry Hobart's house.[42]

However, apart from those craftsmen who moved to the largest towns or university cities where a certain amount of building was almost continually in progress, it is unlikely that many craftsmen undertook to travel without the certain knowledge that building was in progress at their destination. It is difficult to conceive of groups of craftsmen vaguely wandering the countryside in search of work. As knowledge of new building projects probably only travelled a limited distance to reach the ears of interested craftsmen, it remains to explain such extraordinary journeys as that made by the Scampions from London to Montgomery. One possible reason is that the reputation of some craftsmen was so exceptional that they were eagerly sought by prospective builders, and in this respect it is possibly significant that John Scampion was described in glowing terms in the parish register at Montgomery as 'artificiossimi jam architecti novi operis in Castello de Montgomeri'. Other craftsmen were certainly recruited on account of their reputation. Sir Edward Hext, referring to William Arnold, the Somerset mason who had contracted to supervise the erection of Wadham College, Oxford, wrote in 1610

> If I had not tyed him fast to this businesse we shold hardly keepe him; he ys so wonderfully sought being in deede the absolutest & honestest workeman in Ingland.[43]

The subject of patronage and its part in the recruitment of labour has already been dealt with in some detail. It was obviously an important factor in the encouragement of itinerancy among highly skilled craftsmen. The point can be further emphasized by considering the Yorkshire craftsmen working in Oxford in the early seventeenth century. Sir Henry Saville, Warden of Merton College, who originally brought them down to work there, was himself a native of Yorkshire. He had previously employed John and Abraham Akroyd on a number of enterprises in his own county, notably at Bradley Hall and Methley Hall,[44] and it was clearly as a result of his personal knowledge of their skill that he recruited them to work in Oxford. Similarly, when Sir Edward Pytts returned to Worcestershire with John Bentley, another of the Yorkshire craftsmen, it was largely because he was aware that Bentley had 'wrought the newe addition to Sir Thomas Bodleigh his famous library'.[45]

It is difficult to assess the extent to which craftsmen's lives were disrupted by the insecurity of their peripatetic existence. Some, no doubt, were acutely conscious of it; such as the painter from London who found only two days' work at Trentham Hall, Staffordshire, in 1633, and who left such a small impression on the accountant that he was recorded simply as 'London John'.[46] But the effects on many craftsmen must have been largely mitigated by the considerable length of time often taken to build a country house. This meant that the more skilled craftsmen frequently enjoyed long periods of employment on one house. When Robert Smythson appeared at Longleat in 1568, work had already been in progress for over twenty years, yet he stayed for twelve years before moving on to Wollaton, where Sir Francis Willoughby's building provided him with a further

Wadham College, Oxford, built by William Arnold, 'the absolutest & honestest workeman in Ingland'.

eight years' employment. At least ten other masons at Longleat were employed for periods of twelve years or more and Allan Maynard, the principal mason from 1563, was connected with the house for over twenty years. Some of the other craftsmen working at Longleat enjoyed a similar security of employment. William Palmer, a glazier, was employed for sixteen years and the carpenters John Lewis and William Brown worked respectively for twenty-four and twenty-six years on the house. In addition, a number of craftsmen accompanied Smythson to Wollaton, so that John Hills, a mason who had arrived at Longleat with Smythson, was employed by Sir John Thynne for twelve years and then by Sir Francis Willoughby for eight years, and Richard Crispin, the head carpenter at Wollaton, had previously worked at Longleat between 1568 and 1580. Christopher Lovell, a mason who worked for nine years at Longleat and seven years at Wollaton, seems to have found a further period of employment at Hardwick, another house with Smythson connections.[47]

Longleat, with its continual revisions and remodellings spanning a period in excess of thirty years, was something of an exception even in an age when most country houses were necessarily built at a leisurely pace. Nevertheless, a number of other houses provided a similar length of employment for some of the craftsmen working on them. At Hengrave Hall in Suffolk, several masons and bricklayers were employed for periods of nine to twelve years,[48] and one of them, John Lyng, had previously worked at Little Saxham Hall for seven years.[49] Thomas Lem, a mason and bricklayer, worked for Sir Edward Pytts during both his periods of building activity at Kyre Park, Worcestershire, totalling over seventeen years' employment between 1586 and 1617, while John Chaunce of Bromsgrove, the 'Cheiff mason . . . and Survey're of the work', saw almost twenty years' service at the site.[50] Those craftsmen who had achieved positions of responsibility, like Chaunce, were invariably employed for the duration of the work and they consequently enjoyed a greater continuity of employment than the ordinary craftsmen. Walter Madison, the carpenter who directed part of the labour force for Sir John Petre's Old Thorndon Hall, Essex, was present on the site from about 1577 to at least 1594,[51] and Robert Liming, another carpenter by trade, acted successively as surveyor at Hatfield House for five years and at Blickling Hall, Norfolk, for eleven or twelve years.[52]

Such lengthy periods of employment encouraged many of the itinerant craftsmen to bring their families with them and to set up home close to the building site, sometimes in a house provided by their employer. Two pairs of sawyers who travelled from London in 1576 to work at Stiffkey Hall, Norfolk, were accompanied by their wives,[53] as was Thomas Accres when he came to Hardwick at the end of 1594.[54] John Scampion took his bride of a few months with him when he went to work for Lord Herbert at Montgomery, where she died in childbirth and was buried in the parish church.[55] At Longleat, Smythson lived with his wife at the parsonage of Monkton Deverill, which he rented from Sir John Thynne, and Allen Maynard lived in another house rented from Thynne at Woodlands, on the edge of the park.[56] William Arnold and his wife were provided with a house, apparently rent-free, actually on the site of Wadham College, Oxford, in 1610, 'that he may continually attend the worke',[57] but it was more usual for most craftsmen to pay some rent for their accommodation, even if at times it was on favourable terms, such as the tenement in Cambridge leased to Ralph Symons by Emmanuel College in 1586.[58] However, Bess of Hardwick used her extensive landholdings as a means of securing the long-term commitment of her most valued craftsmen. During the building of Hardwick Hall, she provided rent-free farms for John Balechouse who was in overall charge of the works and for the principal mason, Thomas Accres. The fifty-five acre farm at Ashford-in-the-Water she leased to her accomplished plasterer Abraham Smith tied him to the locality from 1589 until at least 1616 and meant that his services were available whenever they were needed.[59]

The effects of the itinerancy that was inevitably the common experience of the building craftsmen can be exaggerated. Many, perhaps most, never moved outside the county of their birth, while for those who did, the upheaval that this implies was often greatly diminished by the length of employment that they could expect at the average country house site, with the opportunity that this provided of setting up a stable home in the neighbourhood like Robert Smythson, Abraham Smith and other favoured craftsmen. Far greater problems for many building craftsmen must have arisen from their position as wage-earners in a society where such a dependence was unusual. Apart from a few contractors working for a fixed sum and the privileged few on annual retainers, the majority of those employed in the building trades were paid either a daily wage or a piece rate dependent upon the actual amount of work that they had executed. The workmen employed by the contractors were paid on a similar basis. Whether paid by the day or by the measure their economic well-being depended on the number of days on which they were offered work. As they were paid only for the days that they had actually worked, the number of years that they were employed on a particular house is an uncertain guide to their economic security. This can be properly assessed only by considering the number of days that they worked in each year that they were employed at the site.

Due to the limitations of the various methods of accounting and the incomplete nature of the documentation, few building accounts are capable of sustaining the close analysis necessary to establish the daily work record of all the craftsmen. This is especially true of the accounts that survive for the early part of the sixteenth century, but by the latter half of the century the methods of book-keeping employed on a number of building sites are sufficiently full and lucid to enable the attempt to be made.

Although some of the accounts for Wollaton Hall, Nottinghamshire, are missing, and parts of those that remain are illegible, there is a complete record of the workmen employed at day rates extending from the last week in October 1584 to the week ending 15 November 1585.[60] The period covered comprises fifty-six weeks, or 336 working days based on a six-day week. As there was a complete break of three days in the first week of August 1585 during which no work was done, the maximum number of working days possible for any workman was 333. Fifty-three masons and stone-layers, and twenty-four carpenters and joiners were employed during the period, but a number of these did not start work until the spring of 1585 when the labour force was considerably enlarged. Consequently only the work-records of the craftsmen already employed in the last week of October 1584 have been set out in Table 1, as the inclusion of those starting later would distort the general picture. Of the twenty-eight workers in stone, five left the site shortly after the beginning of the period, and have also been excluded. The attendance record of the remaining twenty-three men is remarkably high. Over half of them were present on the site for more than fifty weeks, and three of these found some employment in every single week of the period.

Laurence, the most consistently employed of all the masons, missed only twenty-four possible working days, some of which can be accounted for by holidays such as Christmas and Easter which were not specifically mentioned in the account. In fifty-one of the fifty-six weeks he worked for five days or more. The records of several of his colleagues were only slightly inferior to this. Fifteen masons found employment on two-thirds or more of the possible working days, and only Collyar and Styles were absent for long periods. The layers were in a less advantageous position than the more highly skilled masons. During the bad weather of the winter months there was little work for them to do, and none was employed at all between the weeks of 1 December 1584 and 8 February 1585. By the end of February they had all returned and they were employed regularly until the beginning of July, when their employment became more erratic, presumably as a result of the approaching completion of the walls of the fabric. Nevertheless, four of the six layers worked for approximately 200 days and they all found employment in over half of the weeks of the period.

One of the carpenters left the site after eight weeks, but the employment opportunities for the remaining ten woodworkers were almost as good as those for the workers in stone. All of them worked for over half the possible number of weeks, and if the two joiners who disappeared in July 1585 are included, seven of them were employed for more than two-thirds of the working days. As with the stone workers, it was the more skilled craftsmen who found the greatest continuity of employment. Two of the four joiners were absent for only twenty-two-and-a-half days throughout the whole period, and the other two joiners only missed a few days before they departed in July. One of the joiners who replaced them worked for all but five of the remaining days in the period. The carpenters were more susceptible to periods of unemployment, but even so, Sherwin was employed for the full fifty-six weeks, during fifty of which he managed to work for five or more days.

The prospects of regular employment were clearly very good for craftsmen at Wollaton in 1584 and 1585. Building activity was at its height, and this undoubtedly had a beneficial effect on the amount of work available for the workmen at the site. Possibly in the years for which full documentation is lacking the craftsmen suffered long periods of unemployment or worked for fewer days in the week, but this seems unlikely, for the labour force was considerably smaller in those years. The total number of craftsmen working by the day at the end of June 1585 was fifty, whereas in 1582 it was twenty-eight, in 1586 twenty-one, and in 1587 twenty-two, which suggests that extra workmen were hired in the years of greater activity and that the regular work force were fully employed in other years. Thus craftsmen, such as the mason John Hills, who were employed for the full period of the enterprise, probably enjoyed a high degree of job security.

The accounts for Trentham Hall, Staffordshire,[61] provide the opportunity to study the employment pattern for craftsmen employed by the day over a longer period than those for Wollaton. The work began in June 1630 and a full series of

Table 1: Craftsmen employed by the day at Wollaton Hall, October 1584–November 1585

Masons	Weeks present	Weeks absent	Days	6-day weeks	5-day weeks	Comments
Laurence	56	–	309	36	15	
Tobyas	56	–	293	29	16	
Wichenden Jnr.	56	–	307	35	15	
Otes	55	1	293	32	13	
C. Rodes	55	1	291 ½	31	13	
C. Wichenden	54	2	279 ½	22	23	
Berington	54	2	288	32	14	
Symson	53	3	295 ½	35	14	
Stone	53	3	275	27	16	
Hills	52	4	295 ½	34	15	
W. Evenden	52	4	292 ½	33	27	
Coles	51	5	281	33	15	
G. Evenden	45	11	244	26	14	
Vinsent	44	12	239	25	14	
Atkynson	41	15	211 ½	22	12	
Collyar	27	29	129 ½	31	7	Absent January–June 1585
Styles	13	43	70 ½	6	6	Absent December 1584, October 1585
More	8	48	40 ½	3	6	Leaves December 1584
Warde	6	50	33	4	1	Leaves November 1584
Henlay	2	54	11	1	1	Leaves November 1584
Butler	2	54	11	1	1	Leaves November 1584
Myller	2	54	10	1	–	Leaves November 1584
Layers (No work available 7 December 1584–8 February 1585)						
Wodnett	41	15	206 ½	18	13	
Raphell	38	18	203	20	13	
Whitworth	37	19	200	22	12	
Mason	37	19	199 ½	19	14	
Jacke	35	21	182 ½	18	11	
Marshall	28	28	149 ½	14	12	
Joiners						
Hargrave	56	–	310 ½	37	15	
Chester	56	–	310 ½	37	15	
Thicke	37	19	205	24	10	Leaves July 1585
Chadson	36	20	201	23	11	Leaves July 1585
Carpenters						
Sherwin	56	–	302	34	16	
Smallwood	46	10	254	27	15	Absent November and December 1584
R. Crispin	40	16	219	25	13	Absent July–October 1585
Chester	35	21	195	22	11	Absent November 1584, March 1585
Crispin Jnr.	32	24	177	21	9	Absent February–March and August–September 1585
Marshall	8	48	39	4	2	Leaves December 1584

accounts exists from the week ending 23 March 1633 to the completion of the house in February 1639. The masonry work was organized in two distinct ways, with the decorative carving being paid for at piece rates, and the construction of the fabric by the day. Many of the masons were employed at times by both methods, but those masons who were predominantly paid piece rates and who only occasionally worked by the day have not been tabulated in Table 2. Casual masons, who only worked for a few days, have also been excluded. The general pattern, although complicated by occasional piece-payments, is similar to that discernible at Wollaton. In 1633, five out of the six masons who worked solely by the day found employment in more than half the possible weeks, as did three of the masons who also received piece-payments. Butler, the one mason working by the day who worked fewer than half the weeks in the year, did not arrive at the site until late in July, and Vaughan, who only worked for ten weeks at day wages, received almost ten times as much money for his piece-work during the period and was almost certainly working at the site by one method or the other throughout the whole year. Only Chester, who by reason of his general availability seems to have been a local mason, had a noticeably poor employment record. He worked for one day in March, received a small payment for piece-work at the end of June, and was then regularly employed for eight weeks from the beginning of September.

In 1634, all four masons working by the day were employed in over half the weeks that any building activity took place. Two of the masons who also did piece-work were employed by the day for more than half the possible weeks, whereas most of the remainder derived a greater proportion of their income from their piece-work payments. Nicholas Bellamie and Clayton, the two masons with the worst record, had both left the site by the summer and it is possible that they had moved on to find employment elsewhere. The fabric of the house was largely completed by the end of August 1635, and consequently the amount of work available for masons after that date was drastically reduced. Nevertheless, five of the masons were employed for more than half the weeks in the year and if we exclude the eighteen weeks from 22 August, when only occasional masons' work was required, their employment was comparable to previous years. They must have been aware at the time that their work at Trentham was coming to a close and it is possible that some of them had made arrangements for alternative employment after the end of August, although Henry Bellamie, Thomas Griswell, Wright and Vaughan continued to find occasional work at the site until the end of the year.

Those masons who worked for the full three years generally enjoyed a consistently high level of employment. Some, such as Thomas Griswell and Henry Bellamie, were only absent for a few weeks each year and when they were present were predominantly employed for six days in the week. Others, such as Holt and Vaughan, were probably employed with an equal regularity but spent a significant part of their time working at piece rates. Michael Griswell and Wright, who regularly worked for fewer weeks in each year than the other masons employed by the day, were apprentices learning the craft and consequently were always among the first masons to be laid off when there was insufficient work available.

The organization of the carpenters and joiners at Trentham falls into two separate phases. Until the summer of 1635 most of the work was carried out at

Table 2: Masons employed predominantly by the day at Trentham Hall, 1633–5

1633: 40 weeks	Weeks present	Weeks absent	Days	6-day weeks	5-day weeks
T. Griswell	38	2	206	30	2
Mr H. Bellamie	35	5	200	26	3
W. Bellamie	32 *	8	135	13	1
Holt	32 *	8	138 ½	12	4
M. Griswell	27	13	140	18	2
Vaughan	10 *	30	34	2	1
N. Bellamie	24	16	123	14	4
Clayton	21 *	19	95	10	2
Bond	22	18	128	18	3
Butler	12	28	58 ½	6	2
Chester	10 *	30	40 ½	3	1
1634: 50 weeks					
T. Griswell	44	6	248	37	2
Mr H. Bellamie	44	6	231 ½	32	2
W. Bellamie	30 *	20	120	12	1
Holt	28 *	22	113	12	5
M. Griswell	27	23	155	23	1
Vaughan	19 *	31	67 ½	3	3
N. Bellamie	2 *	48	9	–	–
Clayton	3 *	47	14 ½	1	1
Butler	16 *	34	53	4	–
Wright	33	17	199	29	2
1635: 48 weeks					
T. Griswell	31	17	159 ½	20	3
Mr H. Bellamie	28 *	20	136 ½	9	11
W. Bellamie	29	19	148	19	2
Holt	11 *	37	31	1	1
M. Griswell	13	35	73 ½	10	1
Vaughan	24 *	24	79	4	3
Wright	24	24	112	13	1

* Also worked at piece rates in this year

piece rates with only a few small tasks being executed by the day. All the principal craftsmen worked during those three years, some of them being paid very substantial sums, but there is no way of effectively establishing whether any of them were unemployed for long periods during this time. The evidence from their annual incomes suggests that, on the contrary, they enjoyed a high continuity of employment. By 1635, much of the carpentry on the building had been completed and most of the skilled carpenters and joiners left the site. The remaining woodwork was executed by a small group of carpenters who were employed exclusively by the day, and their work record between 1636 and the conclusion of the work in 1639 has been set out in Table 3. Their security of employment was truly remarkable. Bradwall, who was probably the estate carpenter and a permanent member of Sir Richard Leveson's establishment, had been paid an annual salary in the early years of the work. He commenced working by the day in June 1635 and in the remainder of that year was absent for only three weeks. He was consistently employed for the full duration of the building accounts. Walker was initially hired in January 1636 to assist Bradwall. During the following two years he was absent for only one week when work was in progress, but early in 1638 he left the site. Thomas, the other carpenter assisting Bradwell, was almost as consistent. He began work at the end of March 1636 and, apart from one week in September that year, he was employed in every week until 23 September 1637. Although he was occasionally absent during the winter of 1637/8, from 7 April 1638 to 23 February 1639 when the carpenters' work was finished, he was again ever-present. Porter, who was of equal status with Bradwall, similarly missed only five weeks' work from his arrival in June 1637 to his departure in March 1638. Clearly, the small number of carpenters working during the final years of construction of Trentham Hall enjoyed a level of security in their employment fully comparable to that of any modern building craftsman who is equally likely to be temporarily laid off during periods of bad weather or when there is insufficient work available.

Confirmation of the validity of the results obtained from an analysis of the accounts for Wollaton Hall and Trentham Hall is provided by those for the building of Sir Thomas Tresham's Triangular Lodge at Rushton, Northamptonshire.[62] The attendance records for the craftsmen in 1595 have been set out in Table 4 and will only be discussed briefly here. Among the stone-workers, it was again the more skilled freemasons who had the most regular employment pattern. William Tirroll was absent for the whole of July and his brother, Thomas, did not begin work until the second week in March. Hence they appeared on the site only at the beginning of July, and then worked continuously until the end of November. Employment for the roughmasons commenced with the temperate weather in the spring, and extra labour was taken on during the summer months when the work was at its height. The carpenters suffered from lack of work between March and July, but were then fully occupied until the end of December.

There were, of course, other craftsmen apart from masons and carpenters who were employed on every country house building site. The small numbers of painters, glaziers, plumbers and smiths working at any one time, together with the nature of their work, meant that it was not necessary to direct their tasks closely and they were generally paid at piece rates. This makes it difficult to establish in any detail the pattern of their employment. As far as continuity of employment is concerned, however, some of them worked for more years on one house than many of the carpenters and masons. At Trentham Hall, for example, Thomas Leversage, who worked as both a painter and a glazier, was employed in every year from 1633 to 1638, earning quite substantial sums in the first four years, and Zachery Kirkes, another painter, who subsequently decorated the nave ceiling at Staunton Harold Church, Leicestershire, worked from 1633 to 1636. Similarly, the slater found employment in every year, and of the two smiths, one worked for the full period and the other until March 1636. Other craftsmen were employed for shorter periods. The plumbers worked only in 1633 and 1635 and the tiler in 1638. At Wollaton Hall, where the documentation is less complete, the principal painter seems to have worked from the end of 1585 until 1588 and the two smiths

Table 3: Carpenters employed by the day at Trentham Hall, 1636–8

1636: 49 weeks	Weeks present	Weeks absent	Days	6-day weeks	5-day weeks
Bradwall	47	2	227	13	14
Walker	48	1	242 ½	20	15
Thomas	39	10	198 ½	14	15
1637: 50 weeks					
Bradwall	48	2	212 ½	13	14
Walker	50	–	247 ½	21	12
Thomas	45	5	219 ½	23	8
Porter	23	27	104	8	5
1638: 50 weeks					
Bradwall	43	7	169	8	12
Walker	2	48	1 ½	–	–
Thomas	42	8	204	17	12
Porter	6	44	29	3	1

were employed in 1585 and 1586, but the glazier and the plasterers were regularly employed for less than a year. On the whole there appears to have been less work available on any particular building for these craftsmen, but, on the other hand, their specialized skills and the smaller numbers engaged in their crafts probably meant that they were more in demand than all but the most skilled masons and carpenters, and consequently it was easier to find alternative employment.

Similar results have been obtained from an analysis of other building accounts of the period. However, despite the fairly secure picture of employment that can be presented for some craftsmen while engaged on particular buildings, not every building workman was so fortunate. There are examples in every building account of craftsmen working only for a few weeks, and even those craftsmen who were more regularly employed experienced periods without work. Once the house that they were building was completed, there was always the problem of finding work on another site. Some craftsmen, such as Robert Smythson, were of sufficiently high reputation to be immediately offered alternative employment, and some of the other craftsmen undoubtedly moved with them, but many craftsmen must have remained unemployed for an unpredictable length of time, especially if they were reluctant to move out of the area. It must have been a very common experience, and there is evidence of measures taken by some building craftsmen to protect themselves from its effects.

Many of them had small agricultural holdings at which they could work during times of slack, and which could be maintained by their wives and young children when they were fully engaged on their craft. Sometimes these holdings were rented from the country house builders for whom they were working, and these tenancies were no doubt partly granted to ensure the continued services of particularly desirable craftsmen in a period when skilled men were at a premium. However, the combination of agriculture and building seems to have been general throughout the

Table 4: Craftsmen employed by the day at Rushton, 1595

1595: 50 weeks

Freemasons	Weeks present	Weeks absent	Days	6-day weeks	5-day weeks	Comments
Old Tirroll	45	5	233 $\frac{1}{2}$	25	9	
J. Tirroll	45	5	230	24	10	
T. Tirroll	41	9	209	21	11	
W. Tirroll	39	11	201 $\frac{1}{2}$	22	7	
Hence	21	29	117	16	2	begins 3 July
Roughmasons						
Hitchcock Snr.	36	14	182	16	10	begins 5 April
J. Hitchcock	36	14	184	17	10	begins 5 April
Longe	28	22	126	10	6	begins 10 May
Weston	30	20	153 $\frac{1}{2}$	13	10	begins 10 May
Kirke Snr.	18	32	93	7	8	begins 26 July
S. Kirke	18	32	94	8	7	begins 26 July
C. Hitchcock	7	43	39	5	1	works 17 August– 27 September
T. Hitchcock	7	43	38	4	2	works 17 August– 27 September
Carpenters (no work available between March and July)						
Watts	28	22	138 $\frac{1}{2}$	12	9	
his man	27	23	134 $\frac{1}{2}$	10	10	
Ellyott	17	33	78 $\frac{1}{2}$	6	4	
his man	27	23	126 $\frac{1}{2}$	11	7	

industry. In about 1670, Sir William Coventry wrote that few building craftsmen

> rely entirely on their Trade as not to have a small Farm, the Rent of which they are the more able to pay by the gains of their Trade . . .[63]

and there is evidence that this was a well-established practice.

Such by-employments were, of course, a necessary prerequisite for those itinerant craftsmen who were not accompanied by their families to distant sites, for it was only in this way that their families could be supported during the period of their absence; but it is equally probable that they also served as an insurance against unemployment for the families of most building craftsmen. Indeed, some of them seem to have farmed on a fairly large scale. William Thomas, an Oxford plumber who died in 1552, had fifty sheep, nine beasts, and a nag[64] and John King, a carpenter of Ravensden in Bedfordshire, had nine beasts, six bullocks, five pigs, two sheep and a quantity of poultry as well as eight and a half acres under cultivation.[65] But most craftsmen possessed only a few animals or a small amount of land which they worked on a subsistence basis, like the mason Thomas Hill of Wardington in Oxfordshire, who had a cow and 'the crope of a quarterne Lande',[66] or the Halifax mason, Martin Ackroyd, who grew some corn and kept a few beasts to maintain his family while he was working in Oxford.[67]

The expansion of the woollen industry enabled the wives of some craftsmen to undertake spinning and carding, and the inventory of a mason, Richard Rothwell, taken in 1565, included four stones of wool.[68] Another mason, William Ardon of Pavenham in Bedfordshire, kept an ale-house in addition to a small farm,[69] and other craftsmen bought and sold building materials. The income from these activities was probably less important than the security that they provided. Even those craftsmen working on a large country house must have been constantly in fear of unemployment, whether temporary, due to unpredictable factors such as bad weather or a lack of materials, or permanent, due to the completion of the work. The knowledge that they could always supply their families with the basic necessities must have had a profoundly stabilizing effect on their lives.

Despite a decline in their economic position during the period, and despite their itinerant existence and their basic dependence on a money wage, there was a very strong family tradition in the building trades that resulted in several generations following the same craft. At least eleven members of the Grumbold family from Weldon in Northamptonshire are known to have been working as masons in the late sixteenth and seventeenth centuries, and two generations of the Frisbey family from the same area were masons at the turn of the century,[70] while the presence of a mason called William Frysby at Hengrave in 1537 suggests an even longer family involvement in the craft.[71] Elizabeth Frisbey was the first wife of the King's Cliffe mason Thomas Thorpe, whose father had also been a mason, and whose two sons by his second marriage were also to enter the building world.[72] Almost every building account contains several examples of related craftsmen working alongside each other, and among the better-known families we can cite the Smythsons and the Ackroyds already mentioned.

Many sons must have followed their father's craft as a matter of course, out of family tradition or as a result of a lack of local opportunity to do anything else, but for many others there must have been a conscious choice to become building craftsmen. The possibilities of advancement probably attracted some of them and certainly the most successful craftsmen achieved a social status beyond their humble origins. The mason William Arnold was called 'gentleman' in chancery proceedings of 1617,[73] and the Smythsons had achieved gentry status by 1600.[74] John Symonds, the mason extensively patronised by Lord Burghley in the latter part of the sixteenth century, was granted arms in 1591,[75] and the son of Thomas Bertie, another mason, married the widowed Duchess of Suffolk.[76] Other lesser craftsmen were styled 'Mr' on several building sites, apparently with the social meaning of 'mister' rather than the craft meaning of 'master'.[77] However, few could have realistically hoped to rise out of their social class and most of them remained simply wage-earning craftsmen as their fathers had been before them. Nevertheless, the incidence of family continuity in the building crafts suggests that successive generations found the working conditions sufficiently rewarding, despite the unpredictability of employment and remuneration. Indeed, by the 1650s if not earlier, the members of the London Carpenters' Company were even able to recruit a number of apprentices from among the sons of the minor gentry.[78] Wage-earners and artisans they might be but clearly building craftsmen were following a trade which was not without a degree of estimation.

CHAPTER 13

Labourers

The building of a country house was usually a very labour-intensive operation but the precise number of labourers required varied considerably according to the stage which the work had reached. Initially large numbers were needed to clear the site, dig the foundations, and help with the preparation of materials, but once the construction of the building had commenced, far fewer labourers sufficed to serve the craftsmen and prepare their materials. From time to time, as the building progressed, additional labour was temporarily taken on for the erection of scaffolding and other major jobs such as the raising of the roof and the digging of trenches for the connection of the water supply. When the building was nearing completion, the number of labourers again increased to deal with the landscaping of the site and the preparations necessary to make the house ready for occupation.

Consequently, the labouring force usually consisted of a small nucleus of consistently employed workmen who performed a wide variety of tasks and a large number of more casual workers who were engaged at irregular intervals for short periods working on specific jobs. Thus at Trentham Hall one hundred and four different labourers were employed between 1633 and 1638, but only three of them worked in all six years and a further four worked for five years. Sixty-three of the labourers were employed only for a brief period in a single year and they must have viewed the work as a welcome supplement to whatever other employment prospects were available in the neighbourhood.[1] The situation was similar in Northamptonshire where sixty-three labourers worked for Sir Thomas Tresham between 1594 and 1597 at Rushton, of whom twenty-nine were employed only in one year, four were employed for the whole period and two worked for three years.[2]

The regular labourers at Trentham were consistently employed in the early years of the work, but after the completion of the shell of the building in 1635 their prospects of employment became more erratic and they were all subject to fairly long spells of unemployment (Table 5). The Triangular Lodge, which was a much smaller building, provided a more stable pattern of employment for the regular labourers. Watson, indeed, was in the happy position of missing only two weeks' work during the three years that he was employed at the site (Table 6). The number of casual labourers required each year was comparatively high, but it was probably easier on a small enterprise to plan the work efficiently so that the regular labourers were almost fully employed.

Labourers differed from craftsmen in that they brought little in the way of trained technical skill to the building site. There was little need to look further

Trentham Hall, Staffordshire.

than the immediate locality to recruit them in sufficient numbers, unless there were competing demands from other employers at crucial stages in the building process. In the summer of 1589, labourers came some distance from Edensor and Chesterfield to work at Hardwick Old Hall, no doubt as a result of Cavendish connections, and two years later when both the old hall and the new hall were under construction simultaneously, six labourers from Lancashire were taken on. Presumably they were travelling as a group of companions in search of work and they arrived in Derbyshire at just the right time.[3] But in general the evidence for itinerant building labourers is very slight and the majority of them were probably either drawn from the neighbourhood of the site or they were already employed on other duties on the estate of the builder. Many of the casual labourers were employed for short periods at widely spaced intervals and could only have been available if they were local men.

Table 5: Labourers regularly employed at Trentham Hall, 1633–8

	1633: 40 weeks		1634: 50 weeks		1635: 51 weeks		1636: 49 weeks		1637: 50 weeks		1638: 50 weeks	
	weeks	days	weeks	days	weeks	days	weeks	days	weeks	days	weeks	days
Greatbatch	35	151	43	163 ½	38	147 ½	29	128 ½	17	78 ½	45	222 ½
Hassall	24	91 ½	34	146	34	157	30	157 ½	20	83	8	14 ½
Moreton	35	160	47	191	39	165 ½	31	146	3	14		
Rushton	38	215 ½	46	236 ½	27	124	20	97	1	6	7	23
Gervace			10	42	27	119 ½	17	67	20	78	8	19
Chere			24	88	6	18	16	76	25	137	17	71 ½
Plymley	11	51			17	82	18	77	15	48 ½	4	14
Total number employed	31		45		51		27		29		17	

Table 6: Labourers regularly employed at Rushton, 1594–7

	1594: 22 weeks		1595: 50 weeks		1596: 51 weeks		1597: 49 weeks	
	weeks	days	weeks	days	weeks	days	weeks	days
Horner	11	59 ½	33	160 ½	50	234	49	259
Benton	12	66	16	86 ½	35	181 ½	49	256 ½
Watson			48	237	51	246 ½	49	252
Hueson	4	14	14	78	25	122	47	212 ½
Bartle	9	49 ½	42	213 ½	25	108	5	22
Rice	1	4	49	243 ½	25	112 ½		
Total number employed	18		35		32		21	

The tasks that they carried out required little specialized skill and only a few of them seem to have been given the opportunity to learn any of the building crafts. Some of the sons of craftsmen, including John Smythson at Wollaton in April 1585, worked as labourers, but generally only for a few weeks as an introduction to the building site before starting to learn their fathers' craft. Conversely, some craftsmen, such as John Drake, a bricklayer who worked at Old Thorndon Hall, were the sons of labourers.[4] But the only documented example of a man who began his working life as a labourer and later became a craftsman was that of someone called Brykleton who was labouring at Loseley House in 1561 and in 1563 was 'entred to lere' as a mason on the same house.[5] However, for most labourers, the building of a country house was no more than an interlude when there were increased opportunities for employment in the neighbourhood and after the completion of the work even those who were most regularly employed no doubt returned to working on the land.

On most sites the labourers were generally employed by the day, even where the craftsmen were working at piece rates or by contract. This method of working was probably more convenient for many of the tasks that they carried out which required

Hardwick Old Hall, Derbyshire.

close direction, but some of the basic jobs needed less supervision and were occasionally paid for by contract. These jobs invariably involved simple digging which could be easily measured and required few instructions. At Little Saxham Hall and Hengrave Hall, Suffolk, Ingatestone Hall, Essex, and Trentham Hall, Staffordshire, ditching was executed in this way, as was the digging of the foundations at Trentham and Bolsover Castle, Derbyshire, and the trenching for the water supply at Redgrave Hall, Suffolk. Generally the labourers formed temporary associations in gangs to carry out contract work, payment being made to them collectively rather than individually. But sometimes even the minimal organization that this required was beyond them. The four labourers who were working on the foundations at Trentham in 1634 so miscalculated their contract that

> being not able to pforme theire bargaine desire to leave it & take day wage.[6]

Women were occasionally employed as labourers for short periods of time on a number of sites. Their duties were usually light, as at Hengrave Hall where they gathered rushes for thatching, cleaned and swept the rooms as the craftsmen finished work on them, and watched the kilns during firing.[7] At Bolsover Castle, where unusually high numbers of women were employed, their jobs were mainly similar, although some of them also served the craftsmen with materials, as did a woman employed on William Dickenson's house in Sheffield in 1576 and the women who worked at Hardwick Hall.[8] However, on a small number of sites no

Wollaton Hall, Nottinghamshire (RCHME © Crown Copyright).

allowance appears to have been made on account of their sex and they were given heavy tasks as a matter of routine. In June 1587 women helped the labourers unload slate from barges at Grays Thurrock for Old Thorndon Hall, Essex.[9] At Wollaton Hall, Nottinghamshire, they carried limestone and plaster[10] and at Chester they worked a treadmill that operated a crane.[11] The numbers employed were generally small, rarely exceeding two or three women at one time, but at Bolsover as many as ten were employed in some weeks. Apparently there was a shortage of labour in the area, for boys and girls were also regularly employed. In almost every case the women were related to labourers already working on the site and their wages must have been a welcome if irregular supplement to the family budget. Most women worked for only a few days or weeks in any year, but at Trentham Hall, Staffordshire, where they were mainly engaged on weeding in the garden in the spring and summer, a small number was regularly employed for the last three years of the building. A total of five women worked during this period, but the most consistently employed were the wife and daughter of the labourer, Gervace, and indeed between 1636 and 1638 he worked in fewer weeks in the year than his wife.[12] However, in terms of numbers, women were an insignificant element in the labour force on most building sites and the building industry in the Tudor and Jacobean period was still very much a male preserve.

CHAPTER 14

Working Conditions

There is little direct evidence for the number of hours worked each day on country house sites. A shorter day was undoubtedly worked during the winter when there was less daylight, and in the sixteenth century this was generally reflected in a lower wage rate paid during those months, but the actual hours are nowhere specified. The ideal for the sixteenth century was clearly laid down by the Statute of Artificers of 1563,[1] which repeated the terms of earlier statutes of 1495[2] and 1514[3] concerned specifically with masons, in which workmen hired by the day or week were to start work in summer (mid–March to mid–September) at or before 5 o'clock in the morning and to finish between 7 and 8 o'clock in the evening with breaks of no more than two and a half hours during the course of the day. In the winter they were to work 'from the springe of the daye in the mornynge untill the nyght of the same day'. However, the length of the statutory working day is an uncertain guide to the actual practice on private building sites and Sir Roger Pratt seems to imply that by the latter part of the seventeenth century, at least, shorter hours were being worked when he posed the rhetorical question, 'How many bricks will an able workman lay ordinarily in one day, from 6 of ye clock to 6?'[4] Many country houses were built on isolated sites some miles from the nearest village, which must have meant a long walk for most of the craftsmen, and this possibly had an effect on the time that they started work. Robert Smythson, for example, lived five miles away from Longleat and even though he was provided with a horse at his employer's expense, the daily journey must have been quite time-consuming.[5]

In the absence of any clear documentary evidence, it is probably correct to suggest that the normal working day on a country house building site was effectively from dawn to dusk during the winter months and varied in the summer between the extremes of the Statute of Artificers and the shorter day mentioned by Pratt.

The day was punctuated by a number of breaks for eating and drinking, but, again, their exact length and the times of their occurrence are not divulged by any of the private building accounts that have survived. The Statute of Artificers specified

> at every drynkyng one halfe howre, for his Dynner one hower, and for his Slepe when he is allowed to slepe, the which is from the middest of May to the mydest of August, halfe an houre at the most, and at every Breakefast one halfe hower . . .

but it is impossible to know how closely this practice was followed on individual country house sites.

In most accounts the working week ran from Monday to Saturday, when those on daily and weekly wage rates were paid. Sundays were occasionally worked, generally by labourers tending the kilns, which, once lit, had to be attended throughout the night, and there are frequent references to labourers on 'night watche' when they were paid their normal day wage. When the lime-kiln was being burnt for the Hawkfield Lodge at Rushton in October 1597, Sir Thomas Tresham provided beds for the two labourers engaged on 'watching their kill'.[6] Apart from these extra duties associated with the manufacture of bricks and lime, overtime was rare on the majority of country house sites, in contrast to the growing practice in the Royal Works.[7] Speed of construction was not a prime consideration for most private builders and the occurrence of overtime was usually the result of unusual circumstances, as when a number of masons and joiners engaged on interior decoration at Chatsworth worked through the night and on a Sunday prior to the arrival of the queen in 1579.[8] Sir John Thynne, who, at least in the early years at Longleat, was more concerned than most builders with rapid progress, instructed his steward in 1547 that the workmen were to work part of their meal breaks, but the principal motive for this was his determination to reduce the size of the labour force in the autumn.[9] Despite Thynne's continual exhortations of haste to his steward at this period, there is no other record of overtime being worked at Longleat.

Holidays tend to be mentioned in the various building accounts only on the few occasions when individual workmen worked during them. Thus at Bolsover Castle in 1613, eight labourers demolished part of the castle wall that was possibly dangerous 'in the three Christmas holidays'[10] and Sir Thomas Tresham's boon tenants from Rothwell were paid 3s. 6d. in 1595 'in respect of servinge their daies work on good fryday'.[11] Christmas and Easter were observed on all building sites, but it is difficult to ascertain how many other holidays the workmen were allowed each year. An Act of 1552 named 27 days apart from Sundays that were to be observed as holidays, provided always

> that it shall be lawful . . . [for every person] upon the holy-days aforesaid, in harvest, or at any time in the year when necessity shall require, to labour . . . or work any kind of work, at their free wills and pleasure[12]

but it was repealed in the following year,[13] and it is unlikely that it was ever effectively enforced. No doubt the actual practice varied on individual sites. At Kyre Park, Worcestershire, St Luke's Day was specifically mentioned as a holiday in 1611 and St Matthew's Day in 1612.[14] The workmen were not paid for these days, and, as far as it can be determined, this was the common practice on most country house sites during the period, although in 1550 only, the masons working at Redgrave Hall were apparently paid for one day's holiday out of every two that they took.[15]

The lack of payment for holidays meant that in some weeks the workman's income was greatly reduced and to these days must be added those that were lost through bad weather when no work was possible. In September 1612, the labourers digging stone at Kyre Park were paid for only five days in the week 'for one daye they wrought not for Raine'.[16] Longer rainy periods must have resulted in considerable financial hardship. Craftsmen were less vulnerable than labourers to temporary redundancy caused by wet weather, because they could often work inside the house or in their workshops when it was not possible to venture outside. During the wet October of 1561, Sir William Cecil's steward was able to report from Burghley, 'there is some store of ashlar hewen these Rayne days'[17] and masons at Longleat in 1547 were saving work on the interior of the hall to 'do yt in foule wether and nar wynter when they can not worke abrode'.[18]

However, on many houses, building stopped completely during the winter months, and even on those sites where work continued it was generally with a greatly reduced labour force. In 1594, the first year of the construction of Sir Thomas Tresham's Triangular Lodge, the partially built walls were covered with furze as protection against the frost during the week ending 2 November and the labourers were dismissed. The carpenters continued to work at day rates preparing the framework of the roof in their workshop, and six of the freemasons remained on the site carving decorative stonework at piece rates. All the roughmasons and the other six freemasons who had been working in October were made redundant. Work ceased completely in the first week of January 1595 and the only workmen employed during the remainder of the month were a number of labourers searching for building stone. The freemasons and the carpenters returned in the middle of February, but the roughmasons remained unemployed until the milder weather of May enabled the construction of the walls to be restarted. The roof had been erected and tiled by November and consequently there was sufficient work available to occupy most of the labour force until the middle of December. In January 1596, the labourers who were digging stone were again the only workmen employed on the site. Three freemasons returned at the end of February to work on the interior decoration of the lodge at piece rates, but it was the second week of April before there was any work for the roughmasons. Most of the work on the lodge was finished by October of that year, although it was September 1597 before the painter had completed the decoration.[19]

The possibility of frost meant that work on the fabric of the building was generally confined to the period between March and October or November and consequently the craftsmen who were most vulnerable to seasonal redundancy were the less skilled men engaged on laying and other tasks which could only be executed outside. Sometimes other work was found for them under cover, such as the stone layers at Bolsover Castle who spent the winter of 1613 dressing stone,[20] but most of them were usually laid off for the whole winter. The craftsmen who remained tended to be more skilled and capable of decorative work which could be prepared in their workshops or executed in the interior of the house if the construction was sufficiently advanced. Thus during the remodelling of Old Thorndon Hall, Essex, the bricklayers worked only between March and October, but the glaziers, plasterers and joiners continued to be employed throughout the winter.[21] At Redgrave Hall, Suffolk, most of the work stopped shortly after Michaelmas in each year but a few skilled workmen always remained throughout the winter months.[22] At Longleat in 1547, Sir John Thynne determined not to 'kepe oon workman that shall work day work after Michaelmas',[23] but his joiners spent the winter wainscoting the parlour and a chamber[24] and the principal mason was engaged on squaring stone at the quarry at piece rates.[25] Some of the masons at Hatfield worked through the winter of 1610–11 on the sculpture so that it was ready to be set up in the following spring,[26] and a mason at Gawthorpe Hall,

Lancashire, made the moulded 'windowe stuffe' during the winters of 1600–1 and 1601–2. The hall at Gawthorpe was roofed in June 1602 and in subsequent winters a glazier, a plasterer and several joiners were also employed for the duration.[27]

Besides the skilled craftsmen, a number of labourers were also generally retained throughout the winter. When necessary, they were able to serve the craftsmen, but they were principally engaged in replenishing the supply of materials against the recommencement of construction work in the following spring.

Temporary redundancy caused by the weather or the irregular demands for their particular skills must have formed a predictable part of the craftsmen's lives and they were presumably prepared for this. The unexpected occurrence of sickness or injury, however, must have severely strained their resources. When an accident occurred on the site the builder sometimes paid for the necessary medical treatment. Sir Richard Leveson paid 5s. 'to hemings the plaisterer towards the cure of his wounds received by a fall in the Kitchin' at Trentham Hall in 1635,[28] and Sir Roger Townshend gave 11s. in 1619 to the father of one of his workmen who broke a leg during the demolition of Coxford Abbey from which stone was being provided for Raynham Hall, Norfolk,[29] but compensation was not provided for the wages that the victim lost during the period that he was absent from work. Corporate organizations were more benevolent towards their workmen. The Trustees of London Bridge spent the large sum of 58s. 4d. in 1547 on two surgeons, 'for healing of a great wound in the head of John Alerton, Carpenter, hurt at the bridge by default of the old gin', and among other sickness gratuities they made an allowance of 6s. 8d. in 1494

> to oon John Isaac, late servaunt and laborer unto the said bridge, in consideracion of his good and true service doon unto the same bridge by meny yeris past and nowe is fallen blynde and impotent.[30]

The fellows of Trinity College, Cambridge, made several payments in 1601 to a stone carver 'in ye time of his sickness for his relief',[31] but private builders seem to have felt no such obligation. Therefore, the mason at Rushton who fell sick after three days' work in October 1596 but had five days 'allowed him by yor. wo. appointment because of his sickness' was exceptionally fortunate, and he was left to his own devices in the following week when he continued to be absent from work. James Alcot, the carpenter building Hall Court, Herefordshire, by contract, had his diet paid for him when he was ill in June 1609 but, of course, he did not receive any wages.[32]

The extra two days' wages for his sick mason were given by Sir Thomas Tresham as compensation for his misfortune, rather than as a regular sickness payment. Similar philanthropic actions were occasionally taken by other builders. Sir Richard Leveson gave 3s. to a mason working at piece rates in June 1634 'for working a stone yt was broken, wherein he lost 3s.'[33] and Sir William Petre paid a carpenter the large sum of £5 after he had completed the framework of the gallery at Thorndon, Essex, in 1550 'in way of rewarde in recnpance of an harde bargeiyne yt he hadde before at Thorndon'.[34] John Tusle, the carpenter who made the roof of the Shire Hall at Stafford in 1590 for £30, was subsequently given a further £1 'in respect of his hard bargaine'.[35]

Although, as these examples show, some builders were prepared to compensate for the difficulties in accurately estimating for contract work, they were under no obligation to do so, and even when the craftsman had carried out extra work that was not specifically part of his contract it appears that any additional payment was largely at the discretion of the builder. Thus in April 1575 when John Greaves submitted his bill to Lord Paget for carpentry work executed 'over and besydes my bargaynes' at Beaudesert Hall, Staffordshire, he simply stated what he had done

> not vuluinge any porcion thereof but leavinge that and referringe my self therin to yor Lordshippes goodnes and gentlenes . . .

Greaves received £8 'wch his lordshippe off his goodnes paieth'.[36] The wording used by the accountants to record similar payments at other building sites implies that it was general practice for the builder to fix an arbitrary price for extra work. The payment of £1 to a mason at Little Saxham Hall, Suffolk, in August 1507 was

> in ful paiement of his task of xix li. for my first house wt vj*s*.viij*d*. rewarded hym for making there of a window of ij lights[37]

and Richard Rogers, the Southwark stonecarver who made a chimney-piece at Old Thorndon Hall, Essex, in 1590, was paid an additional £2 in 'consideracon of doynge more than bargayne & well doynge of the worke'.[38]

The occasional payment of a bonus or reward to individual craftsmen for well-executed work was fairly common. Usually only small sums were involved, such as the 15*s*. divided among four labourers at Trentham Hall in December 1634 'over & above their wage' for finishing the trenching ready for laying the water supply to the house,[39] or the 4*s*. 4*d*. given to four roughmasons at their completion of a bridge at Rushton in 1595.[40] However, rewards equivalent to several weeks' wages were not uncommon. In the week after the labourers had received their bonus at Trentham, the smith was given £1 'by yor appoyntment after I had paid him for all his locks', and a freemason was also given £1 in January 1509 at Little Saxham Hall 'by way of reward'.[41] When the house was ready for occupation substantial *ex gratia* payments were sometimes made to those craftsmen who had been prominent in the supervision of the work. John Kniveton was given a reward of £10 by Bess of Hardwick in October 1597, immediately after she had moved into Hardwick Hall,[42] and the Earl of Salisbury gave Robert Liming the enormous sum of £100 in 1612 at the completion of Hatfield House.[43]

In addition to their workmanship, craftsmen were also rewarded for ideas that increased efficiency or saved the builder money. The churchwardens of St Mary-the-Great, Cambridge, gave 3*s*. 4*d*. in 1593 to a mason 'for his great pains in saving much scaffolding'[44] and Bess of Hardwick paid £2 in 1596 to the wife of Thomas Accres 'in respect of her husbands devise of sawing blackstone to buy her a gowne withal'.[45] A benevolent concern for the families of her principal craftsmen was characteristic of the later years of Bess of Hardwick's life. In 1592 she had given £2 to the mason Abraham Smith, 'against his weddinge' and when Accres' daughter got married in December 1595, Bess gave her £1 and her mother £5. She also contributed £1 to John Kniveton's wife in February 1597, 'when she was robbed', having two months previously given the labourer John Clarkson ten shillings when he too had been robbed. This was the equivalent of his wages for 20 days' work and must have provided welcome relief.

Indirect bonuses were sometimes found for workmen in the form of tools or clothing. Usually it was the craftsman's responsibility to provide the specialized tools for his particular trade and the only tools supplied by the builder were of a more general nature, such as pickaxes, shovels and pails. This is sometimes made explicit in contracts of employment, such as that between the Earl of Shrewsbury and two masons in 1576, by which the latter were to find 'themselves all maner of toyles to worke with pertayning to their scyence of their owne Costs & chardgs',[46] and is implied by the arrangements made at various sites for the carriage of the tools of those craftsmen who came from a distance. At Trentham Hall, for example, the plumber's son was paid his expenses in June 1635 for going to Bridgnorth to collect the plumbers' tools and, at the completion of their work in September, a labourer returned their tools to the same place.[47] However, on a few occasions, individual craftsmen were given an allowance for their tools by the builder. Two London joiners employed at Old Thorndon Hall in 1587 received 6d. each for their tools[48] and the three masons hired by the year at Loseley House, Surrey, between 1563 and 1566 were provided with all their tools by Sir William More.[49] At Longleat, a saw was bought for the masons in 1572,[50] and stone axes and chisels were provided at Kyre Park, Worcestershire, in 1611,[51] although on both these sites the majority of their tools were supplied by the workmen themselves.

Protective clothing was sometimes provided for those workmen engaged on tasks which placed them at risk of minor injury. The most frequent references are to gloves for carpenters, who were vulnerable to splinters from the great baulks of framing timber that they handled and to blisters from the ropes used to manoeuvre the timbers into position on the building. Some examples have already been given and to these may be added gloves bought for the carpenters at Hengrave Hall in 1532 and 1535[52] and the 2s. 'gyven to the carpenters for gloves

Hatfield House, Hertfordshire.

'A sawe for Blacke stone', drawn by Robert Smythson and possibly devised by Thomas Accres for use at Hardwick Hall in 1596. The other tools in the drawing are a frame saw for panelling, a ladder and a lime sieve (British Architectural Library, RIBA, London).

at the raysinge of the Rofe of the chappell' at Trinity College, Cambridge, in July 1564.[53] Brickmakers were also given gloves to protect their hands when they were firing the kilns at Hengrave Hall and Redgrave Hall, Suffolk.[54]

However, the gloves presented by Lawrence Shuttleworth to six masons, ten labourers, the housekeeper, two maids and eight estate servants including the cow-boy on 26 August 1600, were clearly some sort of symbolic gesture occasioned by the laying of the first stone of Gawthorpe Hall, Lancashire.[55] Such a gift was similar to the practice on some building sites of providing some of the craftsmen in the most responsible positions with a livery in common with other servants in permanent employment. At Kyre Park in 1611, the gesture was unusually elaborate, the 'cheiff mason' being given boots, slippers, a coat, 'cognizance hat band, feather & cognizance of silver'.[56] Another mason at Kyre Park received annually 'a livery to make him a coat'. Generally it was only those craftsmen who were employed on an annual basis, and therefore formed part of the builder's permanent establishment, who were given a livery. The two masons who agreed to serve the Earl of Shrewsbury for a year in January 1575 were to have a 'Coate' in addition to their wages and the contract with two bricklayers at Thorndon Hall, Essex, in 1550 specified a livery coat for each of them.[57] At Loseley House, Surrey, the three permanent masons were given two liveries a year costing 10s. each.[58] Presumably these were equivalent to the winter and summer liveries mentioned at Old Thorndon Hall, Essex.[59] It is possible that the practice of giving a livery to permanent employees was dying out by the end of the period for, while examples from the sixteenth century are common, that from Kyre Park is the only example noted from the following century.

CHAPTER 15

Accommodation and Food

The workmen who came to the site from outside the neighbourhood must often have incurred considerable expenses on their journey, but they were not always reimbursed by their new employer. Such payments seem to have been largely a matter for individual negotiation with no specific obligation on the part of the builder. Indeed, Sir Roger Pratt, in his advice on the best terms for drawing up contracts with workmen, wrote in 1665, 'Nothing to be expected for carriage of tools, or journeys',[1] and the 6s. 8d. divided among thirteen masons who came to Redgrave Hall, Suffolk, in March 1551, 'in rewardes for parte of there charges from London' seems to have been thought of as a considerate gesture on the part of Sir Nicholas Bacon and could hardly have covered their costs.[2] However, some craftsmen were sufficiently in demand to insist upon recompense for the time that they spent in travelling to the site, and they were generally paid a day's wage for each day taken. The only workman who received any travelling expenses at Loseley House, Surrey, was a mason who was specifically summoned from Oxford in 1562 and given 2s. 4d. 'for his costes in comyng from thens'.[3] The plumber from Bridgnorth employed at 2s. a day at Trentham Hall, Staffordshire, was paid 4s. in July 1635 'for 2 dayes coming & going',[4] and at Raynham Hall, Norfolk, in 1620, a limeburner who came from Thetford received 3s. 'for ij daies cominge & returninge as . . . was my Mrs comand to give him'.[5] In some cases, the craftsman was in a strong enough position to demand the repayment of travelling expenses as a necessary condition of his employment. A clause in William Arnold's contract with Sir George Luttrell for additions to Dunster Castle in 1617 included the payment of travelling expenses as part of his remuneration,[6] and one of the conditions laid down by Humphrey Lovell when he sent Robert Smythson and his assistants to Longleat in 1568 was that they were 'to have dayes wages for theare travel whiles they are cominge'.[7]

On arrival at the site, the itinerant workmen were immediately faced with the task of finding accommodation for themselves. Those craftsmen who could reasonably expect a long period of employment often brought their families with them and set up house in the neighbourhood, but there were others who travelled alone or who were employed to execute specific tasks which were unlikely to last for longer than a few months and who required little more than somewhere to eat and sleep when they were not working. The builder, with his local influence and knowledge, was clearly better placed then the men themselves to provide them with lodgings and generally he made all the arrangements. Thus at Hengrave Hall,

Suffolk, in 1526, a joiner and his servant who came from London to work for sixteen days were boarded for three weeks by Sir Thomas Kytson at a cost of 6s., and six men were accommodated for a week by one of the local workmen employed at the site in 1529.[8] The labour force working on the house during these years was mainly drawn from the locality and consequently only the occasional craftsman required accommodation. However, in 1530, the increase in the size of the enterprise and the arrival of a large number of workmen from elsewhere made it necessary to make regular arrangements for board and lodging. Thomas Shethe, the former overseer of the work, was now made solely responsible for boarding and carriage. Although a contract with a mason specified that he

> and all his company yt he setts a worcke for ye said house shall be bordyd at Thomas Shethes for xvj*d.* a week,[9]

Shethe did not actually provide the accommodation, his role being to make the necessary arrangements. Shethe's accounts survive for the period between 1536 and 1538, and at times he was finding accommodation for well over twenty workmen. The cost for each man was 16*d.* for every seven days as set out in the contract mentioned above but there is no indication where they were lodged. The unvarying uniformity of the rates and the large numbers of men involved suggest that they were probably accommodated in the completed part of the house itself, and that the 16*d.* represented the allowance made to Shethe for providing the necessary facilities. The wording of the contract might seem to indicate that it was the contractor's responsibility to pay the 16*d.*, but in the building accounts all the payments to Shethe 'ffor bordyng' were made by the accountant on Sir Thomas Kytson's behalf and, although it is possible that appropriate deductions were made in settling the contractor's bill, there is no evidence for this. Certainly, at Beaudesert Hall, Staffordshire, in 1576, it was the builder who paid the boarding expenses of the craftsmen[10] and this seems to have been the practice on a number of other sites. At Rushton, for example, five masons came twelve miles from Lyveden to work on the cornice of the Triangular Lodge in August 1595. For the first three days they were boarded and paid 16*d.* a day each, but on the fourth day when they had finished their work and had returned home, they were paid only 10*d.*[11] The extra 6*d.* a day allowed for their accommodation corresponds with a similar sum paid by Tresham to two limeburners in August of the following year and can be taken as the going rate in the neighbourhood.

Where accommodation was required for only a short period for a few workmen, as at Rushton, it was usually possible to make arrangements with a local innkeeper or with the wife of one of the local craftsmen. Thus at Haddon Hall, Derbyshire, in November 1549, 2s. 8d. was paid

> unto Wyllm bowryngs wyff for ye borde of henrye wagstagge, Ryc wyght, Tomas noytte and Robarte handerton for iiij dayes workynge at Elkar for great Tymbre for ye howsse,[12]

and the craftsmen employed during the first five years at Redgrave Hall, Suffolk, appear to have lodged at the village inn.[13] As work on the house progressed, the workmen were often provided with sleeping accommodation in those parts which had already been roofed. From 1550, the Redgrave craftsmen were boarded in the house and Trentham Hall, which was begun in 1630, was ready to accommodate the workmen in March 1634.[14] A joiner employed at Old Thorndon Hall was noted to be 'lodging in the house' in 1587,[15] and mention was made at Hardwick Hall in June 1597 of 'the turret where Accres lyeth'. The contract of 1593 for Oldcotes, Derbyshire, specified that Bess of Hardwick was to lend the craftsmen 'sixe beds so long as they shalbe in the sayde works'.[16] No doubt on those sites where there was already an existing house, it was frequently used to provide accommodation for the workmen engaged on building the new house.

Although accommodation, when necessary, was usually arranged by the builder, this was not always the case. When Stephen Chappell, a carpenter, was contracted to execute all the woodwork for the stables at Stiffkey Hall, Norfolk, in 1582, he agreed to find board for himself and his men.[17] Chappell and his men had previously worked on the house from at least 1579, during which period they had generally been boarded by Sir Nathaniel Bacon.[18] It is probable that the change in lodging arrangements was brought about by the virtual completion of the internal decoration of the house towards the end of 1581, which meant that it was no longer desirable to use it as temporary accommodation for the workmen. Having worked in the area for at least three years, Chappell was presumably perfectly capable of making his own arrangements for accommodation, as was no doubt the painter, Thomas Selby, who had worked on several occasions at Bramshill in Hampshire before he petitioned Lord Zouche in 1619 for payment for

> the last peece of work [which] held you peticioner on worke 16 weekes, duringe which tyme your Peticioner borded himself.[19]

However, in the contract made by the mason Roger Palmer of North Buckland, Devon, with Sir Richard Edgecumbe for the building of Mount Edgcumbe, Cornwall, in 1547, the former bound himself to find 'loddgyng' for himself and his men for the duration of the work.[20] It is difficult to understand the reason for the inclusion of this particular clause, unless, perhaps, Palmer had already made a preliminary journey to view the site during which he had secured satisfactory lodgings in the neighbourhood for the number of men that he intended to employ. Palmer certainly appears to have been a very shrewd negotiator and the covenants of his contract were unusually precise. In addition to providing lodging for his men, he was also to find them 'mete and dryngke' but he ensured that they were to have adequate facilities for this by getting Edgecumbe to agree to the unique condition that he would 'bylde make and Cover a Convenyent & Syfficient house or leyney [linhay] for dressyng of their mete'.

The provision of food and drink for workmen varied considerably from site to site. Sir Richard Edgecumbe was not alone in leaving the responsibility for feeding arrangements to his contractor, although he was unusual in providing him with the necessary facilities. None of the workmen employed at Little Saxham Hall, Suffolk, were fed by Thomas Lucas,[21] and neither were those at a number of

Bramshill House, Hampshire.

other country house building sites. During the additions to Syon House, Middlesex, in the early seventeenth century, the few workmen who were fed were craftsmen who had been specially brought in to execute specific tasks,[22] and at Trentham Hall, Staffordshire, only the small number of workmen employed on an annual basis were provided with their 'dyett'.[23] In contrast, most of the day workers at Gawthorpe Hall, Lancashire, were either fed or given an allowance for their 'table' when they were working away from the site, while those working by contract made their own arrangements.[24] Sir John Petre provided food for most of his craftsmen at Old Thorndon Hall, Essex, with the exception of his bricklayers who were mainly local men. However, as the house was predominantly built of brick, the number of craftsmen requiring to be fed at any one time was fairly small. Until the 1580s, he also supplied the food and drink of his labourers, but for some unrecorded reason he had largely discontinued the practice by 1587, although he continued to feed the craftsmen.[25] Similarly, John Talbot fed most of the men working on Grafton Manor, Worcestershire, in 1568, but by 1576 they had to feed themselves.[26] All the small labour force employed to build William Dickenson's house at Sheffield in 1575 were fed by the builder's wife,[27] and Sir William More managed to feed the much larger number of men working on the site at Loseley House, Surrey; his stone-diggers, who were necessarily employed away from the site, were the only workmen who were left to fend for themselves.[28]

As with so many aspects of the administration of the work at Hengrave Hall, Suffolk, the expansion of Sir Thomas Kytson's plans in 1530 resulted in a corresponding change in his attitude towards the feeding of his workmen. From 1525 when the work commenced with a predominantly local labour force, the workmen provided their own food and drink, but in 1530 when large numbers of workmen were imported from outside the district, Kytson reversed the practice and began to feed all his men, including those who had previously been accustomed to providing for themselves.[29] Given the necessity to make arrangements for feeding the new workmen, he no doubt found that it was more efficient to extend the facilities to his established labour force.

A number of factors must have influenced the decision of individual builders as to whether to feed their workmen or not. Breakfast and dinner, which were the main meals of the workmen's day, were both consumed during normal working hours, and consequently some facilities for the preparation of the food on the site were necessary. If the builder undertook to supply and prepare the food, the operation would undoubtedly proceed more quickly and efficiently than if each workman, or group of workmen, made their own individual arrangements; but, on the other hand, the extra administrative burden might not have been acceptable to the builder. The composition of the labour force was probably fairly crucial. Single workmen coming to the site from other areas, living in lodgings, and ideally working six days a week, were poorly placed to supply their own food in a largely subsistence-based local economy, whereas local workmen were in a far better position. This situation seems to be reflected in the change of practice at Hengrave Hall in 1530.

Another factor of some importance was that of finance. When the builder provided his workmen with food and drink, he paid them correspondingly less. Thus at Hengrave, the wages of those workmen employed before 1530 fell by 2d. a day when Kytson began to feed them. On most sites the food was probably the produce of the builder's own estates and, although its use represented a loss of potential profit from selling it on the open market, the most immediate result was an effective reduction in the builder's expenditure on wages. As many builders seem to have had some difficulty in raising sufficient cash for their work, the payment of part of their wage-bill in kind must have seemed an attractive proposition.

The standards of working accommodation varied from site to site, but usually the buildings that were provided were of a fairly makeshift nature. In 1589, shortly after work had commenced at Kyre Park, the carpenter moved a house two and a half miles to the site 'for the masons to work in' and built '2 other Hovells for the masons, brickmakers and a smith to work in'. In 1590 he built a 'house' for drying bricks and squaring timber and another masons' lodge at the quarry, and two years later he moved one of the lodges to a different position on the site. The first period of building at Kyre was completed by 1595 and when work began again in 1611 it was necessary to build another two lodges for the masons, the original structures presumably having been dismantled at the end of the earlier building phase.[30]

Freemasons needed covered workshops protected from the elements in which to dress and carve their stone, but they were not the only craftsmen who were provided with specialized accommodation. At Trentham Hall, Staffordshire, in April 1633, the 'kilnhouse' was whitewashed.[31] This was possibly similar to the lodge built by the Royal Works next to the lime-kiln at Dartford in 1543 'for to laye chalk drye in & for the . . . brekers of chalk to wurk in',[32] a function no doubt also fulfilled by the 'morter howse' constructed at Old Thorndon Hall, Essex, in December 1589.[33] The bricklayers also had a 'howse' at Old Thorndon and at Longleat, in 1563, a workshop was built for the brick maker.[34] At Hardwick Hall 'the old plumery' where the plumber had worked was demolished in 1594,[35] and in John Smythson's survey plan of Worksop Manor, Nottinghamshire, one of the rooms is entitled the 'plomerye'.[36] When work commenced at Raynham Hall, Norfolk, in 1619, one of Sir Roger Townshend's first actions was to construct 'an hovell for the Sawrs',[37] and during the repairs to Aylesbury market house in 1645 a similar building, called the 'sawpitt house', was made.[38] Sawpits must have been particularly vulnerable to flooding during periods of rain and some sort of covering must have been highly desirable.

Most workshops were simple timber-framed structures. The 'cabin' used by the masons employed on the Shire Hall at Stafford in 1590 was constructed of birch poles and had a thatched roof.[39] A carpenter at Trentham Hall spent five days making 'a Cabbyn for ye masons to worke in' in November 1634,[40] and the 'old lodg wher the masons wrought' at Hardwick Hall was taken down by a carpenter and was re-used as a hay house.[41] Essentially, it was only necessary to have a covered-in space and often it was possible to adapt buildings already existing on the site. When Sir Edward Hext wrote to John Lord Petre, in March 1610, about the site proposed for Wadham College, Oxford, he pointed out that it contained

> Many hangyng houses which will serve to hewe our stones in or work in tymber in all weathers,[42]

and at Raynham Hall, an 'old Bearn [was] ther agayne to be builded for a Workehouse'.[43] The loft above the coachhouse at Trentham Hall was perfectly adequate to be used by the painter as a workshop, where he could prepare and store his materials.[44] Those craftsmen who were primarily concerned with fitting out the building were sometimes accommodated in an unoccupied room in the house itself where they could sleep as well as work. The glazier sent to work at the Earl of Shrewsbury's house at Chelsea in 1578 was to have 'good glasse to worke and a room in Shrewsbury House to lye in and to worke it'[45] and at Longleat in an inventory taken in 1580 on the death of Sir John Thynne, when work was still in progress on the house, one of the rooms was noted as the glazier's chamber.[46]

CHAPTER 16
Labour Relations

It would be foolish to look for modern terms of employment on the Tudor or Jacobean building site. Most workmen were engaged on a daily basis and were instantly dismissed when they were no longer required. The policy of many employers was probably similar to that of Lord Burghley whose steward reported in 1578 that:

> there be no moe in woorke then of necessitie must nedes be to performe those works yor L. did appointe, and yet as the same ende I doe discharge the superflouous nombre.[1]

Faced with that sort of attitude, the workmen must have become accustomed to insecurity in their employment, but some employers appear to have been excessively unscrupulous in their dealings with them. Sir John Thynne's instructions to his steward in August 1547 seem particularly harsh:

> I wol not kepe oon workmen that shall work day work after Michaelmas . . . but ye shall not nede to let the workmen themselfs know it.[2]

Employment by the week was comparatively rare, but on the few occasions where it did occur, as at Grafton Manor, Worcestershire, the workmen seem to have been considerably better off, for the employers usually undertook to pay them their full wage irrespective of the availability of sufficient work to occupy them in any particular week. This seems to be the correct interpretation of the phrase 'broken worke and Holle',[3] or its equivalent,[4] used to describe the conditions of employment enjoyed by the weekly workers. However, although their short-term prospects were more secure, they were still subject to summary dismissal.

Those craftsmen who undertook contracts to execute specific tasks for a negotiated sum were in an even better position because their period of employment was reasonably predictable, but perhaps the most fortunate workmen were those who were hired by the year. A small number of workmen were employed on this basis on most building sites. Sometimes they were paid a small retaining fee to which was added wages at the prevailing rate for the work that they actually executed and sometimes they were paid an inclusive annual salary, usually in quarterly instalments. Sir Francis Willoughby used both methods simultaneously at Wollaton in 1585, when he paid Thomas Accres, the marble mason, and Thomas Greenway, the joiner, £30 each for the year and Christopher Lovell, the principal mason, £16, whereas two other masons John Hills and Clement Wynchenden received £1 in addition to their normal day wages.[5] Whichever way they were paid, they were generally employed for the duration of the work, and were treated as permanent members of the builder's household, their position often being marked by the annual gift of a livery. It is probable that some of them remained in the service of the builder after the completion of the house to carry out the necessary maintenance work. Certainly, Thomas Leversage, a glazier, was in receipt of an annual 'pencon for the repare of the windows' of Sir Richard Leveson's two houses at Trentham and Lilleshall during the building of the former,[6] and another glazier, Mark Wells, was paid £5 per annum by the Earl of Middlesex to maintain the glass at Copthall, Essex.[7]

Such workmen could reasonably expect employment throughout the year, and in some cases they were guaranteed work for longer periods. In February 1599, Sir Edward Pytts

Bargayned with Thomas Lem to serve for 7 yeares as my covenant Servant . . . for a mason a brickmaker & bricklayer.[8]

In 1612 he hired another mason, John Chaunce, to be his surveyor 'till the work be finished God will'. When Pytts died in April 1618, his son negotiated a further four-year contract with Chaunce. Very few craftsmen, however, were given contracts of employment covering such a long period of time. The usual contract, such as that between the Earl of Shrewsbury and two masons in 1575,[9] was for no more than a year, which enabled the builder to make an annual review of his labour requirements. Thus, Sir Richard Leveson employed a number of carpenters and labourers on an annual basis in 1633 and 1634. In 1635, as the pace of work slackened, he 'discharged' them, but many of them continued to work at the site at day wages during the following years.[10]

Annual workmen were in a privileged position, but the conditions under which most workmen were employed were generally very much in favour of the builder. The two masons who came from Bromsgrove to work for Sir Edward Pytts at Kyre Park in October 1611 at 11s. a week must have assumed that they were going to be employed for a considerable period, especially as they agreed to 'contynue winter and sommer at that rate' and yet, little over a month later following Pytts' election as Sheriff of the county, they had been dismissed. They, on their part, had bound themselves 'to contynue in the work without going out or changinge during the time I shall sett them to work'. This was a clause common to most contracts of employment and many builders took steps to ensure that it was honoured. The threats made by Sir John Thynne when he heard that his principal mason was working for another builder 'before he have fynished my works without my license for the redres' have already been noticed and when in 1563 a joiner at the same house quarrelled with a workmate and left the site, he got only as far as Mere in Somerset before the steward had him stopped 'and caused hyme to come back agayne'. On his return to the site, the joiner refused to continue with his work so the steward stopped 'his whole wags purposinge therby to stay him at worke'. Undeterred, he again escaped, and this time he was actually working in Dorset before the steward was able to trace him.[11] When two pairs of London sawyers left Stiffkey Hall, Norfolk, in August 1576, after only two weeks' work, Nathaniel Bacon sent his father 'ye bargaine I concluded wth them and ther markes unto it', apparently with the intention of apprehending them in London and taking action against them. Such action could include imprisonment, as is made clear by the documentation for Hall Court, Herefordshire, where John Coke was driven to drafting an indictment in 1609 against Edward Parker and Gilbert Norris, his two masons who had left the site before the completion of their contract. Parker had something of a record for unreliability, having been previously threatened with imprisonment by Sir William Throckmorton for failing to finish another contract.[12]

There is no evidence whatsoever for any form of guild organization among the crafts on country house sites and workmen in dispute with their employer had very little redress. If they left the site, there was always the possibility that they would be caught and forced to return, and if they remained, the terms of any settlement were invariably dictated by the builder to his own advantage. Sir John Thynne exploited this situation to the full in 1574 when he cut the piece rates that he was willing to pay for the carving of the bay windows at Longleat. From 1572, this work had been executed by Allen Maynard and Robert Smythson, but they were understandably reluctant to work at the reduced rates and in 1574 they were replaced by three of the lesser masons. Smythson and Maynard held out for a time, but with their financial resources rapidly dwindling they were forced to capitulate and in 1575 they were back working at the windows at the lower rates.[13]

Despite the shortage of skilled labour, most builders seem to have had sufficient powers of coercion to prevent any strike action, and few workmen were independent enough to do anything more than complain about conditions that they considered to be unsatisfactory. When the accountant at Beaudesert Hall, Staffordshire, drew up the list of payments that he had made in 1575 for the boarding expenses of the workmen, he noted that the principal carpenter 'demandeth more for his men', but there is no indication that his demands were ever met.[14] The only effective form of protest that a workman could make with impunity was to announce his intention to leave when he had completed his period of service, and even this course presumably was open only to those men who had been hired for a specific length of time. When Bess of Hardwick heard that one of her craftsmen at Chatsworth 'sayth he will departe at our Ladeday next', she angrily called him a false knave and ordered her steward to 'have hym bunden in an oblygacyon to avoyde at the same day', but she was powerless to prevent him leaving.[15]

Although some builders appear to have been hard masters, there were many occasions, no doubt, when they were sorely tried by their workmen. As in any age, examples of unsatisfactory workmanship abound. At Little Saxham Hall in October 1506, a brick wall ten yards long and sixteen feet high had to be completely demolished because the bricklayer had skimped the foundations,[16] and at Longleat in 1565, two of the chimneys were crooked as a result of a mistake made by the mason Allen Maynard, who was later to be in dispute with Thynne.[17]

No action seems to have been taken against the craftsmen responsible for these errors, but at Bolsover Castle in 1613, a mason engaged on dressing stone at piece rates had an unspecified sum 'abated for bad scappling'[18] and an incompetent mason at Kyre Park in the same year was grudgingly paid 'for 15 dayes naughty work . . . & so discharged for a bungler'.[19]

The joiner William Bramley seems to have caused Bess recurrent problems at Hardwick. In 1595 there were 'many things yeat unperfect' about his work on the Old Hall, and in January 1599 he was made to put right at his own expense the poor workmanship that he had executed in the High Great Chamber of the New Hall.[20]

Complaints about the behaviour of the workmen are even more numerous. Some of the more general accusations of dilatoriness were, no doubt, intended to placate absent builders who were making unreasonable demands for progress on their stewards, and must be treated with circumspection. However, despite the rhetoric of Bryan Teshe in writing to Sir John Thynne about the Protector Somerset's house at Wulfhall, asking him to

pardon the rudeness of my letter because I write in haste, for if I be absent the tyme of the writing of this letter ther wyl be almost nothing done among the workmen[21]

Bess of Hardwick was notable as a concerned employer during the construction of Hardwick Hall (RCHME © Crown Copyright).

his complaint was probably justified. In the week that the letter was written two labourers had been dismissed for insubordination and one of the other administrators had complained to Thynne about

> such a lewde company of Frenchmen masons as I never saw the lyke. I assure you they be the worst condicyoned people that ever I saw and the dronkenst; for they will drynke more in one day than three days wages will come to, and then lye lyke beasts on the floor not able to stonde.

Drunkenness was also the subject of comment at Kyre Park, where a quarryman was paid for only half a week in 1612 'for the other 3 [days] he spent idelly at Ale', and in the following year he was dismissed for a similar offence.[22] Sir John Thynne had his own share of labour problems at Longleat, although, given his attitude towards his workmen, it is perhaps permissible to feel some sympathy for the carpenters, about whom the steward wrote in 1563,

> I have more adoe wth them then wth all the rest of yowre folks for nether they will apply ther worke or be content with any reasonable allowance . . .[23]

The evidence for unruly and incompetent workmen is, of course, very biased because the documents only survive to give the point of view of the employer and the voice of the employee is seldom heard. It is safe to assume that there were shortcomings on both sides but only the bonus payments made by satisfied clients hint at a happier relationship. The behaviour of every builder like Sir John Thynne needs to be set against the more enlightened attitude of someone like the Countess of Shrewsbury in seeking to arrive at a more balanced picture of labour relations.

CHAPTER 17

Home Life

Building accounts and contracts, by their nature, disclose little about the social conditions of the workmen involved in the construction of country houses. The information to be gained from wills and inventories is valuable, if often incomplete, but the majority of building craftsmen did not need to make such a record in settling their affairs. All that is known about many of them is their mere existence and, in some cases, the wage rate that they were paid while working on a particular building site. This is especially true of the lower ranks of craftsmen. Their more successful fellow-workmen sometimes achieved sufficient wealth or local importance to have left a more substantial record of their life. The evidence that has been accumulated refers largely to these men and it provides a necessarily imperfect picture of their life away from the building site.

The houses lived in by most building craftsmen were indistinguishable from those of agricultural labourers and husbandmen. There is not much information about those craftsmen at the lower end of the social scale, but Thomas Hill, a mason of Wardington in Oxfordshire who died in 1588, inhabited a simple two-roomed building,[1] and Christopher Gold, a glazier who died in Banbury in the following year, lived in a larger town house containing a shop and hall on the ground floor, a chamber over, and a cockloft in the roof.[2] Both these men were worth well under £5 when they died, and the more moderately successful craftsmen generally lived in more spacious accommodation. Giles Haell, a carpenter living at the same time in Oxford, had a hall, shop, and buttery, with a great chamber, a little chamber and another chamber over the shop.[3] In the early seventeenth century, a mason of Writtle in Essex worth just over £6 lived in a house containing a hall, shop and buttery with chambers over the hall and shop,[4] and another mason, worth over three times as much, lived in a similar house in Bedford.[5] In the north Midlands in 1647, the house of Isaac Smith, a mason of Lichfield, with its hall, parlour and kitchen, and two chambers over, provided him with the same kind of accommodation.[6]

In a few cases, existing houses can be identified with particular craftsmen and the physical evidence that they provide helps to elaborate on the documentary information derived from the probate inventories of the comparatively well-off craftsmen. The house of Arthur Grumbold (1603–70), of the well-known family of Northamptonshire masons, still stands in the village of Weldon. It is dated by inscription to 1654, and is built of stone with a thatched roof. There are three rooms on both ground and upper storeys and two rooms in the roof space. It is

Arthur Grumbold's House of 1654 in Great Weldon (RCHME © Crown Copyright).

heated by three separate chimney-stacks and conforms to the through-passage house type common in the Midlands and upland England from the seventeenth century onwards. An equally common equivalent known as the lobby-entry plan could contain the same number of rooms on the principal floors, but was heated by a massive axial stack. Such a house, perhaps, was the one lived in by Henry Rogers, a carpenter of Southill, Bedfordshire, which had in 1613 a hall, lower chamber, buttery and kitchen, with three chambers over.[7] A smaller house of the same form in Weldon was built by another mason, Humphrey Frisbey, in 1643.[8] It consists of two rooms on both floors, on either side of a centrally placed axial chimney-stack, with further accommodation in the attic. It was a logical variation on the larger type noted above, and many sixteenth and seventeenth-century examples are to be found throughout lowland England. Frisbey's house is distinguished from that of a prosperous husbandman merely by virtue of the richness of the architectural decoration, which was no doubt inspired by pride in his own skill, and partly intended as an advertisement for his craftsmanship.

Haunt Hill House, Great Weldon, built for Humphrey Frisbey in 1643 (RCHME © Crown Copyright).

Some of the more prosperous craftsmen lived in a much grander style. William Thomas, an Oxford plumber who died in 1553, had accommodation in his house for both male and female servants, as well as a hall, parlour, buttery, kitchen and three other chambers.[9] Thomas Holt, the carpenter who was in charge of the work on the Schools Quadrangle at the Bodleian Library, Oxford, in 1618 and 1619, lived in a house in Holywell Street similar to some that still survive there. It was three storeys in height, with a hall, kitchen and entry passage on the ground floor, three chambers above, and two cocklofts in the top storey.[10] The most successful men, the surveyors and the craftsmen with more than local reputations, were probably housed in conditions similar to those of the smaller gentry, to whose ranks some of them aspired. The house of John Smythson at Bolsover, for example, included among its principal rooms the hall, parlour, kitchen, chamber over the parlour, middle chamber and closet,[11] and John Hills was living in a house with the descriptive name of Chilwell Hall at the time of his death in 1592.[12] The fifty-five acre farm that Abraham Smith continued to rent from the Earl of Devonshire long after the completion of Hardwick Hall is an indication of the status that could be achieved by the most skilled craftsmen.

Holywell Street, Oxford, where the carpenter Thomas Holt lived.

The furnishings and possessions to be found in their houses predictably reflected the wealth of the individual craftsmen. Apart from the animals and crops owned by those who were farming as a by-occupation, the most important possessions were invariably their furniture and utensils. Thomas Burger, a Bedfordshire carpenter whose total estate in 1620 was only worth £3.19s.3d., had a bed, three chests and a little old cupboard,[13] and Luke Baggat, another carpenter from Oxfordshire, whose most valuable possession was a cow worth £1.6s.8d., had a bed, a table and a form, when he died in 1584.[14] Further up the social scale, Giles Haell had six beds and a truckle bed,[15] and one of the four beds owned by Leonard Dalton, a Witney carpenter, was proudly noted as being joined.[16] Most craftsmen, including some of the poorest, seem to have had a few pieces of pewter or brass. Thomas Hill, the Oxfordshire mason who was worth £4.5s.0d. in 1588, had two brass pots and seven pieces of pewter,[17] and Christopher Gold, a glazier who died in Banbury in 1589, had two pewter dishes among his assets of £3.2s.2d.[18] The pewter and brass of John King, a Bedfordshire carpenter, was worth £3.10s.0d. in 1620, out of a total estate of £78.10s.8d.,[19] and William Thomas, the prosperous Oxford plumber who died in 1553 worth £78.3s.4d., had £8 in plate.[20]

A surprising number of craftsmen had decorative furnishings in some of the rooms of their houses. Thomas Hill might have lived in only two rooms but they must have been considerably brightened by the painted cloth that hung in one of them.[21] Christopher Gold had three painted cloths in his house,[22] and Giles Haell had an unspecified number of cloths and some panelling in the hall of his Oxford home.[23] Leonard Dalton had a panelled hall and painted cloths in some of his other rooms,[24] and in Worcester the joiner Anthony Ould had no doubt panelled the walls of his hall himself. Certainly, the spectacularly glazed town house in Warwick of Nicholas Eyffeler, a wealthy glazier who originally came from Westphalia and who died in January 1592, contained many fine examples of his painted glass, including the arms of Sir Thomas Lucas of Charlecote and Christopher Wright of Hopsford, who had been among his patrons.[25]

It is very difficult to find any information about the food that the workmen might have eaten off their pewter plate. A tantalizing document in the Longleat Archives refers to the diet of six men at the house in May 1567. It mentions cheese and butter, wheat and malt, and arrangements made 'wth Hogetts wif to bake [and] brewe', but unfortunately it has been badly mutilated and is incomplete.[26] At Hardwick in 1590, 'oats and dredge' and peas were used to make bread for the workmen;[27] an inferior mixture which accords with Harrison's comment on the gentility providing sufficient wheat for their own table while their household were

> inforced to content themselves with rie, or barlei, yea, and in time of dearth, manie with bread made either of beans, peason, or otes.[28]

Carters, who were often tenants fulfilling their obligations of boon work, were invariably given a simple meal on arrival at the site. The carriers of stone and tile to Condover Hall in 1587 were refreshed with bread,

> three owlde cheeses . . . fower softe cheeses & butter.[29]

Similarly, the carters bringing timber to the site at Wollaton in the same year were provided with 'a cheise for their breakefaste',[30] and the carters working at the Shire Hall, Stafford, in 1590, were also given bread and cheese,[31] but few of the other building accounts specify the nature of any of the food that was provided for the working craftsmen. The most complete record of the diet of a group of building workmen in the sixteenth century is provided by the diary of Peter Lewys, Proctor of Dublin Cathedral. The masons engaged on the work there in 1564 and 1565 were given two meals a day, which usually consisted of bread, beef and ale, with fish on Fridays, and sometimes cheese, butter and eggs as a substitute for beef at breakfast.[32] Corporate organizations were often able to provide better conditions for their workmen and it is not necessarily possible to draw any general conclusions about the diet of English country house craftsmen from the evidence of an Irish cathedral. Nevertheless, in the absence of any other evidence, it is possible that conditions were not dissimilar.

It is difficult to be precise about the extent to which building craftsmen were literate. Certainly the bills and contracts to which many of them laboriously appended their mark are testimony to a high degree of illiteracy, and the comment of Thomas Stirrup that 'but few of them can write', is indicative of the prevailing situation as late as 1651.[33] Generally, the bills that they submitted were written out by clerks or by the builder's accountant, and if a craftsman managed to sign his name it is probable that often those were the only words that he could write. Some craftsmen, of course, were capable of reading and writing, and drew up their own bills themselves, but they appear to have been in a minority. Usually they were craftsmen such as smiths and glaziers, who worked independently of the main labour force, and provided their own materials. Consequently, they were obliged to document in some way the purchases that they had made, and the details of the work that they had executed. Craftsmen who undertook limited supervisory duties were another group for whom it was an advantage to be able to write. If they were working away from the main site, quarrying stone or felling timber, they were invariably responsible for recording the hours and wages of the workmen under their charge. Thus, William Grumbold kept the accounts for the work carried out at the stone pits for Sir Thomas Tresham during his building at Lyveden in the early seventeenth century. These were then submitted to the accountant who entered them into the main accounts.[34] Most of the craftsmen who graduated to more responsible administrative positions were almost certainly literate, and the ability of some, such as John Thorpe and Robert Stickles, went beyond the mere facility of being able to read and write. However, the majority of artisans were incapable of leaving any written evidence in their own hands, and the only documentation of their existence is in the writing of the professional scribes of the age, the clerks and accountants.

CHAPTER 18

Wages

Largely because of the availability of the evidence, one aspect of building in the period which has long attracted the attention of economic historians, is the subject of wage rates. The basis from which any consideration of wages paid to artisans working on the construction of country houses must commence, is the pioneering study of masons' wages in general made by D. Knoop and G.P. Jones,[1] and the later research into building wages and prices by E.H. Phelps Brown and S.V. Hopkins.[2] Both studies use the figures collected in the late nineteenth century by J.E. Thorold Rogers,[3] and show a remarkable decline in the real wages of building workers, beginning in the early years of the sixteenth century and continuing throughout the period, caused by wage increases lagging behind rapidly rising food prices. A more optimistic view was taken by Donald Woodward in 1981 but his subsequent detailed research into the conditions of building workers in nine northern towns published in 1994 forced him to conclude that the picture presented by Phelps Brown and Hopkins was broadly correct.[4] However, an analysis restricted to the wage rates in the country house sector of the building trade suggests a number of refinements to the detailed validity of their findings and indicates that workers in this specialized branch of the industry fared considerably better than their urban counterparts.

By extrapolating a predominant wage rate from the various annual statistics collected by Thorold Rogers, both Phelps Brown and Hopkins and Knoop and Jones were able to present a simple graph of the progress of wages over a given period of time. Although acceptable as an indication of the general trend of wages, this method tends to disguise the variety and complexity of the actual situation at any particular point,[5] and, based as it is on comparatively few figures largely drawn from one or two areas in southern England, it suggests a general application that is more apparent than real.[6] The country house building accounts that have survived are characterized by a marked regional variation in wage rates. For example, in 1576, the carpenters working on William Dickenson's house in Sheffield were paid the equivalent of 8*d.* a day,[7] while those working for Lord Paget at Beaudesert Hall, Staffordshire, in the previous year, had been paid 9*d.* and 10*d.* a day,[8] and the carpenters employed at Longleat House, Wiltshire, and Old Thorndon Hall, Essex, were receiving 10*d.* a day during the same period.[9] A similar regional variation in wage rates can be discerned at other periods. Undoubtedly, one of the reasons for this lay in the length of employment enjoyed by many building workers at country house sites and which distinguishes them from the jobbing building workers in the towns. Wage rates generally remained at their initial level for the duration of a particular enterprise, and consequently workmen at one house could be receiving a wage agreed as long as ten years before, while those on a newly commenced house were being engaged at a currently higher rate. During the thirty-four years that building was taking place at Longleat, the only general wage increase was in 1568 and can be partly explained by the arrival of a large number of highly skilled workmen in that year,[10] while wage rates at houses which were built in a shorter length of time, such as Wollaton Hall and Trentham Hall, remained stable for the duration of the work.[11]

However, regional differences in wage rates are not solely explicable by the variety of dates at which particular engagements commenced, and the surviving wage assessments drawn up by the local justices in response to the statute of 1563 suggest that there was a general diversity in the prevailing rate from area to area. Master craftsmen in the building trades in Hertford in 1592, for example, were not to take more than 12*d.* a day in summer, and the 'second sort' of craftsmen were to take no more than 10*d.* a day,[12] while the equivalent rates in Wiltshire eleven years later in 1603 were only 11*d.* and 7*d.*[13] Labourers at York in 1563 were assessed at 5*d.* a day,[14] and their more fortunate colleagues at Lincoln in the same year were assessed at 7*d.* a day.[15] Although the publication of a scale of maximum wage rates does not imply its effective enforcement, the variety of scales in different areas does seem to indicate a regional diversity in the rates that were actually being paid, and this conclusion has been emphasized by Woodward in his research into the north of England.

In addition to this regional disparity, different rates were often paid to workers in the same craft on the same site. Thus at Wollaton between 1582 and 1588, four masons were paid at 14*d.* a day, one at 13*d.*, thirty at 12*d.*, four at 11*d.*, nineteen at 10*d.*, and one at 9*d.*, and among the woodworkers, one was paid 14*d.*, another 13*d.*, thirteen were at 12*d.*, seven at 10*d.*, and five at 9*d.*[16] Although 12*d.* a day was clearly the predominant rate for craftsmen on the site, to ignore the other rates being paid simultaneously to some of the other craftsmen would be a misleading simplification of the true situation. The diversity of rates seems to reflect a combination of the degree of skill attained by the individual craftsmen, and possibly their method of recruitment; the inducement of higher wage rates being necessary to attract itinerant craftsmen, with the local men being content to work at a lower rate in return for a period of comparatively secure employment. Whatever the reason, the majority of country house sites from the mid-sixteenth century onwards exhibit a variety of wage rates similar to that at Wollaton, suggesting that tables of predominant wage rates largely based on short-term engagements involving only a few local workmen must be treated with a degree of caution.

The graph of wage rates published by Phelps Brown and Hopkins is a composite figure which makes no distinction between rates paid to the different crafts.[17] Although it tacitly assumes that all craftsmen were paid the same wage, the authors point out in their text that the carpenter 'showed more upward variants, and led the field in the Tudor rise'. As the carpenter provided their most numerous and continuous quotations, they generally followed him when there

Longleat House, Wiltshire (as drawn by Leonard Knyff and engraved by Jan Kip).

was a divergence from the rates paid to the other crafts. However, the evidence from country house accounts, in addition to showing a variety of rates between workmen in the same craft, also demonstrates that there was often a disparity between the rates paid to different crafts, and, in contrast to the assertion of Phelps Brown and Hopkins, the higher rates were generally paid to masons and bricklayers rather than to workers in wood. Thus, at Longleat between 1568 and 1580, the majority of carpenters were paid 10*d.* a day, with 12*d.* and 14*d.* for a few of the more skilled men, while the predominant rates for the masons were 10*d*. and 12*d*., with the skilled men getting 14*d*. and 16*d*.[18] Similarly at Ashley Park, Surrey, between 1602 and 1607, the carpenters working by the day were generally paid 14*d*. with occasional payments at 16*d*. and 12*d*., and the masons and bricklayers were paid 16*d*. and 18*d*. with only a few at 14*d*.[19]

The wage rates for other craftsmen, such as plasterers and tilers, are too fragmentary to allow any consistent comparison, but generally they seem to have been lower than those paid to the masons and bricklayers. At Trentham Hall, Staffordshire, for example, the plasterers were paid 12*d*. a day, whereas the majority of the masons were paid 16*d*.,[20] and at Wollaton the plasterers received 10*d*. in comparison with the predominant rate for masons of 12*d*.[21]

Another factor which detracts from the validity of a predominant wage table is similarly connected with the complexity of the wage structure on many country houses. Such tables can only be constructed from the evidence provided by those workmen who were paid by the day. Piece rate and contract payments from different engagements can never be strictly compared because of the individual methods by which such payments were calculated and the frequent confusion as to the precise number of workmen being paid for a particular piece of work. However, from the late sixteenth century there was a growing trend on the part of many country house builders to pay their skilled craftsmen at piece rates. By the seventeenth century this had become the predominant method of working and on most major houses only the labouring and some of the more routine craftwork were carried out at day rates. Consequently the daily wage rates that exist for the early seventeenth century often refer only to the less-skilled craftsmen and it is probable that this has a depressing influence on the general trend of wages in that period. The striking effect that the contrasting methods of working could have on the annual income of craftsmen working on the same site can be illustrated from the accounts for Trentham Hall, Staffordshire. In 1633 and 1634, Henry Smethley, a carpenter and joiner, was paid respectively £105.11*s*.6*d*. and £130.10*s*.9½*d*, for his piece-work on the house, while his colleague, Ralph Sutton, received £103.8*s*.9*d*. and £64.17*s*.3*d*. during the same period. Out of these sums both men made unspecified payments to two or three assistants, but, even so, a large proportion of the money must have remained to them as income. Between 1635 and 1638, when the more skilled woodworkers had left the site, the remaining carpentry was executed at day rates by John Bradwell, the estate carpenter and two assistants. Although they were employed consistently in almost every week during that period, none of them earned more than £12 in any one year. The predominant day wages for carpenters at Trentham was 12*d*. for Bradwell and 11*d*. for his assistants, but it is arguable that the piece rate payments to Smethley and Sutton are of equal significance in assessing the economic position of the carpenters on the site, especially as the numbers of men receiving such payments between 1630 and 1634 probably exceeded those employed at day rates in the later years of the work. On the few occasions that Smethley worked at day rates he was paid 18*d*. a day, and his men were paid 16*d*., which seems to suggest that the movement towards piece-work certainly conceals a higher general wage-level than is apparent from a consideration of only those workmen who were paid exclusively at day rates.

The wide variety of wage rates that were often paid on a single site, both to the different crafts and to different groups of men within those crafts, makes it difficult to chart the course of wages between 1500 and 1640. In Figure 1, an attempt has been made to show the limits of the movement of wages during that period. For the reasons outlined above, and also on account of the limited number of entries obtainable from country house accounts, it seemed inadvisable to construct a predominant wage rate, but the results of Phelps Brown and Hopkins have been superimposed on the figure for purposes of comparison. There were insufficient entries to usefully include the other crafts so the figure has been confined to the wage rates for masons and carpenters. The practice on some sites of providing food and drink for the workmen, or of paying them less during the winter months, necessitated adjustments to some of the examples. Where the value of meat and drink could be firmly established, as at Hengrave Hall, the entries were adjusted accordingly, but where there was some doubt as to the exact

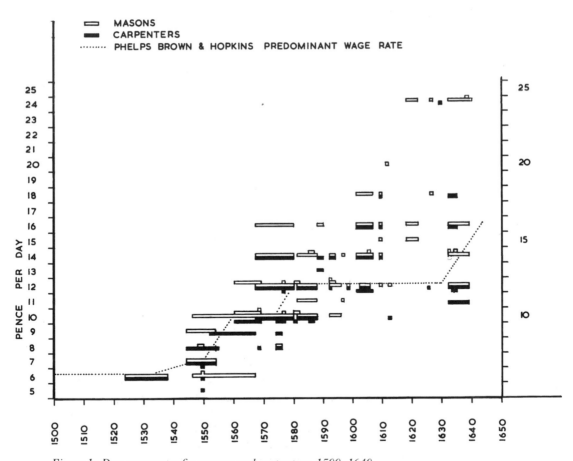

Figure 1: Day wage rates for masons and carpenters, 1500–1640

value that the builder placed on the food he supplied to his workmen, the entries have not been included. Thus the wage rates for Gawthorpe Hall, Lancashire, were not plotted on the figure. Most accounts were of sufficient duration to give both summer and winter wage rates and where there was a divergence between the two, only the higher summer rate has been considered.[22]

There was an unfortunate lack of entries for the early years of the sixteenth century. However, wage rates for craftsmen seem to have been stable at 6d. a day during this period, as they had been for much of the preceding century. The 6d. a day paid to carpenters and masons at Hengrave Hall from 1525 to 1538 accords with the similar sum paid to the craftsmen at Kirby Muxloe Castle, Leicestershire, in the 1480s.[23] The evidence from Hengrave suggests that during this settled period a uniform rate was being paid both to the various crafts and to the men within those crafts. By the middle of the century, wages were beginning to rise. The increase in prices, which had effectively begun some decades before, was clearly beginning to have an influence on wage rates as the consequences of inflation began to bite.[24] Some craftsmen continued to be paid at the former rate, but a divergence in wages between individual workmen within the same craft was becoming apparent, creating maximum and minimum wage scales on most sites. Thus at Longleat, some masons were being paid 10d. a day, while others were only receiving 6d. By the third quarter of the century wages had continued to rise and the maximum and minimum rates at Longleat were now 16d. and 10d. In some parts of the country, however, wage rates remained at a lower level. In 1575 and 1576, for example, the masons and carpenters in Sheffield were paid 8d. a day, and the carpenters at Beaudesert Hall, Staffordshire, received 9d. and 10d. But, as these are the first entries from the Midlands and the north of England, it is impossible to know whether wages were slow to rise in these areas or whether they had risen from a comparatively lower base and thus represented an improvement similar to that noted for the southern and eastern parts of the country.

In the last quarter of the sixteenth century, craftsmen's wages appear to have stabilized for a period at the level to which they had been moving in the previous decade. The various rates paid to the different groups of craftsmen at Longleat in the 1570s are approximately similar to those paid at Wollaton in the 1580s, and to Sir Thomas Tresham's workmen in Northamptonshire in the 1590s. Minor upward movements were certainly taking place during this period, but the general pattern was for the lowest wage scales to disappear gradually while the maximum scales of 14d. and 16d., first discernible at Longleat in 1568, were not exceeded until the early years of the seventeenth century. During that century, the maximum rate rose from 18d. a day in the first decade to 24d. by the end of the second decade, at which level it appears to have remained until the Civil War. The differential between the highest and lowest wage scale appears to have increased considerably in the early seventeenth century, so that of the masons consistently employed at Trentham Hall, Staffordshire, in the 1630s, some were being paid 24d. a day while others were receiving only half that sum. However, the day wage rates for the early seventeenth century are less representative than those available for the previous century, for on all the recorded accounts much of the work was carried out at piece rates and consequently the day rates generally reflect the routine work executed by the less skilled craftsmen. Occasionally, some of the piece-workers were employed for a short period at day rates and they were invariably paid on a higher wage scale. It seems probable that these wages are indicative of a higher general level of wages than is apparent from the rates paid to those workmen who were exclusively employed by the day.

The movement of country house wages during the period broadly reflects the same trends plotted by Phelps Brown and Hopkins, with increases in the 1550s and '70s, and a period of comparative stability in the late sixteenth and early seventeenth centuries. In general, however, wage rates seem to have been higher than their predominant rate indicates, especially in the early seventeenth century when the market seems to have been moving to a higher level at an earlier date than they allow. It is possible that such higher rates were peculiar to the country house sector of the building trade, where the difficulties of attracting sufficient numbers of skilled workmen might have compelled the builders to pay higher wages. But it is perhaps significant that in the Royal Works, where the prerogative of impressment enabled the Crown to overcome any temporary shortages of labour, the wage rates were similar to those being paid on country house sites. Therefore it seems likely that, in long-term engagements at least, Phelps Brown and Hopkins consistently underestimated the level of wage rates from the middle of the sixteenth century onwards.

The wage rate for labourers working on country house sites have been set out in Figure 2.[25] As might be expected, these follow the same general pattern as has been outlined for masons and carpenters, with increases occurring during approximately the same periods. Although for much of the sixteenth century the wage rates agree fairly closely with those given by Phelps Brown and Hopkins, it appears that the movement towards a higher level had begun in parts of the country by 1590, and once again it is possible that they underestimated the extent of the increase in the early seventeenth century. In this respect, it is apposite to note that the purchasing power of the wages paid to agricultural labourers during the first four decades of the century seems to have been considerably higher than the purchasing power of the wages of building craftsmen suggested by Phelps Brown and Hopkins.[26]

The reluctance to project a predominant wage rate from the variety of figures collected for craftsmen and labourers makes it impossible to construct an index of wages for the period, and consequently no strict comparison with prices can be attempted. However, using as a guide the graph showing the price of a composite unit of consumables in southern England compiled by Phelps Brown and Hopkins,[27] it is clear that despite the improvement in wages from the mid-sixteenth century onwards, prices had consistently risen faster and that the economic position of the wage-earner in 1640 was markedly worse than it had been in 1500. The exact extent of this decline is more difficult to assess. Little is known about the precise nature of individual expenditure during the period, and the compilation of an aggregate price-index is correspondingly arbitrary. In addition, the only statistics surviving in sufficient numbers to enable such an index to be constructed are for wholesale prices and it is not at all certain that

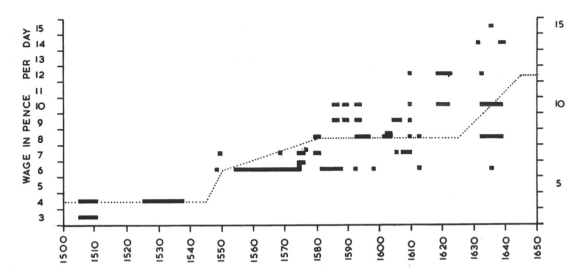

Figure 2: Day wage rates for labourers, 1500–1640

retail prices rose quite so often or so fast. This doubt is especially pertinent to those goods which required processing and therefore contained an element of labour charge in their retail price, for wages, as has been suggested above, often remained relatively stable for a considerable period of time.

Although the graph compiled by Phelps Brown and Hopkins probably represents the most successful attempt that can be made on the available evidence to show the course of prices, it is instructive to compare it with the monetary equivalent of a craftsman's food and drink over the same period. At Hengrave Hall in the 1530s it was valued at 2*d.* a day, but by the 1550s, in Essex, Sir William Petre was assessing it at 3*d.*, a sum which was similar to that existing at Longleat during the same decade. In the 1560s it had risen to 4*d.* at Longleat, which was also the prevailing rate at Grafton Manor, Worcestershire, and Loseley House, Surrey. Its value then seems to have remained at this level through the 1570s in Sheffield and into the 1580s at Old Thorndon Hall, Essex. In the various surviving wage assessments, the value of meat and drink was calculated at 3*d.* in Northamptonshire in 1560,[28] and in Buckinghamshire in 1562,[29] and then at 4*d.* or 5*d.* in all the succeeding assessments, down to that of Hertford in 1631 where it had risen to 5*d.* or 6*d.*[30] Such figures, of course, are only a very rough guide, as they probably represent only a theoretical value that the builder placed on produce largely derived from his own demesne, and they fail to take account of any possible lowering in the quality of the diet provided. But they do, perhaps, indicate that the rise in wholesale prices was not felt quite so strongly at a local level.

According to the evidence presented by Phelps Brown and Hopkins, by 1640 prices had risen to some five or six times their level in 1500, while the wage of a building craftsman had approximately doubled over the same period. This represents a catastrophic economic deterioration and even if it is assumed that building craftsmen were unusually prosperous at the beginning of the sixteenth century, it is difficult to accept a decline of such magnitude in their real wages without any attendant evidence of widespread starvation and distress. In the absence of such evidence, it is perhaps reasonable to doubt whether the impact of the price rise on wage-earners was quite as disastrous as has been generally assumed. In addition to the evidence for a higher level of wages and a slower rise in some retail food prices, it is possible that alterations in their working conditions enabled the building craftsmen to maintain a reasonable standard of living. Unfortunately, there is insufficient information available about such factors as the number of holidays taken by the workmen, so that it is not possible to speculate whether a decline in the number of religious festivals and saints' days after the Reformation, for example, provided them with an opportunity to earn more money during the year. However, there are indications that some improvements were taking place in their earning potential, for the reduction in their wages during the winter months, which had been almost universal practice in the sixteenth century, occurred only rarely in the early seventeenth century. As the original motive for a lower wage was that fewer hours of work were possible during the shorter winter days, the abolition of the practice effectively provided the workmen with a seasonal wage increase.

In addition, many building workmen were able to supplement their wages from other sources. The evidence for by-occupations among the building trades has already been discussed and it is relevant to point out that any agricultural surplus which they were able to sell would have benefited from the rising prices and thus helped to offset the deterioration in their real wages. However, too much emphasis must not be placed on such ameliorating factors. The building worker was primarily a wage-earner, and over a period of a century and a half he was faced by a consistent and rapid rise in prices. There is no doubt that on the whole his economic position declined, but for those workers engaged on building country houses at least, there are reasonable grounds to suggest that the extent of this decline was not as great as the wage and price statistics of Thorold Rogers would seem to indicate. It is most unlikely that the economic position of the workmen employed in other branches of the building trade was radically different, but further research into the original sources is necessary before this more general conclusion can be confirmed.

Part V

CONCLUSION

Mount Edgcumbe

Most gentry in England at this day, have some knowledge in the Theory of Architecture.

JOHN WEBB, 1660

CHAPTER 19

Specialization and Professionalism

The important changes that took place in the way that country houses were designed and constructed during the period of almost 150 years with which this study is concerned have already been documented and discussed. The common themes which characterize the period are a growing awareness of architecture as an art form capable of intellectual analysis and appreciation and an increased specialization in the practical processes of construction. To a certain extent, both these themes reflect the gradual acceptance by the men who were building the more important country houses, of Renaissance and humanist ideas. They spring from the Renaissance concept of architecture as a liberal art, to be ranked with the traditional arts of grammar, dialectic, rhetoric, geometry, arithmetic, astrology and music, and as such worthy of the educated attention of someone of gentle birth. But it was only by emphasizing its intellectual and theoretical basis that architecture was able to aspire to this position. From the middle of the sixteenth century onwards, there is growing evidence from the correspondence of the builders themselves and from the publication of authors such as Shute, Wotton and Bacon that such an emphasis was taking place. By the seventeenth century, the liberal status of architecture had been accepted in some quarters of educated society, especially by those close to the Court and familiar with the ideas of Inigo Jones, but the majority of·builders, although they were fully aware of the fashionable aspects of architectural style, were still incapable of appreciating its deeper philosophical content. However, although it was often imperfectly understood, the concept of the liberal architect whose primary role was confined to the design of a building based on a knowledge of architectural theory was sufficiently established by 1640 for it to exercise a growing influence on the remainder of the century.

In common with the changes that were taking place in the processes of design, there was a similar trend towards a more clearly defined method of administering a building enterprise. Although architecture might aspire to become a liberal art, building, the transformation of architectural ideas into a three-dimensional form, was indisputably a mechanical pursuit. However, efficiency, and the growing adoption of piece-work as the best method of working, demanded that the everyday supervision of the work should be conducted by someone who was versed in the specialized techniques of building administration. The emergent status of the architect prevented him from combining his designing role with that of surveyor of the work, although his occasional attendance at the site was often necessary to ensure the successful execution of his design. The more literate craftsmen, however, were familiar with all the practical aspects of building, including the supervision of other workmen and the mathematical competence necessary to calculate piece-work. The same social barrier between architecture and building, which denied them the opportunity to become architects in any acceptable sense of the word, meant that the only opening for their talents was in the field of supervision, and consequently the construction of many of the more important country houses of the late sixteenth and early seventeenth centuries was directed by specialized building surveyors who had risen from a training in one of the crafts.

The functional and social distinction between architects and surveyors was still in a very tentative state by the beginning of Civil War, but the intellectual and practical conditions which were to crystallize the distinction were intensifying. In essence, they were symptomatic of a growing professionalism in building, whereby the more specialized requirements of architectural design and methods of working prompted the employment of acknowledged experts to create and administer a building as well as to execute it. Something of the stage that this process had reached by the early seventeenth century can be seen from the arrangements that Sir Edward Pytts made in 1611 for the construction of additions to Kyre Park, Worcestershire. The design was commissioned from John Bentley, who was known to Pytts for his work on the Schools Quadrangle at Oxford, but the administration of the work was put into the hands of John Chaunce, a Bromsgrove mason previously employed by Pytts as a working craftsman and who was now termed 'Surveyr of the work & workmen'.[1] Similarly, the Earl of Danby employed Nicholas Stone to design his house at Cornbury, Oxfordshire, in 1631, and although the terms of Stone's employment included the direction of the workmen, this function was in practice fulfilled by Gabriel Stacey, who had worked for Stone in a similar capacity at the Botanic Gardens in Oxford.[2]

The administrative opportunities available to the more talented and literate craftsmen did not represent a new departure from medieval practice. Master craftsmen had always played a prominent role in the organization of most building enterprises, but the limits of their responsibility were now being circumscribed by the emergence of the architect as a separate and socially superior agent in the building process. There were other changes at a craft level which were similarly contingent on the acceptance of Renaissance ideas. Not only were many of the motifs of architectural decoration now derived from literary sources, but new criteria of correctness were imposed upon their execution. Not every craftsman had access to these sources or was capable of adapting to new ideas that had been implanted from outside rather than developed organically within the traditions of his craft. Inevitably, such craftsmen were restricted to the more straightforward aspects of their craft, while their more literate and adaptable fellows increasingly specialized in decorative work. It is probable that the wide variety in wages within particular crafts which characterized most building operations from the middle of the sixteenth century onwards was, at least in part, a reflection of this differential in skill and knowledge.

The sixteenth and early seventeenth centuries are best viewed as a period of transition. None of the developments outlined above can be said to have been universally accepted by 1640. Many country houses continued to be designed and built by traditional methods, and few builders were aware of the theoretical implications behind the new styles that they consciously adopted. But, even so, important changes had taken place during the period which were to receive more precise definition after the Restoration. The Renaissance might not have been fully assimilated, but the Middle Ages had clearly ended.

Notes

1. The Motives for Building

1. Thomas Smith, *Discourse of the Commonweal of this Realm of England* (1549); *Harrison's Description of England in Shakespere's Youth*, ed. F.J. Furnivall (New Shakespere Soc., vi, 1877) p. 341; C. Platt, *Medieval Southampton* (1973), p. 27.

2. G. Goodman, *The Court of James I*, ed. J. Brewer (London, 1839), i. p. 199.

3. *Camden Soc.*, ix (1840), p. 42.

4. G.C. Tyack, 'Country House Building in Warwickshire, 1500–1914' (Oxford Univ. B.Litt. thesis, 1970), p. 5.

5. L. Stone, *The Crisis of the Aristocracy, 1558–1641* (Oxford, 1957), p. 551.

6. The term 'builder' has been used throughout to refer to the patrons for whom the houses were built.

7. For an elaboration of this theme, see E. Mercer, 'The Houses of the Gentry', *Past and Present*, 5 (1954), pp. 11–32; idem.; *English Art 1556–1625* (Oxford, 1962), pp. 12–59.

8. E.S. Hartshorne, *Memorials of Holdenby* (Newcastle, 1868), p. 16.

9. E.R. Sandeen, 'The Building Activities of Sir Nicholas Bacon' (Chicago Univ. Ph.D. thesis, 1959), p. 142. Hereafter cited as Sandeen.

10. For a fuller discussion of this intellectual aspect of the period, see M. Girouard, *Robert Smythson and the Architecture of the Elizabethan Era* (London, 1966), pp. 35–92. Hereafter cited as Girouard, *Smythson*.

11. *The Letters of John Chamberlain*, ed. N.E. McClure (Philadelphia, 1939), i. 83.

12. Hist. MSS. Comm., *Cecil*, xv, p. 383.

13. Sir John Soane's Museum, The Book of Architecture of John Thorpe, T56, T58, T145–6, T151, T30 & 50.

14. RIBA Library, Drawings Collection, Smythson Collection, II/10, I/8.

15. BL., MSS. Facs. 372 (i). I am indebted to Sir John Summerson for discussions on the problems of this plan.

16. *The Chamberlain Letters*, ed. E.N. Thomson (London, 1966), p. 61.

17. See also Warmwell House, Dorset, of *c.* 1618.

18. Sir John Soane's Museum, *op. cit.*, T156.

19. BL., Addit. MSS. 39832.

20. J.A. Gotch, *A Complete Account . . . of the Buildings Erected in Northamptonshire by Sir T. Tresham, 1575–1605* (Northampton, 1883) gives the most complete reading of these sometimes obscure emblems and inscriptions. See also G. Isham 'Sir Thomas Tresham and his Buildings', *Northants. Antiquarian Soc.*, lxv (1964–5).

21. Dorset CRO, MW/M4, f. 24.

22. BL., Addit. MSS. 54332.

23. M. Girouard, 'Elizabethan Architecture and the Gothic Tradition', *Architectural History*, 6 (1963), pp. 23–40.

24. This paragraph is based on the interpretation of Smith's building activities given in P.J. Drury, '"A Fayre House, Buylt by Sir Thomas Smith": The Development of Hill Hall, Essex, 1557–81', *Jour. B.A.A.*, cxxxvi (1983), pp. 98–123.

25. The Earl of Ilchester, *The House of the Hollands, 1605–1820* (London, 1937); Leeds City Library, TN/EA/13/74.

26. Unpublished account by the author prepared for the Historic Buildings Board of the Greater London Council.

27. A. Oswald, 'Chantmarle, Dorset', *Country Life*, cvii (1950), pp. 1966–71. Dorset CRO MW/M4 f. 22v.

28. J. Spedding, *The Letters and the Life of Francis Bacon* (London 1872), vii, p. 114.

29. The most detailed account of Bacon's buildings is Sandeen. A microfilm copy is

deposited in the Bodleian Library, Oxford, 1959 Chicago 9.

30. J. Nichols, *The Progresses and Public Processions of Queen Elizabeth* (London, 1823), i, p. 205n.

31. F. Peck, *Desiderata Curiosa* (2nd edn, London, 1779), p. 25.

32. H.G. Leask, 'Early Seventeenth-century Houses in Ireland', in *Studies in Building History*, ed. E.M. Jope (London, 1961), p. 244.

33. *The Loseley Manuscripts*, ed. A.J. Kempe (London, 1836), pp. 265–6.

34. L. Stone, *The Crisis of the Aristocracy*, 1558–1641 (Oxford, 1965), p. 454.

35. L. Stone, 'The Building of Hatfield House', *Arch. Jour.*, cxii (1955), pp. 100–28.

36. Girouard, *Smythson*, p. 98.

37. *Ibid.*, p. 118.

38. E.S. Hartshorne, *Memorials of Holdenby* (Newcastle, 1868), p. 16.

39. Mrs Baldwin-Childe, 'The Building of the Manor House of Kyre Park, Worcestershire, 1588–1618', *The Antiquary*, xxi–ii (1890).

40. BL., Addit. MSS. 39830–6.

2. Sites

1. F.G. Emmison, *Tudor Secretary, Sir William Petre at Court and Home* (London, 1961), p. 27.

2. C. Stanley-Millson and J. Newman, 'Blickling Hall: The Building of a Jacobean Mansion', *Architectural History*, 29 (1986), pp. 1–42.

3. M. Howard, *The Early Tudor Country House* (London, 1987), p. 17.

4. J. Ward, *Old Thorndon Hall* (Chelmsford, 1972).

5. Mrs Baldwyn-Childe, 'The Building of the Manor House of Kyre Park, Worcestershire', *The Antiquary*, xxvi (1890), p. 202.

6. Dorset CRO, MW/M4 f. 24v.

7. W. Minet, *Hadham Hall* (Colchester, 1914), p. 63.

8. J.C. Rogers, 'The Manor and Houses of Gorhambury', *St Albans and Herts: Architectural and Archaeological Soc. Trans.*, new ser. iv (1933), pp. 35–112.

9. Quoted in Girouard, *Smythson*, p. 84.

10. Essex CRO, D/DP Q13/3/13.

11. J. Summerson, 'The Building of Theobalds, 1564–85', *Archaeologia*, xcvii (1959), p. 108.

12. BL., Addit. MSS. 54332.

13. Rogers, *op. cit.*

14. Howard, *op. cit.*, Chapter 7.

15. Beds. CRO, TW 11/110.

16. Cambridge Univ. Lib., Hengrave Hall Deposit 80.

17. A. Simpson, *The Wealth of the Gentry, 1540–1660* (Cambridge, 1961), p. 53.

18. S.D. Spittle, 'Madingley Hall', *Arch. Jour.*, cxxiv (1967), p. 225.

19. Sandeen, p. 188.

20. BL., Egerton MSS. 2599, ff. 159–60; Essex CRO, D/D ST T1; PRO, C142/86/74.

3. Design and Designers

1. N. Pevsner, 'The Term "Architect" in the Middle Ages', *Speculum*, xvii (1942), p. 549.

2. L.F. Salzman, *Building in England Down to 1540* (2nd edn., Oxford, 1967), pp. 228, 420. Hereafter cited as Salzman.

3. Winchester City Archives, St John's Hospital Accounts, 69 & 70 (1462–3), *Ibid.*, 65 (1459–60). I owe both these references to the kindness of Dr D. J. Keene.

4. J. Shute, *The First and Chief Groundes of Architecture* (London, 1563), preface.

5. J. Strype, *The Life of the Learned Sir Thomas Smith* (Oxford, 1820 edn), p. 171.

6. Cambridge Univ. Lib., Hengrave Hall Deposit, 80.

7. Strype, *op. cit.*, p. 171.

8. R. Willis and J.W. Clark, *The Architectural History of the University of Cambridge and of the Colleges of Cambridge and Eton* (Cambridge, 1886), ii, p. 693n. Hereafter cited as Willis and Clark.

9. *Ibid.*, ii, p. 251 *et passim*.

10. I.G. Philip, 'The Building of the Schools Quadrangle', *Oxoniensia*, xii (1948), p. 42.

11. T.W. Hanson, 'Halifax Builders in Oxford', *Trans. Halifax Antiq. Soc.* (1928), pp. 253–317.

12. Dorset CRO, MW/M4 f. 24v.

13. *The Account Book of Nicholas Stone*, ed. W.L. Spiers (Walpole Soc., vii, 1919), p. 65.

14. Northants. CRO, IC 4957.

15. As an illustration of the process, see J.H. Harvey, 'The Origin of the Perpendicular Style', in *Studies in Building History*, ed. E.M. Jope (London, 1961), pp. 134–65.

16. *Ibid.*, p. 134.

17. J. H. Harvey, *English Medieval Architects* (London, 1954).

18. *Harrison's Description of England in Shakespere's Youth*, ed. F.J. Furnivall (New Shakespere Soc., series vi. 1877) p. 238. Only Vitruvius and Serlio were mentioned in the

1577 edition. The name of Alberti was added for the edition of 1587. It is revealing that Harrison only identifies him by his Christian names, suggesting, perhaps, that he had not actually read him.

19. BL., Addit. MSS. 39830, f. 191 v. For a list of other architectural libraries see Lucy Gent, *Picture and Poetry 1560–1620* (Leamington Spa, 1981).

20. Hist. MSS., Comm., *Portland*, ix, p. 152.

21. The collection, which is kept at Hatfield, is available in facsimile at BL., MSS. Facs. 372 (1 and 2).

22. Mrs Baldwyn-Childe, 'The Building of the Manor House of Kyre Park, Worcestershire', *The Antiquary*, xxii (1890), p. 53.

23. Linda Campbell, 'Documentary Evidence for the Building of Raynham Hall', *Architectural History*, 32 (1989), p. 56.

24. G. Tyack, *Warwickshire Country Houses* (Chichester, 1994), p. 48.

25. H.L. Bradfer-Lawrence, 'The Building of Raynham Hall', *Norf. Arch.*, xxiii, (1927), p. 125.

26. *The Account Book of Nicholas Stone*, ed. W.L. Spiers (Walpole Soc., vii, 1919), p. 3.

27. Baldwyn-Childe, *op. cit.*, p. 53.

28. For example, T34 and T141. See *The Book of Architecture of John Thorpe* ed. J. Summerson (Walpole Soc., xl, 1966), p. 29.

29. T71–2, and T75–6. *Ibid.*, pp. 67–8.

30. RIBA Library, Drawings Collection, Smythson Collection, 1/25. See also *The Smythson Collection*, ed. M. Girouard (*Architectural History*, v, 1962), p. 38.

31. Devon CRO, 404 M/61–2.

32. Summerson, *op. cit.*, pp. 7–8.

33. K.J. Höltgen, 'An Unknown Manuscript Translation by John Thorpe of du Cerceau's *Perspective*', in E. Chaney and P. Mack (eds), *England and the Continental Renaissance* (Woodbridge, 1990). J. Summerson, 'Three Elizabethan Architects', *Bull. of the John Rylands Lib.* xl. (1957), pp. 216–21.

34. BL., Addit. MSS, 39831 ff. 3–4.

35. BL., Landsdowne 84/10.

36. *The Loseley Manuscripts*, ed. A.J. Kempe (London 1836), p. 304. For a recent discussion of the role of the patron see Maurice Howard, '"His Lordship was the Chiefest Architect": Patrons as Builders in 16th-century England' in Giles Worsley, ed., *The Role of the Amateur Architect* (Georgian Group Symposium, 1993), pp. 7–13.

37. *The Account Book of Nicholas Stone*, ed.

W.L. Spiers (Walpole Soc., vii, 1919), p. 104.

38. Longleat Archives, R.O.B., I, 121. 18 June 1547.

39. *Ibid.*, R.O.B., I, 19. 16 April 1547.

40. *Ibid.*, R.O.B., I, 70. 7 May 1547.

41. *Ibid.*, R.O.B., I, 120. 18 June 1547.

42. *Ibid.*, R.O.B., I, 141. 22 June 1547.

43. In June 1547, for example, he sought clarification of Thynne's wishes for treating the roof of a tower. *Ibid.*, R.O.B., I. 127.

44. *Ibid.*, R.O.B., I, 199. Undated, but probably 1546.

45. *Ibid.*, R.O.B., III, 197.

46. *Ibid.*, p. 213.

47. *Richard Carew of Antony: The Survey of Cornwall etc.*, ed. F.E. Halliday (London, 1953), p. 175.

48. Girouard, *Smythson*, p. 68

49. Sandeen, p. 178.

50. BL., Addit. MSS. 27, 278, f. 24v.

51. J.R. Wigfull, 'Extracts from the Note-book of William Dickenson', *Trans. Hunter Arch. Soc.*, ii (1921), pp. 189–200. Campbell, *op. cit.*

52. J.A. Gotch, 'The Renaissance in Northamptonshire', *Trans. R.I.B.A.*, new ser., vi (1890), pp. 104–6.

53. Essex CRO, D/DP Q13/11: Sir Edward Hext to John Lord Petre, 19 Mar. 1609/10.

54. Willis and Clark, ii, p. 172.

55. 'Extracts from the Registers of the Parish of Much Wenlock', *Trans. Shropshire Arch. Soc.*, xi (1888), p. 15.

56. H. Avray Tipping, 'Condover Hall', *Country Life*. xliii, (1918), p. 513.

57. Mrs Baldwyn-Childe, 'The Building of the Manor House of Kyre Park, Worcestershire', *The Antiquary*, xxi–ii (1890).

58. For Stickells and Adams, see J. Summerson, 'Three Elizabethan Architects', *Bull. of the John Rylands Lib.*, xll (1957), pp. 202–28. Bradshaw, who was Surveyor of the Royal Works 1547–64, provided plans for Sir William Petre at East Thorndon, Essex, in 1550, Essex CRO, D/DP A10 f. 81 and f. 85.

59. D.J. Gordon, 'Poet and Architect: The Intellectual Setting of the Quarrel between Ben Jonson and Inigo Jones', *Courtauld and Warburg Journal*, xii (1949), pp. 152–78.

60. For an important discussion of Dee's preface see F.A. Yates, *Theatre of the World* (London, 1969).

61. H.M. Colvin, *Biographical Dictionary of British Architects, 1600–1840* (London, 1978), p. 871.

62. *'Brief Lives' Chiefly of Contemporaries, set*

down by John Aubrey between the years 1669 &
1696, ed. A. Clark (Oxford, 1898), i. p. 78.
63. *The Architecture of Sir Roger Pratt*, ed. R.T.
Gunther (Oxford, 1928), p. 60.
64. Colvin, *op, cit.*, p. 543.
65. *Ibid.*, p. 596.
66. W.J. Williams, 'Wills of Freemasons and
Masons', *The Masonic Record*, xvi (1936), pp.
171–236.
67. *Ibid.*, p. 223.
68. *Ibid.*, p. 234.
69. *The Book of Architecture of John Thorpe*, ed.
J. Summerson (Walpole Soc., xl, 1966), p. 4.
70. RIBA Library, Drawings Collection,
Smythson Collection, I/3–4, 7, 9–15, 17, 20,
24.
71. *Ibid.*, III/6–8, 13.
72. Williams, *op. cit.*, p. 204.
73. *Ibid.*, p. 234.
74. Girouard, *Smythson*, p. 200.
75. Noting his intention to see 'every place of
mark where curiosities are used' before starting
to build at Petworth. Hist. MSS. Comm., *Cecil*,
xv, p. 383.
76. Willis and Clark, ii. p. 490.
77. G. Batho, 'Notes and Documents on
Petworth House, 1574–1632', *Sussex. Arch.
Coll.*, xcvi, (1958), pp. 108–34.
78. BL., Addit. MSS. 7097, ff. 175, 175v, 178
& 192v.
79. Campbell, *op. cit.*, pp. 56–8.

4. *Methods of Undertaking*

1. *Wren. Soc.*, v. (1928), 20.
2. Cambridge Univ. Library, Hengrave Hall
Deposit 80.
3. Longleat Archives, R.O.B., ii, f. 177.
4. BL., Egerton MSS. 2816.
5. J. Lister and W. Brown, 'Seventeenth
Century Builders' Contracts' *Yorks. Arch. Jour.*,
xvi (1902), pp. 109–10.
6. S.D. Kitson, 'The Heraldic Glass of
Gilling Castle, Yorks., and Bernard
Dinninghof', *Jour. British Soc. of Master Glass
Painters*, iii (1929), pp. 55–8.
7. Willis and Clark, ii, pp. 248–63.
8. W.H. Godfrey, 'An Elizabethan Builder's
Contract', *Sussex Arch. Coll.*, lxv. (1924), pp.
219–24.
9. G.R. Batho, 'The Percies at Petworth,
1547–1632', *ibid.*, xcv (1957), p. 12.
10. Cornwall CRO, Mount Edgcumbe MSS.,
MTD/48/10.
11. Longleat Archives, R.O.B., ii, f. 117.

12. BL., Addit. MSS. 25302, f. 153.
13. Beds. CRO, TW818.
14. Lister and Brown, *op. cit.*, pp. 109–10.
15. Cambridge Univ. Library, Hengrave Hall
Deposit 81.
16. B. Gerbier, *A Brief Discourse Concerning the
Three Chief Principles of Magnificent Building . . .*
(London, 1662), p. 26.
17. B. Stallybrass, 'Bess of Hardwick's
Buildings and Building Accounts', *Archaeologia*,
lxiv (1913), p. 366.
18. Willis and Clark, ii, pp. 257–8.
19. Surrey CRO, Acc. 1030, f. 99v. BL., Addit.
MSS. 69,869.
20. BL., Addit. MSS. 7079, ff. 174–200.
21. Longleat Archives, T.P., lxviii, Bk. 60,
f. 43.
22. Dorset CRO, MW/M4, f. 24v. See Roger
Pratt; '. . . it is to be observed, that the higher
they go, the greater the price will be, by reason
of the trouble of the materials, which are carried
up to them . . .', *The Architecture of Sir Roger
Pratt*, ed. R.T. Gunther (Oxford, 1928), p. 52.
23. W.E. Preston, 'A Sixteenth Century
Account Roll of the Building of a House at
Chevet', *Yorks. Arch. Jour.*, xxxii (1934), pp.
326–30.
24. Staffs. CRO, D593 R/1/2.
25. *Wren Soc.*, v. (1928), p. 20.
26. B. Gerbier, *Counsel and Advise to All
Builders . . .* (London, 1663), p. 61.
27. Gunther, *op. cit.*, pp. 87–8.

5. *The Administrative and Executive Labour Force*

1. Beds. CRO, TW 818.
2. D. Knoop and G.P. Jones, 'The
Carreglwyd Building Account, 1636', *Trans.
Anglesey Antiq. Soc.* (1934), pp. 27–43.
3. Mrs Baldwyn-Childe, 'The Building of the
Manor House of Kyre Park, Worcestershire,
1588–1628', *The Antiquary*, xxi–ii (1890), pp.
202–264 and 24–50.
4. BL., Addit. MSS 7097, ff. 174–200.
5. Cambridge Univ. Lib., Hengrave Hall
Deposit 80.
6. See D. Knoop and G.P. Jones, *The
Medieval Mason* (3rd edn., Manchester, 1967),
pp. 38–9.
7. E.R. Sandeen, 'The Building of Redgrave
Hall, 1545–54', *Proc. Suffolk Inst. of
Archaeology*, xxix, pt. 1 (1961), pp. 1–33.
8. Essex CRO, D/DP A 18–22.
9. BL., Addit. MSS. 39832 f. 57.

10. J. Strype, *The Life of the Learned Sir Thomas Smith, kt. D.C.L.* (Oxford, 1820), p. 171.

11. G.R. Batho, 'Henry, Ninth Earl of Northumberland, and Syon House Middlesex, 1594–1632', *Trans. Ancient Monuments Soc.*, new ser., iv (1956), p. 104.

12. Longleat Archives, R.O.B., i & ii.

13. Cambridge Univ. Library, Hengrave Hall Deposit 80.

14. B. Stallybrass, 'Bess of Hardwick's Buildings and Building Accounts', *Archaeologia*, lxiv (1913), p. 359.

15. For the house at Great Bedwyn see J.E. Jackson, 'Wulfhall and the Seymours', *Wilts. Arch. Mag.*, xv (1875), pp. 178–86; for the remainder of Somerset's building, see BL., Egerton MSS. 2815.

16. For Salisbury House, see *Survey of London*, *xviii. The Strand* (1937), pp. 120–3; for the New Exchange, see L. Stone, 'Inigo Jones and the New Exchange', *Arch. Jour.*, cxiv (1957), pp. 106–21; for Hatfield House, see L. Stone, 'The Building of Hatfield House', *ibid.*, cxii (1955), pp. 100–28.

17. N. Briggs, 'The Foundation of Wadham College, Oxford', *Oxoniensia*, xxi (1956), pp. 67–8.

18. *The Architecture of Sir Roger Pratt*, ed. R.T. Gunther (Oxford, 1928), p. 48.

19. Girouard, *Smythson*, p. 54.

20. Longleat Archives, R.O.B., iii, 161. William Spicer to the Earl of Leicester, 15 July 1571.

21. Notts. Univ. Library, Mi A 60/1–7. For the other details of his career, and that of John and Huntingdon Smythson, see Girouard.

22. J. Summerson, 'Three Elizabethan Architects', *Bull, of the John Rylands Library*, xl (1957), p. 201.

23. *Ibid.*, p. 216.

24. *The Book of Architecture of John Thorpe*, ed. J. Summerson (Walpole Soc., xl, 1966), p. 11.

25. *The Account Book of Nicholas Stone*, ed. W.L. Spiers (Walpole Soc., vii, 1919), pp. 70, 10, 11.

26. A. Oswald, *Country Houses of Dorset* (2nd edn, London, 1959), pp. 25–30.

27. Dorset CRO, MW/M4 f 24V.

28. M. Airs, 'Lawrence Shipway, Freemason', *Architectural History*, 27 (1984), pp. 368–75.

29. M. Airs, 'Blickling Hall', *Archaeological Journal*, 137 (1980), p. 336.

30. Mrs Baldwyn-Childe, 'The Building of the Manor House of Kyre Park, Worcestershire', *The Antiquary*, xxi–ii (1890). Willis and Clark, ii, p. 475n.

31. J. Evans, 'Extracts from the Private Account Book of Sir William More of Loseley . . .', *Archaeologia*, xxxvi (1855), pp. 284–310.

32. Staffordshire CRO, D593 R/1/2.

33. Beds. CRO, TW 818.

34. D. Knoop and G.P. Jones, 'The Carreglwyd Building Account, 1636', *Trans. Anglesey Antiq. Soc.* (1934), pp. 27–43.

35. D. Knoop and G.P. Jones, 'The Bolsover Castle Building Account for 1613', *Ars Quatuor Coronatorum*, xlix (1939), pp. 24–80.

36. H.L. Bradfer-Lawrence, 'The Building of Raynham Hall', *Norfolk Archaeology*, xxiii, pts 1 and 2 (1927), pp. 93–146.

37. BL., Addit. MSS 39832.

38. J. Dent, *Quest for Nonsuch* (London 1962), p. 261.

39. *The Chronicle of Calais* (Camden Soc., 1846), p. 17.

40. W.L. Rutton, 'Sandgate Castle, AD 1539–1540', *Archaeologia Cantiana*, xx (1893), pp. 228–57.

41. PRO, E101/483/16.

42. Salzman, pp. 37–9.

43. J.E. Jackson, 'Wulfhall and the Seymours', *Wilts. Arch. Mag.*, xv (1875), p. 181.

44. BL., Egerton MSS 2815.

45. J. Dent, *Quest for Nonsuch* (London, 1962), pp. 263–4.

46. Rutton, *op, cit.*

47. PRO, E101/483/16.

48. Willis and Clark, ii, p. 198.

49. *Ibid.*, pp. 469–70.

50. Longleat Archives, R.O.B., 1, 117. Thynne to Dodd, 18 June 1547.

51. Salzman, p. 575.

52. *Records of the Worshipful Company of Carpenters*, ii, p. 155.

53. P.S. Spokes and E.M. Jope, 'The Priory, Marcham, Berks', *Berks. Archaeological Jour.*, lvii (1959), pp. 93–4.

54. L. Stone, 'Inigo Jones and the New Exchange', *Arch. Jour.*, cxiv (1957), p. 114.

55. William Salt Library, Stafford. D1721/1/4.

56. Mrs Baldwyn-Childe, 'The Building of the Manor House of Kyre Park, Worcestershire', *The Antiquary*, xxi–ii (1890).

57. J. Evans, 'Extracts from the Private Account Book of Sir William More of Loseley . . .', *Archaeologia*, xxxvi (1855), p. 296.

58. J.A. Gotch, 'The Renaissance in Northamptonshire', *Trans, R.I.B.A.*, vi, new ser. (1890), p. 105.

59. Longleat Archives, R.O.B., ii, 31. Sharington to Thynne, 25 June 1553.

60. *Ibid.*, R.O.B., i, 135. Thynne to Dodd, 21 June 1547.

61. Sandeen, *op. cit.*, MW/M4 f. 23.

62. *Ibid.*, p. 186.

63. Dorset, CRO, MW/M4 f. 23.

64. Staffs. CRO, D593 R/1/2.

65. G.R. Batho, 'The Percies at Petworth, 1574–1632', *Sussex Arch. Coll.*, xcv (1957), p. 14.

66. Essex CRO, D/DP A 22.

67. J. Evans, *op cit.*, p. 296.

68. BL., Addit. MSS. 39832.

69. Essex CRO, D/DP A19.

70. Willis and Clark, ii, p. 571.

71. Staffs. CRO, D593 R/1/2.

72. B. Stallybrass, 'Bess of Hardwick's Buildings and Building Accounts', *Archaeologia*, lxiv (1913), p. 378.

73. Longleat Archives, R.O.B., ii, 87. Cavendish to Thynne, 30 March (1555?).

74. *Ibid.*, ii, 129. Elizabeth St Loe to Thynne, 25 April 1560.

75. Girouard, *Smythson*, pp. 75, 77.

76. A. Oswald, *Country Houses of Dorset* (2nd edn, London, 1959), p. 26.

77. H.A. Tipping, 'Condover Hall, Shropshire', *Country Life*, xliii (1918), p. 513.

78. Stallybrass, *op. cit.*, pp. 352, 356.

79. J.W. Burgon, *The Life and Times of Sir Thomas Gresham* (London, 1831), ii, p. 257.

80. E.R. Sandeen, 'The Building of Redgrave Hall, 1545–54', *Proc. Suff. Inst. of Arch.*, xxix, pt. 1 (1961), p. 23.

81. Dorset CRO, MW/M4 f. 24V.

82. Cranfield Papers. Quoted in J. Harris, 'A History of the Burlington-Devonshire Collection and an Analysis of the English Drawings' (typescript catalogue of the collection in the RIBA Library, 1960), p. 90.

83. Girouard, *Smythson*, pp. 80–1.

84. Longleat Archives, R.O.B., iii, 61.

85. Mrs Baldwyn-Childe, 'The Building of the Manor House of Kyre Park, Worcestershire', *The Antiquary*, xxi (1890), pp. 202–5. The masons had probably been working at Weston Hall, Warwickshire, for Ralph Sheldon, whose steward, R. Richmond, had travelled to Kyre earlier in the month.

86. S.D. Kitson, 'The Heraldic Glass of Gilling Castle, Yorks, and Bernard Dinninghof', *Jour. Brit. Soc. of Master Glass Painters*, iii (1929), pp. 55–8.

6.   *Preparation of the Work*

1. Mrs Baldwyn-Childe, 'The Building of the Manor House of Kyre Park, Worcestershire, 1588–1618', *The Antiquary*, xxi (1890), pp. 202–5.

2. J. Evans, 'Extracts from the Private Account Book of Sir William More of Loseley . . .', *Archaeologia*, xxxvi (1855), p. 296.

3. *The House and Farm Accounts of the Shuttleworths*, ed. J. Harland (Chetham Soc., xxxv, 1856), pp. 126–30.

4. Bedfordshire CRO, TW 818.

5. Shrewsbury Public Library, Deeds 6883.

6. Sandeen, p. 157 *et seq.*

7. Sir Balthazar Gerbier, *A Brief Discourse Concerning the Three Chief Principles of Magnificent Building, viz. Solidity, Conveniency, and Ornament* (London, 1662), p. 26.

8. E.R. Sandeen, 'The Building of the Sixteenth-century Corpus Christi College Chapel', *Proc. of the Cambridge Antiq. Soc.*, lv (1961), pp. 23–35.

9. Willis and Clark, ii, p. 172.

10. See, for example, the abandonment of the economy measures proposed at Hatfield in 1609. L. Stone, 'The Building of Hatfield House', *Arch. Jour.*, cxxi (1955), pp. 115–16.

11. *Ibid.*, p. 107n.

12. Sandeen, pp. 318–19.

13. J.A. Gotch, 'The Renaissance in Northamptonshire', *Trans. R.I.B.A.*, new ser. vi (1890), p. 108.

14. H.C. Maxwell Lyte, *A History of Dunster* (London 1909), ii, p. 366.

15. G. R. Batho, 'Notes and Documents on Petworth House, 1574–1632', *Sussex Arch. Coll.*, xcvi (1958), pp. 113–29.

16. *Ibid.*, pp. 108, 109.

17. G. R. Batho, 'Henry, Ninth Earl of Northumberland and Syon House, Middlesex, 1594–1632', *Trans. Ancient Mons Soc.*, new ser. iv (1956), pp. 102–4.

18. G. R. Batho, 'The Percies at Petworth, 1574–1632', *Sussex Arch. Coll.*, xcv (1957), p. 16.

19. *The Architecture of Sir Roger Pratt*, ed. R.T. Gunther (Oxford, 1928), p. 46.

20. Cornwall CRO, Mt. Edgcumbe MS MTD/48/10.

21. Willis and Clark, ii, p. 253.

22. BL., Addit. MSS. 25302 f. 153.

23. Hist. MSS. Comm., *Various*, iii, p. li.

24. S.D. Kitson, 'The Heraldic Glass of Gilling Castle, Yorks, and Bernard Dinninghof', *Jour. Brit. Soc. Master Glass Painters*, iii (1929), pp. 55–8.

25. Essex CRO, D/DP A 19.

26. Longleat Archives, R.O.B. I, 287–9. Thynne to Dodd, 2 October 1547.

27. J.A. Gotch, 'The Renaissance in Northamptonshire', *Trans. R.I.B.A.*, new ser. vi (1890), p. 106.

28. Essex CRO, D/DP A 20 & A 22.

29. J. Strype, *The Life of the Learned Sir Thomas Smith* (Oxford 1820), p. 171.

7. The Realization of the Design

1. Longleat Archives, R.P. Box lxviii, Book 59, f. 59. The first payment to Adrian Gaunt, the joiner, was in December 1567 and the model seems to have been completed in June 1568. It is doubtful whether 'the frame' mentioned in a mason's contract of *c.* 1530 for Hengrave Hall, Suffolk, was anything more than a drawing or plan. Cambridge Univ. Library, Hengrave Hall Deposit 81. For models in Renaissance Italy see Henry A. Milton and Vittorio Magnago Lampugnani (eds), *The Renaissance from Brunelleschi to Michelangelo* (London, 1994), pp. 19–73.

2. PRO, PROB 11/65/45. Will of Henry Wriothesley, 2nd Earl of Southampton, dated 29 June 1581, refers to the 'modell made by Adams . . . for the buildinge of the saide house'.

3. At Syon House in 1602 the carpenter made a model for the staircase; G.R. Batho, 'Syon House; The First Two Hundred Years', *Trans. London and Middx. Arch. Soc.*, xiv (1958), p. 13. In Oxford a model was made of a proposed staircase to the library in 1632–4; I.G. Philip, 'The Building of the Schools Quadrangle', *Oxoniensia*, xiii (1948), p. 47. During the alterations to Kirby Hall, Northants, a model for a staircase was made in 1639; *The Account Book of Nicholas Stone*, ed. W.L. Spiers (Walpole Soc., vii, 1919), p. 125.

4. Willis and Clark, ii, p. 475. Howard Colvin, *Unbuilt Oxford* (New Haven and London, 1983), pp. 9–11.

5. G.H. Chettle, *The Queen's House, Greenwich* (14th Monograph of The London Survey Committee, 1937), p. 102; PRO, SP 14/108, no. 55.

6. H.L. Bradfer-Lawrence, 'The Building of Raynham Hall', *Norf. Arch.*, xxiii (1927), p. 135.

7. Willis and Clark, i, pp. 206–8.

8. W.H. Godfrey, 'An Elizabethan Builder's Contract', *Sussex Arch. Coll.*, lxv (1924), pp. 201–23.

9. RIBA Library, drawings collection, Smythson Collection, III/1(2). I am grateful to Dr Mark Girouard for pointing out the significance of this drawing.

10. Sandeen, p. 178.

11. J.E. Jackson, 'Wulfhall and the Seymours', *Wilts. Arch. Mag.*, xv (1875), p. 180.

12. Willis and Clark, i, pp. 608–13.

13. B. Stallybrass, 'Bess of Hardwick's Buildings and Building Account', *Archaeologia*, lxiv (1913), p. 357.

14. J.W. Burgon, *The Life and Times of Sir Thomas Gresham* (London, 1831), ii, p. 257.

15. *The Account Book of Nicholas Stone*, ed. W.L. Spiers (Walpole Soc., vii, 1919), p. 70.

16. H.L. Bradfer-Lawrence, 'The Building of Raynham Hall', *Norf. Arch.*, xxiii (1927), p. 128.

17. Sir John Soane's Museum, Thorpe Collection T1–9. Illustrated in *The Book of Architecture of John Thorpe*, ed. J. Summerson (Walpole Soc., xl, 1966), plates 1–4.

18. Trentham Hall, Staffs; Staffs. CRO, D593 R/1/2, 5 April 1634.

19. Trinity College, Cambridge, 1566; Willis and Clark, ii, p. 570.

20. Essex CRO, D/DP A 18.

21. Sandeen, p. 189.

22. BL., Addit. MSS 39832, f. 26.

23. *Ibid.*, f. 50.

24. L. Stone, 'The Building of Hatfield House', *Arch. Jour.*, cxii (1955), pp. 114–18.

25. BL., Addit. MSS. 7097, ff. 176v & 195v.

26. P.J. Drury, 'No Other Palace in the Kingdom will compare with it: The Evolution of Audley End, 1605–1745', *Architectural History*, 23 (1980), pp. 1–39: *idem.*, '"A Fayre House Buylt by Sir Thomas Smith": The Development of Hill Hall, Essex, 1557–81,' *Journal of the British Archaeological Association*, cxxxvi (1983), pp. 98–123.

27. Staffs. CRO, D593 R/1/2. 13 June 1635. Willis and Clark, ii, p. 155.

28. Cornwall CRO, Mt. Edgcumbe MS MTD/48/10.

29. For example, H.C. Maxwell Lyte, *A History of Dunster* (London, 1909), ii, p. 366.

30. J. Nichols, *The Progresses and Public Processions of Queen Elizabeth* (London, 1823), i, p. 205.

31. *The Architecture of Sir Roger Pratt*, ed. R.T. Gunther (Oxford, 1928), pp. 60–1.

8. Financing and Expenditure

1. Staffs., CRO, D593 R/1/2.

2. BL., Egerton MSS 2815.

3. J.E. Jackson, 'Wulfhall and the Seymours', *Wilts. Arch. Mag.*, xv (1875), pp. 178–86.

4. L. Stone, 'The Building of Hatfield House', *Arch. Jour.*, cxii (1955), p. 114n.

5. L. Stone, *The Crisis of the Aristocracy, 1558–1614*, (Oxford, 1965), p. 554.

6. R.G. Braybrooke, *The History of Audley End*, (London, 1836), p. 72.

7. G.R. Batho, 'Notes and Documents on Petworth House, 1574–1632', *Sussex Arch. Coll.*, xcvi (1958), p. 112.

8. A. Hamilton-Thompson, 'The Building Accounts of Kirby Muxloe Castle', 1480–84', *Leicester. Arch. Soc. Trans.*, xi (1913–14), pp. 193–345.

9. BL., Egerton MSS 2815.

10. J. Summerson, 'The Building of Theobalds, 1564–1585', *Archaeologia*, xcvii (1959), p. 110.

11. Essex CRO, D/DP A18–22.

12. L. Stone, *The Crisis of the Aristocracy, 1558–1641*, (Oxford, 1965), pp. 554–5.

13. BL., Addit. MSS 7097, ff. 174–200. The total cost recorded in this account book is £1,425.3s.0½d., and not £719.3s.0½d. as stated in J. Gage, *Thingoe Hundred* (London, 1838), p. 151.

14. Cambridge Univ. Lib., Hengrave Hall Deposit 80. The recorded expenditure in these account books is £3,036.3s.8d., but the accounts for 1538 and 1539 are missing.

15. E.R. Sandeen, 'The Building of Redgrave Hall, 1545–1554', *Proc. Suff. Inst. of Arch.*, xxix, pt. 1 (1961), pp. 1–33. The total expenditure shown in the building accounts was £1,253.2s.5¾d.

16. J.C. Rogers, 'The Manor and Houses of Gorhambury', *St Albans and Herts. Architectural and Archaeological Soc. Trans.*, new ser. iv (1933), p. 108.

17. J. Evans, 'Extracts from the Private Account Book of Sir William More, of Loseley . . .', *Archaeologia*, xxxvi (1855), 284–310. The estimate for Toddington was made in a survey of 1642: BL, Addit MSS 22,253,f.12ᵛ.

18. The total cost given in the accounts was £48.6s.11½d., J.R. Wigfull, 'House Building in Queen Elizabeth's Days', *Trans. Hunter Arch. Soc.*, iii (1925), pp. 68–73.

19. M.E. Finch, *The Wealth of Five Northamptonshire Families, 1540–1640* (Northants, Record Soc., xix, 1956), p. 183. Between September 1593 and May 1600 his recorded expenditure was £971.0s.11d.

20. Beds. CRO, TW 818. I am grateful to Nicholas Cooper for drawing my attention to the Hall Court accounts in BL, Addit. MS. 69,874.

21. H.L. Bradfer-Lawrence, 'The Building of Raynham Hall', *Norf. Arch.*, xxiii (1927), pp. 93–146. These figures are incomplete but they include the cost of abandoning the original foundations.

22. BL., Harl. MSS. 6853, f. 450. It is possible that this sum was exaggerated as it was quoted to justify a price of £2,500 for the sale of the house.

23. Surrey CRO, Acc. 1030. The actual cost including landscaping was £3,119.4s.7½d.

24. B. Cozens-Hardy, 'Some Norfolk Halls', *Norf. Arch.*, xxxii (1961), p. 188.

25. Dorset CRO, MW/M4, f. 24b.

26. Staffs. CRO, D593 R/1/2.

27. BL., Addit. MSS. 54332.

28. Leeds City Library, TN/EA/13/74.

29. *The Architecture of Sir Roger Pratt*, ed. R.T. Gunther (Oxford, 1928), p. 14.

30. Staffs. CRO, D593 R/1/1.

31. Gunther, *op cit.*, p. 167.

32. BL., Addit. MSS. 39832, f. 32.

33. *Ibid.*, f. 33.

34. *Ibid.*, ff. 90, 93v, 107, 110.

35. Notts. Univ. Library, Mi A60/5.

36. J. Evans, 'Extracts from the Private Account Book of Sir William More of Loseley . . .', *Archaeologia*, xxxvi (1855), pp. 294–310.

37. Sandeen, pp. 32–3. Only £28 was spent in 1549, but this can be accounted for by Kett's rebellion of that year.

38. Staffs. CRO, D593 R/1/2.

39. *The Architecture of Sir Roger Pratt*, ed. R.T. Gunther (Oxford, 1928), p. 172.

40. *Ibid.*, p. 8.

41. Sandeen, pp. 191–3.

42. Girouard, *Smythson*, p. 139.

43. Beds. CRO, TW 818 and TW 11/110.

9.   *The Principal Materials*

1. Sandeen, p. 189.

2. BL., Addit. MSS 39832, f. 40v.

3. *The House and Farm Accounts of the Shuttleworths*, ed. J. Harland (Chetham Soc., xxxv, 1856), p. 160.

4. G.R. Batho, 'Henry, Ninth Earl of Northumberland and Syon House, Middlesex, 1594–1632'. *Trans. Ancient Mons. Soc.*, new ser. iv (1956), pp. 103–4.

5. J.E. Jackson, 'Wulfhall and the Seymours', *Wilts. Arch. Mag.*, xv (1875), p. 181.

6. PRO, SP14/57, f. 108.

7. Sandeen, pp. 189 and 190.

8. BL., Harleian MSS. 98/16.

9. *The House and Farm Accounts of the Shuttleworths*, ed. J. Harland (Chetham Soc., xxxv, 1856), pp. 125–74.

10. J. Evans, 'Extracts from the Private Account Book of Sir William More, of Loseley . . .', *Archaeologia*, xxxvi (1855), pp. 284–310.

11. BL., Addit. MSS 39832.

12. Staffs. CRO, D593 R/1/2.

13. G. Patrick, 'Burghley House and the First Lord Burghley', *Jour. British Arch. Assoc.*, xxxv, (1879), p. 265.

14. Longleat Archives, R.O.B., i, ii, and iii.

15. Dorset CRO, MW/M4, f. 24b.

16. L. Stone, 'The Building of Hatfield House', *Arch. Jour.*, cxii (1955), pp. 108–9; L. Stone, 'Inigo Jones and the New Exchange', *ibid.*, cxiv (1957), p. 115; *Survey of London xviii. The Strand* (1937), p. 121.

17. BL., Landsdowne MSS. 43/14.

18. M. Howard, *The Early Tudor Country House* (London, 1987), pp. 139, 163–4. D. McKeen, *A Memory of Honour, The Life of William Brooke, Lord Cobham* (Salzburg, 1986), pp. 449, 450–1.

19. Girouard, *Smythson*, p. 78.

20. Mrs Baldwyn-Childe, 'The Building of the Manor House of Kyre Park, Worcestershire, 1588–1618', *The Antiquary*, xxi (1890), p. 263.

21. Essex CRO, D/DF A22.

22. Mrs Baldwyn-Childe, *op. cit.*, p. 205.

23. BL., Addit. MSS 7097, ff. 174–200.

24. Cambridge Univ. Library, Hengrave Hall Deposit 80.

25. H.L. Bradfer-Lawrence, 'The Building of Raynham Hall', *Norf. Arch.*, xxiii (1927), pp. 93–146.

26. Beds. CRO, TW 818.

27. G.R. Batho, 'Notes and Documents on Petworth House, 1574–1632', *Sussex Arch. Coll.*, xcvi (1957), pp. 113–29.

28. Longleat Archives, R.O.B., iii, f. 113.

29. H.M. Colvin, 'Haunt Hill House, Weldon' in *Studies in Building History*, ed. E.M. Jope (London, 1961), p. 224.

30. L. Stone, 'The Building of Hatfield House', *Arch. Jour.*, cxii (1955), p. 109.

31. J. Evans, 'Extracts from the Private Account Book of Sir William More, of Loseley . . .', *Archaeologia* xxxvi (1855), pp. 284–310.

32. J.R. Wigfull, 'House Building in Queen Elizabeth's Days', *Trans. Hunter Arch. Soc.*, iii (1925), p. 68.

33. Longleat Archives, R.O.B., iii, f. 79 & f. 169.

34. Beds. CRO, TW 818.

35. From a MS history of the family compiled by Edward Strong in 1716 and printed in R. Clutterbuck, *The History and Antiquities of the County of Hertford* (London 1815), i, p. 167n.

36. H.L. Bradfer-Lawrence, 'The Building of Raynham Hall', *Norf. Arch.*, xxiii (1927), p. 128. It is interesting to note that the father of William Arnold, the West Country mason, was also called Arnold Goverson.

37. D. Knoop and G.P. Jones, 'The Sixteenth Century Mason', *Ars Quatuor Coronatorum*. i. (1937), p. 199n.

38. *Idem.*, 'The English Medieval Quarry', *Econ. Hist. Rev.*, ix (1938), p. 30.

39. Cambridge Univ. Library, Hengrave Hall Deposit 80.

40. Staffs. CRO, D593/R/1/2.

41. Beds. CRO, TW 818.

42. Mrs Baldwyn-Childe, 'The Building of the Manor House of Kyre Park, Worcestershire, 1588–1618', *The Antiquary*, xxi (1890), p. 204.

43. Longleat Archives, R.O.B., i. f. 228.

44. Staffs. CRO, D593 R/1/2.

45. Longleat Archives, R.O.B., ii, f. 179.

46. *Ibid.*, iii, f. 39.

47. BL., Addit, MSS 39832, f. 85.

48. *Ibid.*, f. 93.

49. D. Knoop and G.P. Jones, *The Medieval Mason* (3rd. edn., Manchester, 1967), pp. 12, 71.

50. J. Evans, 'Extracts from the Private Account Book of Sir William More, of Loseley . . .', *Archaeologia*, xxxvi (1855), p. 308.

51. G.R. Batho, 'The Percies at Petworth, 1574–1632', *Sussex, Arch. Coll.*, xcv (1957), p. 11.

52. Longleat Archives, R.O.B., ii, f. 31. Sharington to Thynne, 25 June 1553.

53. *The Account Book of Nicholas Stone*, ed. W.L. Spiers (Walpole Soc., vii, 1919), pp. 42, 68, 82, 101–2, 104, 105, 134.

54. Beds. CRO, TW 818.

55. BL., Addit. MSS. 25302, f. 153.

56. *The Lismore Papers*, ed. A.B. Grosart (v, 1886), p. 37. I owe this reference to the kindness of Dr Mark Girouard.

57. A. Clifton-Taylor, *The Pattern of English Building* (2nd edn, London, 1965), p. 213.

58. W.G. Hoskins, *Devon* (London 1954), p. 166.

59. Sandeen, pp. 23–4.

60. Mrs Baldwyn-Childe, 'The Building of the Manor House at Kyre Park, Worcestershire, 1588–1618', *The Antiquary*, xxi & xxii (1890), pp. 263–4, 24.

61. BL., Addit. MSS. 7097. f. 184v.

62. L. Stone, 'The Building of Hatfield House', *Arch. Jour.*, cxii (1955), p. 107.

63. H.L. Bradfer-Lawrence, 'The Building of Raynham Hall', *Norf. Arch.*, xxxiii (1927), pp. 93–146.

64. 'no semel breke . . . to be told'. BL., Addit. MSS. 7097, f. 176.

65. Sandeen, p. 27.

66. J. Evans, 'Extracts from the Private Account Book of Sir William More, of Loseley . . .', *Archaeologia*, xxxvi (1855), p. 295.

67. Mrs Baldwyn-Childe, *op. cit.*, p. 24.

68. Willis and Clark, i, p. 419n.

69. BL., Addit. MSS. 7097, f. 176.

70. Sandeen, p. 23.

71. *Eastbury Manor House*, Barking. 11th monograph of London Survey Committee (1917), p. 20.

72. E.M. Jope, 'Cornish Houses, 1400–1700', in *Studies in Building History* (London, 1961) p. 212.

73. B. Gerbier, *Counsel and Advise . . .* (London, 1663), p. 56.

74. H.L. Bradfer-Lawrence, 'The Building of Raynham Hall', *Norf. Arch.*, xxxiii (1927), p. 103.

75. Walter Guy had previously been making bricks for Sir William Petre at Ingatestone Hall in the 1550s; Essex CRO, D/DP A 10–11.

76. In addition to Little Saxham Hall, Redgrave Hall, Loseley House, Old Thorndon Hall, Hatfield House, and Raynham Hall already mentioned, see also Gorhambury House, Herts. (J.C. Rogers, 'The Manor and Houses of Gorhambury', *St Albans and Herts. Architectural and Archaeological Soc. Trans.*, new ser., iv. (1933), p. 108), Kirkby-in-Ashfield, Derbys. (*The Chamberlain Letters*, ed. E.M. Thompson (London, 1966), p. 27), Condover Hall, Salop. (Shrewsbury Public Library, Deeds 6885), and Broome House, Kent (BL., Addit. MSS. 54332).

77. Staffs. CRO, D 593 R/1/2, 30 May 1635.

78. Longleat Archives, R.O.B., iii.

79. Mrs Baldwyn-Childe, 'The Building of the Manor House of Kyre Park, Worcestershire, 1588–1618', *The Antiquary*, xxi and xxii (1890).

80. M. Howard, *The Early Tudor Country House* (London, 1987), pp. 131–5 and 'Laughton Place: A Manorial and Architectural History, with an Account of Recent Restoration and Excavation', *Sussex Arch. Coll.*, 129 (1991), pp. 142–9.

81. Raby Castle, Barnard MSS, box 2, bundle 1, no. 1; W.A. Singleton, 'Traditional House-types in Rural Lancashire and Cheshire', *Trans. Hist. Soc. of Lancs. and Cheshire*, civ (1952), pp. 90–1.

82. A.W. Clapham, 'The Court House, or "Old Town Hall", at Barking', *Trans. Essex Arch. Soc.*, xii (1912), pp. 295–8.

83. Bodleian Library, Rawl. MSS. A195c, ff. 369–783.

84. T.H. Clarke and W.H. Black, *Eastbury Illustrated . . .* (London, 1834), p. 12.

85. Beds. CRO, TW 818.

86. H.L. Bradfer-Lawrence, 'The Building of Raynham Hall', *Norf. Arch.*, xxiii (1927), 106, 107.

87. Sandeen, p. 34.

88. Notts. Univ. Library, Mi A 60/6. f. 9.

89. Mrs Baldwyn-Childe, 'The Building of the Manor House of Kyre Park, Worcestershire, 1588–1618', *The Antiquary*, xxii (1890), p. 25.

90. J.Evans, 'Extract from the Private Account Book of Sir William More, of Loseley . . .', *Archaeologia*, xxxvi (1855), p. 306.

91. A. Clifton-Taylor, *The Pattern of English Building* (2nd edn, London, 1965), p. 29.

92. I.C. Philip, 'The Building of the Schools Quadrangle', *Oxoniensia*, xiii (1948), p. 45.

93. Willis and Clark, i, p. 205.

94. *Ibid.*, i., 207; il., 252; ii., iii.

95. Longleat Archives, R.O.B., i, f. 121. Thynne to Dodd, 18 June 1547.

96. Staffs. CRO, D593 R/1/2.

97. BL., Addit. MSS. 39832, f. 68v.

98. Longleat Archives, R.O.B., i, f. 135. Thynne to Dodd, 21 June 1547.

99. *Ibid.*, f. 121.

100. *Ibid.*, R.O.B., iii, f. 161. William Spicer to Earl of Leicester, 15 July 1571.

101. BL., Addit. MSS. 7097, ff. 174–200.

102. Cambridge Univ. Library, Hengrave Hall Deposit 80.

103. Longleat Archives, R.O.B., ii, f. 263. Thynne to Hertford, 15 June 1567.

104. Notts. Univ. Library, Mi A60/6, f. 4v.

105. *Ibid.*, Mi A 60/4, f. 8.

106. *Ibid.*, Mi A 60/5, f. 4.

107. Sandeen, pp. 183–5.

108. *Plymouth Building Accounts of the Sixteenth and Seventeenth Centuries.* ed. E. Welch (Devon & Cornwall Record Soc., new ser., xii, 1967), p. xiii.

109. *The House and Farm Accounts of the Shuttleworths*, ed. J. Harland (Chetham Soc., xxxv, 1856), p. 172.

110. G.R. Batho, 'Notes and Documents on Petworth House, 1574–1632', *Sussex Arch. Coll.*, xcvi (1957), pp. 113–29.

111. For example, the statute of 7 Ed. VI c. 7; *Tudor Economic Documents*, ed. R.H. Tawney and E. Power (London, 1924), i, p. 238. The other examples of scarcity given by the same authors similarly relate to wood as a fuel or as a ship-building material.

112. *Harrison's Description of England*, ed. F.J. Furnivall (New Shakespere Soc., series vi, pt. 1, 1877), p. 233.

113. J. Norden, *The Surveyors Dialogue* (London, 1607), p. 214.

114. R. Reyce, *Breviary of Suffolk*, ed. Lord Francis Hervey (London, 1902), p. 50.

115. On this point, see also G. Hammersely, 'The Crown Woods and their Exploitation in the Sixteenth and Seventeenth Centuries', *Bull. Inst. Hist. Research*, xxx (1957), pp. 136–61.

116. William Salt Library, Stafford, D. 1721/1/4.

117. Shrewsbury Public Library, Deeds 6883, f. 12.

118. J.B. Lawson, 'John Sandford of Shrewsbury and Pitchford, Carpenter; Builder of Pitchford Hall, 1549', *Trans. Shropshire Arch. Soc.*, lxiv (1983–4), pp. 119–20.

119. Old Thorndon Hall, Essex; Essex CRO, D/DP A21: Redgrave Hall, Suffolk.

120. Staffs. CRO, D593 R/1/2.

121. William Salt Library, Stafford, D. 1721/1/4.

122. Staffs. CRO, D593 R/1/2.

123. J.R. Wigfull, 'House Building in Queen Elizabeth's Days', *Trans. Hunter Arch. Soc.*, iii (1925), p. 70.

124. *The House and Farm Accounts of the Shuttleworths*, ed. J. Harland (Chetham Soc., xxxv, 1856), p. 143.

125. E.M. Jope and G.C. Dunning, 'The Use of Blue Slate for Roofing in Medieval England', *The Antiquaries Jour.*, xxxiv (1954), pp. 209–17; E.W. Holden, 'Slate Roofing in Medieval Sussex', *Sussex Arch. Coll.*, ciii (1965), pp. 66–78.

126. Devon CRO, L1258 m/vol. i. D84 no. 73.

127. Longleat Archives, R.O.B., iii, f. 175.

128. Essex CRO, D/DP A20.

129. L. Stone, 'The Building of Hatfield House', *Arch. Jour.*, cxii (1955), p. 109.

130. *'Brief Lives', Chiefly of Contemporaries set down by John Aubrey, between the Years 1669 & 1696*. ed. A. Clark (Oxford, 1898), i, p. 81.

131. G. R. Batho, 'Notes and Documents on Petworth House, 1574–1632', *Sussex Arch. Coll.*, xcvi (1958), p. 128.

132. Surrey CRO, Acc. 1030, f. 101.

133. J. Mills, 'Peter Lewys: His Work and Workmen', *Jour. Roy. Soc. Antiqs. of Ireland*, xxxi (1901), p. 100. Girouard mentions Welsh slate at Longleat (*Smythson*, p. 59), but I have been unable to check the reference in the documents.

134. A. Clifton-Taylor,. *The Pattern of English Building* (2nd edn, London, 1965), p. 121.

135. E.M. Jope in *Oxoniensia*, xiv (1949), p. 94.

136. J. Evans, 'Extracts from the Private Account Book of Sir William More, of Loseley . . .', *Archaeologia*, xxxvi (1855), p. 309.

137. G.R. Batho, 'Notes and Documents on Petworth House, 1574–1632', *Sussex Arch. Coll.*, xcvi (1958), p. 124.

138. B. Stallybrass, 'Bess of Hardwick's Buildings and Building Accounts', *Archaeologia*, lxiv (1913), p. 366.

139. BL., Addit. MSS. 54332.

140. Cambridge Univ. Library, Hengrave Hall Deposit 80.

141. BL., Addit. MSS 7097, f. 195.

142. Bodleian Library, Rawl, MSS. D781, ff. 170–8.

143. Longleat Archives, R.O.B., i, f. 149.

144. PRO, E101/463/23, f.1.

145. Bodleian Library, Rawl. MSS. D784. 4 February – 4 March 1543.

146. BL., Addit. MSS. 39832, ff. 88–95.

147. BL., Addit. MSS. 7097, f. 174v.

148. J. Evans, 'Extracts from the Private Account Book of Sir William More, of Loseley . . .', *Archaeologia*, xxxvi (1855), p. 297.

149. H.L. Bradfer-Lawrence, 'The Building of Raynham Hall', *Norf. Arch.*, xxiii (1927), pp. 110, 137.

150. BL., Addit. MSS. 39832, f. 86.

151. Staffs, CRO, D593 R/1/2.

152. Essex. CRO, D/DP A10, f. 48.

153. Essex, CRO, D/DP A22.

154. W. Minet, *Hadham Hall* (Colchester, 1914), p. 17.

155. BL., Addit. MSS 54332.

156. Essex. CRO, D/DP A22.

157. Salzman, p. 153.

158. BL., Addit. MSS. 7097, f. 182.

159. J. Evans, 'Extracts from the Private Account Book of Sir William More of Loseley . . .', *Archaeologia*, xxxvi (1855), p. 309.

160. Essex CRO, D/DP A20.

161. Shrewsbury Public Library, Deeds 6885, f. 8v.

162. J. Humphreys, 'The Elizabethan Estate Book of Grafton Manor', *Trans. Birmingham Arch. Soc.*, xliv (1918), p. 22.

163. E.A. Gee, 'Oxford Masons, 1370–1530', *Arch. Jour.*, cix (1952), p. 56.
164. BL., Egerton MSS. 2815.
165. Staffs. CRO, D593 R/1/2.
166. A. Hamilton-Thompson, 'The Building Accounts of Kirby Muxloe Castle, 1480–84', *Leics. Arch. Soc. Trans.*, xi (1913–20), p. 203.
167. Mrs Baldwyn-Childe, 'The Building of the Manor House of Kyre Park, Worcestershire', *The Antiquary*, xxii (1890), p. 25.
168. H.L. Bradfer-Lawrence, 'The Building of Raynham Hall', *Norf. Arch.*, xxiii (1927), p. 131.
169. Staffs. CRO, D593 R/1/2.
170. *The House and Farm Accounts of the Shuttleworths*, ed. J. Harland (Chetham Soc., xxxv, 1856), p. 139.
171. D. Knoop & G.P. Jones, 'The Bolsover Castle Building Accounts, 1613', *Ars Quatuor Coronatorum*, xlix (1939), pp. 24–79.
172. BL., Addit. MSS. 39832, f. 30ᵛ.
173. Bradfer-Lawrence, *op. cit.*, p. 133.
174. Salzman, pp. 286–7.
175. Girouard, *Smythson*, p. 59.
176. Sandeen, p. 35.
177. Salzman, p. 182.
178. D.W. Crossley, 'Glass Making in Bagot's Park, Staffordshire, in the Sixteenth Century', *Post-Med. Arch.*, i. (1967), pp. 44–83.
179. *Idem.*, 'The Performance of the Glass Industry in Sixteenth-century England', *Ec. Hist. Rev.*, 2nd serv., xxv (1972), p. 429. The most detailed study of the English glass industry in the sixteenth and seventeenth centuries is E.S. Godfrey, *The Development of English Glassmaking 1560–1640* (Oxford, 1975). See also Crossley, *Post-Medieval Archaeology in Britain* (Leicester, 1990) and G.H. Keynon, *The Glass Industry of the Weald* (Leicester, 1967).
180. Godfrey, *op. cit.*, p. 51.
181. *Plymouth Building Accounts*. ed. E. Welch (Devon & Cornwall Record So., new ser., xii 1967), p. 94. Colin Platt, *The Great Rebuildings of Tudor and Stuart England* (London, 1994), p. 18.
182. R.S. Smith, 'Glass-making at Wollaton in the Early Seventeenth Century', *Trans. Thoroton Soc.* (1962), pp. 24–34.
183. Willis and Clark, ii, p. 572.
184. BL., Addit. MSS 46, 461, f. 46ᵛ. Staffs. CRO, D593 R/1/2. 25 January 1633/4.
185. *The Architecture of Sir Roger Pratt*, ed. R.T. Gunther (Oxford 1928), p. 72.
186. Kent CRO, U269 A505/1.
187. G.J. Eltringham, 'The Extension of the Carpenters' Company Hall, 1572', *Guildhall Miscellany*, i, no. 4 (1955), 32. Cambridge Univ. Library, Hengrave Hall Deposit 80.
188. PRO, E101/463/23, f. 1.
189. J. Humphreys, 'The Elizabethan Estate Book of Grafton Manor', *Trans. Birmingham Arch. Soc.*, xliv (1918), pp. 34, 40, 17.
190. BL., Addit. MSS. 7097, f. 182.
191. Cambridge Univ. Library, Hengrave Hall Deposit 80.
192. BL., Addit. MSS 39836, f. 363.
193. W.H. Cope, *Bramshill* (London, 1883), p. 121; Kent CRO, *op. cit.*
194. B. Stallybrass, 'Bess of Hardwick's Buildings and Building Accounts', *Archaeologia*, lxiv (1913), p. 383.
195. BL., Addit. MSS. 7097, ff. 174–200; Cambridge Univ. Library Hengrave Hall Deposit 80.

10. The Supply of Materials

1. J.W. Burgon, *The Life and Times of Sir Thomas Gresham* (London, 1831), ii, p. 117.
2. Dorset CRO, MW/M4, f. 24v.
3. Mrs Baldwyn-Childe, 'The Building of the Manor House of Kyre Park, Worcestershire', *The Antiquary*, xxii (1890), p. 25.
4. For example from the Earl of Hertford in 1567. Longleat Archives, R.O.B., ii. f. 263.
5. J. Evans, 'Extracts from the Private Account Book of Sir William More of Loseley . . .', *Archaeologia*, xxxvi (1855), p. 294.
6. J. Nichols, *The Progresses and Public Processions of Queen Elizabeth* (London, 1823), i. 524: Hist. MSS. Comm., *Hatfield*, xi, p. 358.
7. Kent CRO, U269 A505/1.
8. *Plymouth Building Accounts*, ed. E. Welch (Devon & Cornwall Record Soc., new ser., xii. 1967), p. 60.
9. PRO, E101/463/23, f. lv.
10. PRO, SP28/207, ff. 51, 34, & 38. I am grateful to Dr John Broad for drawing my attention to this document.
11. H.L. Bradfer-Lawrence, 'The Building of Raynham Hall', *Norf. Arch.* xxiii (1927), pp. 93–146.
12. Essex CRO, D/DP A19 and D/DP A21.
13. BL., Addit. MSS. 7079, ff. 183v., 185, 189v.
14. S.D. Kitson, 'The Heraldic Glass of Gilling Castle, Yorks., and Bernard Dinninghof', *Jour. Brit. Soc. Master Glass Painters*, iii (1929), pp. 55–8.
15. J.C. Rogers, 'The Manor and Houses of Gorhambury', *St Albans and Herts. Architect. and Archaeol. Soc. Trans.*, new ser., iv (1933), pp. 35–112.

16. D. Knoop and G.P. Jones, 'The Bolsover Castle Building Account for 1613', *Ars Quatuor Coronatorum*, xlix (1939), pp. 24–79.
17. L. Stone, 'The Building of Hatfield House', *Arch. Jour.*, xxii (1955), p. 107.
18. Salzman, p. 577.
19. Devon CRO, L1258 M/Vol. 1, Devon G5 No. 4.
20. PRO, E101/463/13.
21. J. Evans, 'Extracts from the Private Account Book of Sir William More of Loseley . . .', *Archaeologia*, xxxvi (1855), pp. 296–308.
22. J.C. Rogers, 'The Manor and Houses of Gorhambury', *St Albans and Herts. Architect. and Archaeol. Soc. Trans.*, new ser., iv. (1933), p. 41.
23. Stone, *op. cit.*, 108; L. Stone, 'Inigo Jones and the New Exchange', *Arch. Jour*, cxiv (1957), p. 115.
24. BL., Harl. MSS. 6853, f. 450.
25. H.l. Bradfer-Lawrence, 'The Building of Raynham Hall', *Norf. Arch.*, xxiii (1927), p. 101.
26. Sandeen, p. 188., T.H. Swales, 'The Redistribution of the Monastic Lands in Norfolk at the Dissolution', *Norf. Arch.*, xxxiv (1966), p. 27.
27. For the most comprehensive view of the impact of the dissolution on the fabric and planning of the country house, see M. Howard, *The Early Tudor Gentry House* (London, 1987).

11. The Transport of Materials

1. BL., Addit. MSS. 7097, f. 174v.
2. J. Evans, 'Extracts from the Private Account Book of Sir William More of Loseley . . .', *Archaeologia*, xxxvi (1855), p. 303.
3. L. Stone, 'The Building of Hatfield House', *Arch. Jour.*, cxii (1955), p. 108.
4. Longleat Archives, R.O.B., i, f. 371. Dodd to Thynne, 20 June 1549.
5. *Ibid.*, R.O.B., ii, f. 147. George Walker to Thynne, 15 March 1562.
6. Hist. MSS. Comm., *Hatfield*, xi, p. 358.
7. BL., Addit. MSS. 7097. f. 182.
8. Beds. CRO, TW 818.
9. Mrs Baldwyn-Childe, 'The Building of the Manor House of Kyre Park, Worcestershire, 1588–1618', *The Antiquary*, xxi. (1890), 205. *The House and Farm Accounts of the Shuttleworths*, ed. J. Harland, Chetham Soc., xxxv (1856), pp. 147–8.
10. R.S. Smith, 'Glass Making at Wollaton in the early Seventeenth Century', *Trans. Thoroton Soc.* (1962), p. 28.

11. Harland *op. cit.*, p. 137.
12. BL., Addit. MSS. 39832.
13. Mrs Baldwyn-Childe, *op cit.*, p. 205.
14. E.R. Sandeen, 'The Building of the Sixteenth Century Corpus Christi College Chapel', *Proc. Cambridge Antiq. Soc.*, lv (1961), pp. 23–35.
15. Longleat Archives, R.O.B., iii. f. 14.
16. *Ibid.*, ii. f. 147, where Thynne's tenants at Upton Scudamore refused him carriage until they had completed sowing.
17. *Ibid.*, iii. f. 14.
18. BL., Addit. MSS. 39832, ff. 59, 60, 63, *et passim*.
19. Notts. Univ. Library, Mi A 60/6, f. 4v.
20. Staffs. CRO, D593 R/1/2. 29 March and 5 April 1634.
21. J. Evans, 'Extracts from the Private Account Book of Sir William More of Loseley . . .', *Archaeologia*, xxxvi (1855), pp. 284–310.
22. Dorset CRO, MW/M4, f. 24v.
23. Longleat Archives, R.O.B., i. ff. 165–6. Thynne to Dodd, 4 July 1547.
24. *Ibid.*, f. 287. Thynne to Dodd, 2 October 1547.
25. *Ibid.*, f. 299. Thynne to Dodd, 8 November 1547.
26. J.A. Gotch, 'The Renaissance in Northamptonshire', *Trans. R.I.B.A.*, new ser., vi (1890), p. 104.
27. Longleat Archives, R.O.B., ii. f. 257. Thomas Vyttery to Thynne, 22 May 1567.
28. Girouard, *Smythson*, p. 59.
29. BL., Addit. MSS. 39832, f. 81.
30. Mrs Baldwyn-Childe, *op. cit.*, xxii, p. 53.
31. B. Stallybrass, 'Bess of Hardwick's Buildings and Building Accounts', *Archaeologia*, lxiv (1913), p. 186.
32. Staffs. CRO, D593 R/1/2.
33. H.L. Bradfer-Lawrence, 'The Building of Raynham Hall', *Norf. Arch.*, xxiii (1927), pp. 111, 114.
34. BL., Addit. MSS 7097, f. 176v.
35. Longleat Archives, R.O.B., i, f. 136. Thynne to Dodd, 21 June 1547.
36. Notts. Univ. Library, Mi A 60/6,. f. 4v.
37. William Salt Library, Stafford, D1734/3/4/101.
38. Leeds City Library, TN/EA/13/39.
39. *The House and Farm Accounts of the Shuttleworths*, ed. J. Harland (Chetham Soc., xxxv, 1856), pp. 147, 165.
40. Hist. MSS. Comm., *Rutland*, iv, p. 405.
41. L. Stone, 'The Building of Hatfield House', *Arch Jour.*, cxii (1955), p. 108.

42. Essex CRO, D/DP A21.

43. Mrs Baldwyn-Childe, 'The Building of the Manor House of Kyre Park, Worcestershire', *The Antiquary*, xxii (1890), p. 52.

44. *Ibid.*, p. 25.

45. J. Mills, 'Peter Lewys; His Work and Workmen', *Jour. Royal Soc. of Antiqs. of Ireland*, xxxi (1901), p. 101.

46. PRO, E36/251, f. 233.

47. H.L. Bradfer-Lawrence, 'The Building of Raynham Hall', *Norf. Arch.*, xxiii (1927), p. 129.

48. *Ibid.*, p. 131.

49. Longleat Archives, R.P., Box lxviii, Bt. 59, f. 12.

50. Sandeen, p. 82.

51. BL., Addit. MSS. 39832, f. 92.

52. Bradfer-Lawrence, *op cit.*

53. E. Ridout, 'The Account Book of the New Haven, Chester, 1567–8', *Trans. Hist. Soc. Lancs & Cheshire*, lxxx (1928), pp. 86–128.

54. C. Hewett, *English Cathedral and Monastic Carpentry* (Chichester, 1985), pp. 189–99.

55. H.A. Milton and V.M. Lampugnani (eds), *The Renaissance from Brunelleschi to Michelangelo* (London, 1994), pp. 478–93.

56. John Bold, *John Webb* (Oxford, 1989), p. 168.

12. Craftsmen

1. Mrs Baldwyn-Childe, 'The Building of the Manor House of Kyre Park, Worcestershire', *The Antiquary*, xxii (1890), p. 51.

2. *Ibid.*, xxi (1890), p. 262.

3. BL., Addit. MSS. 7097, ff. 174–200.

4. Willis and Clark, ii, pp. 347–8.

5. Cambridge Univ. Library, Hengrave Hall Deposit 80.

6. BL., Addit. MSS. 7097, f. 199.

7. *Churchwarden's Accounts of St Mary the Great, Cambridge*, ed. J.E. Foster (Cambridge Antiquarian Soc., xxxv, 1905), p. 14.

8. Willis and Clark, ii, pp. 243–5.

9. *Ibid.*, pp. 453–4.

10. BL., Addit. MSS. 7097, ff. 174–200; Cambridge Univ. Library, Hengrave Hall Deposit 80.

11. Cambridge Univ. Library, Hengrave Hall Deposit 80.

12. Sandeen, p. 57.

13. *Ibid.*, pp. 50, 52.

14. B. Stallybrass, 'Bess of Hardwick's Buildings and Building Accounts', *Archaeologia*, lxiv (1913), Appendix iii, pp. 393–8. David Durant and Philip Riden (eds) *The Building of Hardwick Hall* (Part 1, Derbyshire Record Soc.,

iv, 1980: Part 2, ix, 1984).

15. J.R. Wigfull, 'House Building in Queen Elizabeth's Days', *Trans. Hunter Arch. Soc.*, iii (1925), pp. 68–75.

16. Notts. Univ. Library, Mi A60/3–7; Stallybrass, *op cit.*, p. 293.

17. Girouard, *Smythson*, pp. 122–3.

18. See the payment at Hardwick in May 1596 to 'Lovells wyffe' for polishing stone. Stallybrass, *op cit.*, p. 379.

19. Devon CRO, 404 M/B1–3.

20. K. and C. French, 'Devonshire Plasterwork', *Trans. Devon. Assoc.*, lxxxix (1957), pp. 124–44. J. and J. Penoyre, *Decorative Plasterwork in the Houses of Somerset, 1500–1700* (Taunton, 1994), pp. 41–4.

21. William Salt Library, Stafford, D1734/3/4/143–4, *Ibid.*, p. 101.

22. *Ibid.*, D1721/1/4.

23. W.H. Godfrey, 'An Elizabethan Builder's Contract', *Sussex Arch. Coll.*, lxv (1924), pp. 211–23.

24. G.R. Batho, 'The Percies at Petworth, 1574–1632', *Sussex Arch. Coll.*, xcv (1957), p. 12.

25. Leeds City Library, TB/EA/13/74.

26. Surrey CRO, Acc. 1039, f. 114.

27. Survey of London, xxxvi, *The Parish of St Paul, Covent Garden* (1970), pp. 274, 282.

28. BL., Harl. MSS. 1653.

29. Survey of London, *passim*.

30. Kent CRO, U269 A505/1 & A508/3.

31. *Idem.*, U269 A462/5.

32. Survey of London, *op cit.*, p. 279.

33. *Idem.*, 14th monograph, *The Queen's House, Greenwich* (1937), p. 104.

34. R. Edwards and P. Ward-Jackson, *Ham House* (4th edn, London, 1959), p. 36.

35. Girouard, *Smythson*, p. 50 *et seq.*, Adrian Woodhouse, 'In Search of Smythson', *Country Life*, clxxv (19 December 1991), pp. 56–8.

36. T.W. Hanson, 'Halifax Builders in Oxford', *Trans. Halifax Antiq. Soc.* (1928), pp. 253–317; Mrs Baldwyn-Childe, 'The Building of the Manor House of Kyre Park, Worcestershire', *The Antiquary*, xxi (1890), p. 202.

37. Willis and Clark, ii, p. 693n. *et passim*.

38. Girouard, *Smythson*, p. 54.

39. *Ibid.*, p. 57, and information kindly communicated by David N. Durant.

40. J.D.K. Lloyd, 'The New Building at Montgomery Castle', *Archaeologia Cambrensis*, cxiv (1965), pp. 60–8.

41. Mrs Baldwyn-Childe, *op cit.*, p. 204.

42. H.L. Bradfer-Lawrence, 'The Building of Raynham Hall', *Norf. Arch.*, xxiii (1927), p. 116.

43. N. Briggs, 'The Foundation of Wadham College, Oxford', *Oxoniensia*, xxi (1956), pp. 67–8.

44. T.W. Hanson, 'Halifax Builders in Oxford', *Trans. Halifax Antiq. Soc.*, (1928), pp. 253–317.

45. Mrs Baldwyn-Childe, *op cit.*, p. 202.

46. Staffs. CRO, D593 R/1/2.

47. Longleat Archives, *passim*. His presence at Hardwick is based on a payment to his wife in May 1596 for polishing stone.

48. Cambridge Univ. Library, Hengrave Hall Deposit 80.

49. BL., Addit. MSS. 7097.

50. Mrs Baldwyn-Childe, 'The Building of the Manor House of Kyre Park, Worcestershire', *The Antiquary*, xxi–ii (1890).

51. Essex CRO, D/DP A18–22.

52. L. Stone, 'The Building of Hatfield House', *Arch. Jour.*, cxii (1955), pp. 103–4.

53. Sandeen, p. 186.

54. B. Stallybrass, 'Bess of Hardwick's Buildings and Building Accounts', *Archaeologia*, lxiv (1913), p. 379.

55. J.D.K. Lloyd, 'The New Building at Montgomery Castle', *Archaeologia Cambrensis*, cxiv (1965), p. 67.

56. Girouard, *Smythson*, p. 58 and *idem*. 'New Light on Longleat: Allen Maynard, a French Sculptor in England in the 16th Century', *Country Life*, xxx (1956), pp. 594–7.

57. N. Briggs, 'The Foundation of Wadham College, Oxford', *Oxoniensia*, xxi (1956), p. 69.

58. Willis and Clark, ii, p. 693.

59. Durant and Riden, *op cit.*

60. Notts. Univ. Library, Mi A60/3.

61. Staffs. CRO, D593 R/1/2.

62. BL., Addit. MSS. 39832.

63. 'An Essay Concerning the Decay of Rents and their Remedies', BL., Sloane MSS. 3828, f. 208. I am most grateful to Dr John Broad for drawing my attention to this document.

64. *Household and Farm Inventories in Oxfordshire, 1550–1590*, ed. M.A. Havinden (Oxfordshire Record Soc., xliv, 1956), pp. 42–3.

65. *Jacobean Household Inventories*, ed. F.G. Emmison (Beds. Hist. Record Soc., xx, 1938), p. 59.

66. Havinden, *op cit.*, p. 258. A Land was usually a strip in the open field of approximately half an acre.

67. T.W. Hanson, 'Halifax Builders in Oxford', *Trans. Halifax Antiq. Soc.*, (1928), p. 316.

68. W.J. Williams, 'Wills of Freemasons and Masons', *The Masonic Record*, xvi (1936), p. 224.

69. Emmison, *op cit.*, p. 60.

70. H.M. Colvin, 'Haunt Hill House, Weldon', in *Studies in Building History*, ed. E.M. Jope, (London 1961), p. 224.

71. Cambridge Univ. Library, Hengrave Hall Deposit 80.

72. *The Book of Architecture of John Thorpe*, ed. J. Summerson (Walpole Soc., xl, 1966), p. 4.

73. A. Oswald, *Country Houses of Dorset* (2nd edn., London 1959). p. 28.

74. Girouard, *Smythson*, p. 133.

75. J. Summerson, 'Three Elizabethan Architects', *Bull. John Rylands Library*, xl (1957), p. 213.

76. J. Harvey, *English Medieval Architects* (London, 1954), p. 32.

77. See, for example, Christopher Lovell at Wollaton, Notts. Univ. Library, Mi A60/4. f. 9.

78. *Records of the Worshipful Company of Carpenters*, ed. B. March (i, 1913), pp. 3, 23, 27, 34, 36.

13. Labourers

1. Staffs. CRO, D593 R/1/2.

2. BL., Addit. MSS. 39832.

3. D.N. Durant and P. Riden, *The Building of Hardwick Hall*, Part 1 (Derbys. Record Soc., iv, 1980), p. xx.

4. Essex CRO, D/DP A 18–20.

5. J. Evans, 'Extracts from the Private Account Book of Sir William More of Loseley . . .', *Archaeologia*, xxxvi (1855), pp. 284–310.

6. Staffs. CRO, D593 R/1/2.

7. Cambridge Univ. Library, Hengrave Hall Deposit 80.

8. Knoop and Jones, *op cit.*, pp. 36–7; J.R. Wigfull, 'House Building in Queen Elizabeth's Days', *Trans. Hunter Arch. Soc.*, iii (1925), pp. 72–3: Durant & Riden, *op cit.*, Part 2, p. xlix.

9. Essex CRO, D/DP A20.

10. Notts. Univ. Library, Mi A60/5, f. 11.

11. E. Ridout, 'The Account Book of the New Haven, Chester, 1567–8', *Trans. Hist. Soc. of Lancs. & Cheshire*, lxxv (1928), pp. 86–128.

12. Staffs. CRO, D593 R/1/2.

14. Working Conditions

1. 5 Eliz. I.c.4.

2. 11 Henry VII, c. 22.

3. 6 Henry VIII, c. 3.

4. *The Architecture of Sir Roger Pratt*, ed. R.T. Gunther (Oxford, 1928), p. 229.

5. Girouard, *Smythson*, p. 58.
6. BL., Addit. MSS. 39832, f. 119.
7. D. Knoop and G.P. Jones, 'Overtime in the Age of Henry VIII', *Economic History*, iv (1938), pp. 13–20.
8. B. Stallybrass, 'Bess of Hardwick's Buildings and Building Accounts', *Archaeologia*, lxiv (1913), pp. 13–20.
9. Longleat Archives, R.O.B., i, f. 141. Thynne to Dodd 22 June 1547.
10. D. Knoop and G.P. Jones, 'The Bolsover Castle Building Account for 1613', *Ars Quatuor Coronatorum*, xlix (1939), p. 34.
11. BL., Addit. MSS. 39832, f. 42.
12. 5 & 6 Edward VI, c. 3.
13. I Mary Sess, 2, c. 2.
14. Mrs Baldwyn-Childe, 'The Building of the Manor House at Kyre Park, Worcestershire', *The Antiquary*, xxii (1890), p. 50.
15. Sandeen, p. 47.
16. Mrs Baldwyn-Childe, *op cit.*, p. 52.
17. J.A. Gotch, 'The Renaissance in Northamptonshire', *Trans. R.I.B.A.*, new ser., vi (1890), p. 105.
18. Longleat Archives, R.O.B., i, f. 206. Dodd to Thynne, undated but probably 1547.
19. BL., Addit. MSS. 39832.
20. Knoop and Jones, *op cit.*
21. Essex CRO, D/DP A19–22.
22. Sandeen, p. 46.
23. Longleat Archives, R.O.B., i, f. 237. Thynne to Dodd, 3 August 1547.
24. *Ibid.*, f. 299.
25. *Ibid.*, f. 228.
26. L. Stone, 'The Building of Hatfield House', *Arch. Jour.*, cxii (1955), p. 120.
27. *The House and Farm Accounts of the Shuttleworths*, ed. J. Harland, (Chetham Soc., xxxv, 1856), pp. 133, 141.
28. Staffs. CRO, D593 R/1/2.
29. H.L. Bradfer-Lawrence, 'The Building of Raynham Hall', *Norf. Arch.* xxiii (1927), p. 102.
30. C. Welch, *History of the Tower Bridge* (London, 1894), p. 53.
31. Willis and Clark, ii, pp. 482n., 487n.
32. BL., Addit. MSS. 39832, f. 93; *idem.* 69, 874.
33. Staffs. CRO, D593 R/1/2.
34. Essex CRO, D/DP A10, f. 80.
35. William Salt Library, Stafford, D1721/1/4.
36. *Ibid.*, D1734/3/4/101.
37. BL., Addit. MSS. 7097, f. 182v.
38. Essex CRO, D/DP A21.
39. Staffs. CRO, D593 R/1/2.
40. BL., Addit. MSS. 39832, f. 63.

41. BL., Addit. MSS. 7097, f. 192.
42. B. Stallybrass, 'Bess of Hardwick's Building and Building Accounts', *Archaeologia*, lxiv (1913), p. 383.
43. L. Stone, 'The Building of Hatfield House', *Arch. Jour.*, cxii (1955), p. 104.
44. D. Knoop and G.P. Jones, 'The Sixteenth Century Mason', *Ars Quatuor Coronatorum*, I (1937), p. 209.
45. Stallybrass, *op cit.*, 379. A contemporary 'sawe for Blacke stone' is illustrated in R.I.B.A. Drawings Collection, Smythson Collection, 11/26.
46. J.A. Wigfull, 'Extracts from the Note-Book of William Dickenson', *Trans. Hunter Arch. Soc.*, ii (1921), p. 192.
47. Staffs. CRO, D593 R/1/2.
48. Essex CRO, D/DP A20.
49. J. Evans, 'Extracts from the Private Account Book of Sir William More of Loseley . . .', *Archaeologia*, xxxvi (1855), p. 303.
50. Longleat Archives, T.P. Box lxviii, Bk. 60, f. 30.
51. Mrs Baldwyn-Childe, 'The Building of the Manor House of Kyre Park, Worcestershire', *The Antiquary*, xxii (1890), p. 26.
52. Cambridge Univ. Lib., Hengrave Hall Deposit 80.
53. Willis and Clark, ii, p. 569.
54. Sandeen, *op cit.*, p. 48.
55. *The House and Farm Accounts of the Shuttleworths*, ed. J. Harland (Chetham Soc., xxxv, 1856), p. 130.
56. Mrs Baldwyn-Childe, *op cit.*, p. 51.
57. Essex CRO, D/DP A10, f. 85.
58. Evans, *op cit.*, p. 303.
59. Essex CRO, D/DP, A19 and A22.

15. *Accommodation and Food*

1. *The Architecture of Sir Roger Pratt*, ed. R.T. Gunther (Oxford 1928), p. 88.
2. Sandeen, p. 62.
3. J. Evans, 'Extracts from the Private Account Book of Sir William More of Loseley . . .', *Archaeologia*, xxxvi (1855), p. 296.
4. Staffs. CRO, D593 R/1/2.
5. H.L. Bradfer-Lawrence, 'The Building of Raynham Hall', *Norf. Arch.*, xxiii (1927), p. 122.
6. A. Oswald, *Country Houses of Dorset* (2nd edn, London, 1959), p. 28.
7. Longleat Archives, R.O.B., iii, f. 61.
8. Cambridge Univ. Lib., Hengrave Hall Deposit 80.
9. *Ibid.*, Hengrave Hall Deposit 81.

10. William Salt Library, Stafford, D1734/3/4/143.
11. BL., Addit. MSS. 39832, f. 54.
12. F.H. Cheetham, *Haddon Hall* (London, 1904), p. 32.
13. Sandeen, p. 43.
14. Staffs. CRO, D593 R/1/2.
15. Essex CRO, D/DP A20.
16. B. Stallybrass, 'Bess of Hardwick's Building and Building Accounts', *Archaeologia*, lxiv (1913), p. 379. D. Durant and P. Riden, *The Building of Hardwick Hall, Part 2* (Derbys. Record Soc., ix, 1984), p. lxxvii.
17. *Camden Miscellany* xvi (Camden Soc., 3rd serv., lii, 1936), p. 50.
18. Sandeen, pp. 202–3.
19. W.H. Cope, *Bramshill* (London, 1883), p. 121.
20. Cornwall CRO, MTD/48/10.
21. BL., Addit. MSS. 7097, ff. 174–200.
22. G.R. Batho, 'Henry Earl of Northumberland and Syon House, Middlesex, 1594–1632', *Trans. Ancient Mons. Soc.*, new ser. iv (1956), p. 104.
23. Staffs. CRO, D/DP A18–22.
24. *The House and Farm Accounts of the Shuttleworths*, ed. J. Harland (Chetham Soc., xxxv, 1856), pp. 125–74.
25. Essex CRO, D/DP A18–22.
26. J. Humphreys, 'The Elizabethan Estate Book of Grafton Manor', *Trans Birmingham Arch. Soc.*, xliv (1918), 1–24. BL., Addit. MSS. 46461.
27. J.R. Wigfull, 'House Building in Queen Elizabeth's Days', *Trans. Hunter Arch. Soc.*, iii (1925), pp. 68–73.
28. J. Evans, 'Extracts from the Private Account Book of Sir William More of Loseley . . .', *Archaeologia*, xxxvi (1855), pp. 284–310.
29. Cambridge Univ. Lib., Hengrave Hall Deposit 80.
30. Mrs Baldwyn-Childe, 'The Building of the Manor House of Kyre Park, Worcestershire', *The Antiquary*, xxii (1890), pp. 24, 25, 51.
31. Staffs. CRO, D593 R/1/2.
32. Bodleian Library, Oxford, MS. Rawl, D784, f. 38.
33. Essex CRO, D/DP A21.
34. Longleat Archives, R.O.B., ii, f. 156. Walker to Thynne, 14 April 1563.
35. Stallybrass, *op. cit.*, p. 376.
36. R.I.B.A., Drawings Collection, Smythson Collection III/17.
37. Bradfer-Lawrence, *op. cit.*, p. 107.
38. PRO, SP28/207, f.14.
39. William Salt Library, Stafford, D1721/1/4.
40. Staffs. CRO, D593 R/1/2.
41. Stallybrass, *op. cit.*, p. 376.
42. N. Briggs, 'The Foundation of Wadham College, Oxford', *Oxoniensia*, xxi (1956), p. 69.
43. Bradfer-Lawrence, *op. cit.*, p. 125.
44. Staffs. CRO, D593 R/1/2.
45. Stallybrass, *op. cit.*, p. 355.
46. Longleat Archives, R.O.B., iii, f. 237.

16.   *Labour Relations*

1. J.A. Gotch, 'The Renaissance in Northamptonshire', *Trans. R.I.B.*, new ser. vi (1890), p. 108.
2. Longleat Archives, R.O.B., i, f. 237. Thynne to Dodd, 3 August 1547.
3. Used with reference to a carter employed by the week at Gawthorpe Hall in July 1601, *The House and Farm Accounts of the Shuttleworths*, ed. J. Harland (Chetham Soc., xxxv, 1856), p. 137.
4. For example, 'broke & hole' at Loseley in 1562, and 'broken & hole' at Old Thorndon Hall in 1590.
5. Notts. Univ. Library, Mi A 60/4. f/ 7.
6. Staffs. CRO, D593 R/1/2.
7. Kent CRO, U269 A505/1.
8. Mrs Baldwyn-Childe, 'The Building of the Manor House of Kyre Park, Worcestershire', *The Antiquary*, xxi (1890), p. 264.
9. J.R. Wigfull, 'Extracts from the Note-Book of William Dickenson', *Trans. Hunter Arch. Soc.*, ii (1921), p. 192.
10. Staffs. CRO, D593 R/1/2.
11. Longleat Archives, R.O.B., ii, ff. 155, 169, 179.
12. Sandeen, p. 186. BL., Addit. MSS. 69,869 and 69,880.
13. Girouard, *Smythson*, pp. 60–1.
14. William Salt Library, Stafford, D/1743/3/4/143.
15. B. Stallybrass, 'Bess of Hardwick's Buildings and Building Accounts', *Archaeologia*, lxiv (1913), p. 352.
16. BL., Addit. MSS. 7097, f. 179.
17. Longleat Archives, R.O.B., ii, f. 209. Vyttery to Thynne, 9 December 1565.
18. D. Knoop and G.P. Jones, 'The Bolsover Castle Building Account for 1613', *Ars Quatuor Coronatorum*, xlix (1939), p. 46.
19. Mrs Baldwyn-Childe, *op. cit.*, p. 51.
20. D. Durant and P. Riden, *The Building of Hardwick Hall, Part 2* (Derbys. Record. Soc., ix, 1984), p. lxviii.

21. J.E. Jackson, 'Wulfhall and the Seymours', *Wilts. Arch. Mag.*, xv.
22. Mrs Baldwyn-Childe, *op. cit.*, pp. 51–2.
23. Longleat Archives, R.O.B., ii, f. 147. Walker to Thynne. 15 March 1562/3.

17. Home Life

1. *Household and Farm Inventories in Oxfordshire* 1550–1590, ed. M.A. Havinden (Oxfordshire Record Soc., xliv, 1965), p. 258.
2. *Ibid.*, p. 282.
3. *Ibid.*, p. 261.
4. F.W. Steer, *Farm and Cottage Inventories of Mid-Essex* (Chelmsford, 1950), p. 71.
5. *Jacobean Household Inventories*, ed. F.G. Emmison (Bedfordshire Historical Record Soc., xx, 1938), p. 86.
6. *Probate Inventories of Lichfield and District*, 1568–1680, ed. D.G. Vaisey (Staffs. Record Soc., Collections for a History of Staffs., 4th ser., v, 1969), pp. 72–3.
7. Emmison, *op cit.*, p. 132.
8. H.M. Colvin, 'Haunt Hill House, Weldon', *Studies in Building History*, ed. E.M. Jope (London, 1961), pp. 223–8.
9. Havinden, *op cit.*, pp. 42–3.
10. T.W. Hanson, 'Halifax Builders in Oxford', *Trans. Halifax Antiq. Soc.* (1928), p. 341.
11. Girouard, *Smythson*, p. 200.
12. Notts. CRO, PRNW. A transcript of his will was kindly supplied to me by David N. Durant.
13. Emmison, *op. cit.*, p. 55.
14. Havinden, *op cit.*, p. 169.
15. *Ibid.*, p. 262.
16. *Ibid.*, p. 129.
17. *Ibid.*, p. 258.
18. *Ibid.*, p. 282.
19. Emmison, *op. cit.*, p. 59.
20. Havinden, *op cit.*, pp. 42–3.
21. *Ibid.*, p. 258.
22. *Ibid.*, p. 282.
23. *Ibid.*, pp. 261–2.
24. *Ibid.*, p. 129.
25. *Probate Inventories of Worcester Tradesmen*, 1545–1614, ed. A.D. Dyer (Worcester Hist. Soc., new ser., v, 1967), pp. 43–5; C. Platt, *The Great Rebuildings of Tudor and Stuart England* (London, 1994), pp. 18–19.
26. Longleat Archives, R.O.B., ii, f. 258. Vyttery to Thynne, 22 May 1567.
27. B. Stallybrass, 'Bess of Hardwick's Buildings and Building Accounts', *Archaeologia*, lxiv (1913), p. 389.
28. *Harrison's Description of England.*, ed. F.J. Furnivall (New Shakespere Soc., ser. vi, 1877), p. 153.
29. Shrewsbury Public Library, Deeds 6883, f. 22.
30. Notts. Univ. Library, Mi A60/6, f. 4v.
31. William Salt Library, Stafford, D1721/1/4.
32. J. Mills, 'Peter Lewys: His Work and Workmen', *Journ. Royal Soc. of Antiqs. of Ireland*, xxxi (1901), p. 105.
33. T. Stirrup, *The Artificers Plain Scale . . .* (London, 1651), p. 2.
34. BL., Addit. MSS. 39836, ff. 288–96.

18. Wages

1. D. Knoop and G.J. Jones, *The Medieval Mason* (Manchester, 1933).
2. E.H. Phelps Brown and Sheila V. Hopkins, 'Seven Centuries of Building Wages', *Economica*, new ser., xxii (1955), pp. 195–206; idem., 'Seven Centuries of the Prices of Consumables, compared with Builders' Wage-rates', *Economica*, new ser., xxiii (1956), pp. 296–314. Reprinted together with a number of other relevant articles in idem., *A Perspective of Wages and Prices* (London, 1981).
3. J.E. Thorold Rogers, *A History of Agriculture and Prices in England*, 7 vols. (Oxford, 1866–1902).
4. Knoop and Jones, *op cit.*, p. 185; Phelps Brown and Hopkins, 'Seven Centuries of the Prices of Consumables . . .', *op cit.*, p. 300; D. Woodward, 'Wage Rates and Living Standards in Pre-Industrial England', *Past & Present*, No. 91 (1981), pp. 28–46; 'The Determination of Wage Rates in the Early Modern North of England', *Ec. Hist. Rev.*, xlvii, no. 1 (February 1994), pp. 22–43.
5. Phelps Brown and Hopkins were well aware of this criticism, but, even so, they based their conclusions on their predominant wage graph and not on the more complex figure that they constructed for builders' wages in Oxford, 1500–1600.
6. Almost half of Thorold Rogers' builders' wages for the period down to 1620 came from the city of Oxford, and the remainder were predominantly derived from Cambridge and the southern counties. Woodward's results from the north, when they are fully published, will provide a useful comparison.
7. J.R. Wigfull, 'House Building in Queen Elizabeth's Days', *Trans. Hunter Arch. Soc.*, iii

(1925), pp. 68–73. They were actually paid a wage of 4*d*. with an equal amount for their 'meat'.

8. William Salt Library, Stafford, D/1734/3/4/143, 144.

9. Longleat Archives, T.P. Box lxviii, Book 60; Essex CRO, D/DP A18.

10. Longleat Archives, *passim*.

11. The workmen at Old Thorndon Hall, Essex, enjoyed periodic rises, but work was going on at this house for an even longer period of time than at Longleat.

12. W.J. Hardy, *Hertford County Records. Sessions Rolls, 1581–1698.* (Hertford, 1905), pp. 58–60.

13. Hist. MSS. Comm., *Various*, i, pp. 162–7.

14. *York Civic Records, vi*, ed. A. Raine (Yorks. Arch. Soc. Records Ser., cxii, 1946), pp. 58–60.

15. V.C.H. *Lincoln*, ii (1906), p. 329.

16. Notts. Univ. Library, Mi A60/1–7.

17. E.H. Phelps Brown and S.V. Hopkins, 'Seven Centuries of Building Wages', *Economica*, new ser., xxii (1955), p. 197.

18. Longleat Archives, *passim*.

19. Surrey CRO, Acc. 1030.

20. Staffs. CRO, D593 R/1/2.

21. Notts. Univ. Library, *op cit*.

22. The statistics for Figure 1 have been provided by the following houses (arranged in chronological order of surviving accounts):

Little Saxham Hall, Suffolk, 1505–11.
Hengrave Hall, Suffolk, 1525–38.
Redgrave Hall, Norfolk, 1545–54.
Longleat House, Wilts, 1547–81.
Wulfhall, Wilts, 1549
East Thorndon Hall, Essex,1550–5.
Grafton Manor, Worcs, 1568–9, 1576.
Beaudesert Hall, Staffs, 1575.
Wm. Dickenson's House, Sheffield, 1575–6.
Old Thorndon Hall, Essex, 1577, 1580–1, 1586–7, 1589–90, 1593–4.
Stiffkey Hall, Norfolk, 1579–80.
Wollaton House, Notts, 1582–8.
Condover Hall, Salop, 1592, 1598.
Lyveden, Northants, 1593–7.
Ashley Park, Surrey, 1601–7.
West Horsley Place, Surrey, 1603–4.
Brigg Milne Dam, Yorks, 1605.
Harrold House, Beds, 1608–10.

Syon House, Middx, 1609–10.
Knole, Kent, 1612.
Bolsover Castle, Derbys, 1613.
Raynham Hall, Norfolk, 1619–22.
Copthall, Essex, 1623, 1627, 1630–1, 1635.
Goldicote House, Worcs, 1626.
Temple Newsam, Yorks, 1632.
Trentham Hall, Staffs, 1633–9.
Milcote House, Warwicks, 1634.
Sezincote House, Gloucs, 1635.
Carreglwyd, Anglesey, 1636.
Holland House, Kensington, 1638–40.

23. A. Hamilton-Thompson, 'The Building Accounts of Kirby Muxloe Castle, 1480–84', *Leics. Arch. Soc. Trans.*, xi (1913–14), pp. 193–345.

24. E.H. Phelps Brown and S.V. Hopkins, 'Seven Centuries of the Prices of Consumables, compared with Builders' Wage-rates', *Economica*, new ser., xxxiii (1956), p. 299.

25. Compiled from the same houses as Figure 1.

26. J. Thirsk, ed., *The Agrarian History of England and Wales, iv. 1500–1640* (Cambridge, 1967), Table xvi, p. 865.

27. E.H. Phelps Brown and S.V. Hopkins, *op cit.*, p. 299.

28. B.H. Putnam, 'Northamptonshire Wage Assessments of 1560 and 1667', *Econ. Hist. Rev.*, i (1927), pp. 131–2.

29. W.A.S. Hewins, 'Regulation of Wages by the Justices of the Peace', *Economic Journal*, viii (1898), pp. 131–2.

30. H. Bentley, 'A Rate for Servants' Wages Made at Easter Sessions, 7 Charles I', *East Herts. Arch. Soc. Trans.*, xiii, part 2 (1952–4), pp. 167–71. For a list of other assessments in print, see C. Read, *Bibliography of British History: Tudor Period, 1485–1603* (2nd edn, Oxford, 1959), pp. 242–3.

19. Specialization and Professionalism

1. Mrs Baldwyn-Childe, 'The Building of the Manor House of Kyre Park, Worcestershire', *The Antiquary*, xxii (1890), p. 51.

2. *The Account Book of Nicholas Stone*, ed. W.L. Spiers (Walpole Soc., vii, 1919), p. 70.

Select Bibliography

The extensive manuscript and secondary sources that have been used to substantiate specific points are fully documented in the footnotes and only modern books and articles which provide useful background information or recently printed documents are listed here.

BOOKS

Malcolm Airs, *The Buildings of Britain: Tudor and Jacobean*, Barrie & Jenkins (London, 1982)

Malcolm Airs (ed), *The Tudor and Jacobean Great House*, Department for Continuing Education (Oxford, 1994)

M.E. Blackman, *Ashley House Building Accounts, 1602–7* (Surrey Record Society, xxix, 1977)

John Bold and Edward Chaney (eds), *English Architecture Public and Private*, Hambledon Press (London, 1993)

H.M. Colvin (ed), *The History of the King's Works, Vol III, 1485–1660 (Pt I)*, HMSO (London, 1975)

H.M. Colvin (ed), *The History of the King's Works, Vol IV, 1485–1660 (Pt II)*, HMSO (London, 1982)

D.N. Durant, *Bess of Hardwick*, Weidenfeld & Nicolson (London, 1977)

D.N. Durant and P. Riden (eds), *The Building of Hardwick Hall, Pt I* (Derbys. Record Soc., iv, 1980)

D.N. Durant and P. Riden (eds), *The Building of Hardwick Hall, Pt II* (Derbys. Record Soc., ix, 1984)

Oliver Fairclough, *The Grand Old Mansion*, Birmingham Museums & Art Gallery (Birmingham, 1984)

Boris Ford (ed), *The Cambridge Guide to the Arts in Britain: Renaissance and Reformation*, Cambridge University Press (Cambridge, 1988)

Alice Friedman, *House and Household in Elizabethan England*, University of Chicago Press (Chicago & London, 1989)

Mark Girouard, *Robert Smythson & The Elizabethan Country House*, Yale University Press (New Haven & London, 1983)

Mark Girouard, *Life in the English Country House*, Yale University Press (New Haven & London, 1978)

S.J. Gunn and P.G. Lindley (eds), *Cardinal Wolsey*, Cambridge University Press (Cambridge, 1991)

Maurice Howard, *The Early Tudor Country House: Architecture and Politics, 1490–1550*, George Philip (London, 1987)

Timothy Mowl, *Elizabethan & Jacobean Style*, Phaidon (London, 1993)

Colin Platt, *The Great Rebuildings of Tudor and Stuart England*, UCL Press (London, 1994)

A. Hassell Smith and Gillian Baker (eds), *The Papers of Nathaniel Bacon of Stiffkey, Vol. I, 1556–1577* (Norwich, 1979), *Vol. II, 1578–1585* (Norwich, 1983), *Vol. III, 1586–1595*, University of East Anglia (Norwich, 1990)

D. Starkey (ed), *Henry VIII, A European Court in England*, Collins & Brown (London, 1991)

John Summerson, *Architecture in Britain, 1530–1830*, Yale University Press (9th edn, New Haven & London, 1993)

Simon Thurley, *The Royal Palaces of Tudor England*, Yale University Press (New Haven & London, 1993)

J. Ward and K. Marshall, *Old Thorndon Hall*, Essex County Council (Chelmsford, 1972)

ARTICLES

Malcolm Airs, 'The Designing of Five East Anglian Country Houses, 1505–1637', *Architectural History*, 21, 1978.

Malcolm Airs, 'Lawrence Shipway, Freemason', *ibid.*, 27, 1984.

A. Baggs, 'Two Designs of Simon Basil', *idem.*

Linda Campbell, 'Documentary Evidence for the Building of Raynham Hall', *ibid.*, 32, 1989.

H.M. Colvin, 'Beaudesert Staffordshire', *Trans. Ancient Mons. Soc.*, 29, 1985.

Rosalys Coope, 'The "Long Gallery": its' Origins, Development, Use and Decoration', *ibid.*, 32, 1989.

P.J. Drury, 'No other Palace in the Kingdom will compare with it: The Evolution of Audley End, 1605–1745', *ibid.*, 23, 1980.

P.J. Drury, '"A Fayre House, Buylt by Sir Thomas Smith": The Development of Hill Hall, Essex, 1557–81', *Jour. B.A.A.*, cxxxvi, 1983.

Oliver Fairclough, 'John Thorpe and Aston Hall', *Architectural History*, 32, 1989.

J. Manco, M. Greenhalf & M. Girouard, 'Lulworth Castle in the Seventeenth Century' *ibid.*, 33, 1990.

John Newman, 'The Elizabethan and Jacobean Great House: A Review of Recent Research', *Archaeol. Jour.*, 145, 1988.

Caroline Stanley-Millson and John Newman, 'Blickling Hall: The Building of a Jacobean Mansion', *Architectural History*, 29, 1986.

Index

Numbers in italics denote illustrations.